Global Health and Human Rights

The right to health, having been previously neglected, is now being deployed more and more often in litigation, activism and policy-making across the world. International bodies such as the WHO, UNAIDS, World Bank and WTO are increasingly using or being evaluated with reference to health rights, and international NGOs frequently use the language of rights in campaigning and in more concrete litigation.

This book brings together an impressive array of internationally renowned scholars in the areas of law, philosophy and health policy to interrogate critically the development of rights-based approaches to health. The volume integrates discussion of the right to health at a theoretical level in law and ethics, with the difficult substantive issues where the right is relevant, and with emerging systems of global health governance. The contributions to this volume will add to our theoretical and practical understanding of rights-based approaches to health.

John Harrington is Professor of Law at the University of Liverpool, UK.

Maria Stuttaford is a Senior Research Fellow at the Institute of Health at the University of Warwick, UK.

Routledge Research in Human Rights Law

Available titles in this series include:

The Right to Development in International Law
The case of Pakistan
Khurshid Iqbal

Forthcoming titles in this series include:

The European Convention on Human Rights and its New Contracting Parties
Democratic transition and consolidation in the European Jurisprudence
James A. Sweeney

The Right to Religious Freedom in International Law
Between group rights and individual rights
Anat Scolnicov

Children and International Human Rights Law
The right of the child to be heard
Aisling Parkes

Emerging Areas of Human Rights in the 21st Century
The role of the Universal Declaration of Human Rights
Marco Odello and Sofia Cavandoli

Human Rights Monitoring Mechanisms of the Council of Europe
Gauthier de Beco

The Human Right to Water
Its application in the Occupied Palestinian Territories
Amanda Cahill

International Human Rights Law and Domestic Violence
The effectiveness of international human rights law
Ronagh McQuigg

The EU as a 'Global Player' in Human Rights
Jan Wetzel

Global Health and Human Rights

Legal and philosophical perspectives

Edited by John Harrington and Maria Stuttaford

Routledge
Taylor & Francis Group
LONDON AND NEW YORK

First published 2010
by Routledge
2 Park Square, Milton Park, Abingdon, Oxon OX14 4RN

Simultaneously published in the USA and Canada
by Routledge
270 Madison Avenue, New York, NY 10016

Routledge is an imprint of the Taylor & Francis Group, an informa business

Typeset in BaskervilleMT by
RefineCatch Limited, Bungay, Suffolk

British Library Cataloguing in Publication Data
A catalogue record for this book is available from the British Library

Library of Congress Cataloging-in-Publication Data
Global health and human rights : legal and philosophical perspectives / edited by John Harrington and Maria Stuttaford.
p. cm.
Includes bibliographical references.
1. Right to health care. I. Harrington, John, 1969– II. Stuttaford, Maria.
K3260.3.G58 2010
362.101—dc22 2009049057

ISBN13: 978–0–415–47938–7 (hbk)
ISBN13: 978–0–203–85063–3 (ebk)

Contents

Notes on contributors

Upendra Baxi is Emeritus Professor of Law and Development at the University of Warwick and was Vice-Chancellor of the University of Delhi from 1990 to 1994. Among his publications are *Human Rights In a Posthuman World* (OUP 2007) and *The Future of Human Rights* (OUP 2002).

Roger Brownsword is Professor of Law at King's College, London. He is a member of the Nuffield Council on Bioethics and has been a specialist adviser to the House of Lords Select Committee on Stem Cells. His publications include *Rights, Regulation, and the Technological Revolution* (OUP 2008) and *Consent in the Law* (Hart 2007, with Deryck Beyleveld).

Lisa Forman is Assistant Professor at the Dalla Lana School of Public Health, University of Toronto, and Director of the Comparative Program on Health and Society, Munk Centre for International Studies, University of Toronto. She has published on the role of human rights in increasing access to AIDS medicines, with particular reference to developments in South Africa, and also on the right-to-health implications of the TRIPs agreement.

John Harrington is Professor of Law at the University of Liverpool and Director of the Medicine, Law and Bioethics Unit there. He has written on health and the law in East Africa and on the legal implications of health care reform in the UK.

Paul Hunt is Professor of Law at the University of Essex. From 2002 to 2008 he served as United Nations Special Rapporteur on the Right of Everyone to the Highest Attainable Standard of Health. His publications include *Reclaiming Social Rights: International and Comparative Perspectives* (Dartmouth 1996).

Sheldon Leader is Professor of Law at the University of Essex. His research includes work on the links between economic actors and social justice. He has been Legal Adviser to Amnesty International UK, is director of the Essex Business and Human Rights Centre, and relevant publications include 'Inflating Consent, Inflating Function, and Inserting Human Rights', in *Capitalism and Human Rights* eds J. Dine and A. Fagan (Edward Elgar Publishing Ltd: 2005); and 'The Collateral Protection of Rights in a Global Economy' 53 *New York Law School Law Review* issue 4 (2009).

Benjamin Mason Meier is Assistant Professor of Global Health Policy at the University of North Carolina, Chapel Hill. He has written on the interaction between human rights and public health, the right to development and global health inequities.

Aoife Nolan is a Lecturer in Law at Queens University Belfast. She was formerly a Senior Legal Officer with the ESC Rights Litigation Programme of the Centre on Housing Rights and Evictions (COHRE) Geneva. She has published on economic and social rights, with a particular focus on the rights of children.

Paul O'Connell is a Lecturer in Law at the University of Leicester. He has published on the right to health implications of globalisation and the privatisation of health services.

Maria Stuttaford is a Senior Research Fellow at the Institute of Health University of Warwick and an honorary lecturer at the Universities of Cape Town and St Andrews. She has published on human rights approaches to promoting health equity, on access to the underlying determinants of health and on the role of civil society organisations in achieving the right to health.

Brigit Toebes is an Honorary Lecturer at the University of Aberdeen School of Law and currently based in Copenhagen as an Independent Researcher and Consultant on Human Rights, including for the Danish Institute for Human Rights. She has published on the legal implications of the right to health and on the connection between health systems and the right to health.

Acknowledgements

Many of the chapters in this volume were originally presented in the course of a UK Economic and Social Research Council (ESRC)-funded seminar series entitled 'Global Health and Human Rights: Theory, Process and Substance' (2007–2008) (RES-451-25-4320). We would like to thank all participants at the seminars, held at Liverpool, Edinburgh and Warwick, for their lively and informative contributions. The series was co-convened by the editors of this volume along with Professor Gillian Lewando-Hundt, University of Warwick. We extend our warmest thanks to her for her role in making the series a success. Karen van Rompaey administered the series efficiently and enabled the co-convenors to focus on the academic content of the series. Kayte Kelley of the Liverpool Law School ensured the success of the seminar at Liverpool. We are particularly grateful to our editor at Routledge, Khanam Virjee, for her patience and her advice at crucial points. Thanks are also due to Vishwas Devaiah for his help in the editing process.

1 Introduction

John Harrington and Maria Stuttaford

1 Themes

In the last decade, the human right to health has moved to the centre of political debate and social policy across the globe. Civil society organizations have put this right at the heart of campaigns for health justice at national and global levels. It features prominently in the output of the United Nations (UN) and regional human rights bodies, as well as national courts and legislatures; national constitutions increasingly include explicit recognition of the right to health. Long neglected in the legal academy, many scholars now labour to develop its normative content, to contextualize its application and to evaluate it from the point of view of moral philosophy and theories of justice. This has been a remarkable transformation.

The right to health has certainly been a feature of international human rights law since the Second World War. The Universal Declaration of Human Rights (1948) states that 'everyone has the right to a standard of living adequate for the health and well-being of himself and of his family, including food, clothing, housing and medical care and necessary social services' (Art 25.1). The Preamble to the Constitution of the World Health Organization (WHO 1948) contains a similar affirmation. These principles were given legal force in the International Covenant on Economic, Social and Cultural Rights (ICESCR) (1966).[1] In Art 12.1 ICESCR States Parties 'recognize the right of everyone to the enjoyment of the highest attainable standard of physical and mental health'. The right is similarly recognized in Art 5(e)(iv) of the Convention on the Elimination of All Forms of Racial Discrimination (1965), Arts 11.1(f) and 12 of the Convention on the Elimination of All Forms of Discrimination against Women (1979) and Art 24 Convention on the Rights of the Child (1989). However, notwithstanding this pedigree, the right to health was relegated to secondary status as a social and economic right for much of the postwar period; it was fatally identified with Soviet ideology during the Cold War. Widespread political hostility was underpinned by juristic and philosophical scepticism. For many, the very idea of a right to health suffered from vagueness, incoherence and incompleteness, especially when compared with more established civil and political rights (see Evans 2002). How could States guarantee to make everyone healthy? How could any limit be set to this obligation? What of other State priorities? Scarcity of resources was inevitable and could not be wished away by fine-sounding principles. As a result, the right played little positive role in the creation of welfare States in Europe and North America or in the endeavours of the developmental State in Africa, Asia and Latin America.

Ironically, the fortunes of the right to health have been transformed in the period after the end of the Cold War, just as State socialism was overwhelmed by a reinvigorated, globalizing capitalist system. The right seems to have been freed from the stigma of association with the Eastern Bloc. At the same time, it has gained in relevance as a response to the collective and individual trauma caused by a drastic reduction of social guarantees in many countries (MacDonald 2005). Moreover, multiple health catastrophes in the developing world – some relatively new, like HIV/AIDS, some of long standing like tuberculosis, diarrhoea and malaria – have at last called forth the concern and engagement of lawmakers, activists and professionals (Thomas and Weber 2004). The right to health has been deployed to give normative force to claims for access to essential medicines and for international solidarity in combating disease (Sell 2002).

These political changes have been supported by a number of important legal developments. In 2000, the UN Committee on Economic, Social and Cultural Rights (CESCR) published General Comment 14, an extensive and authoritative interpretation of Art 12 ICESCR. This work of elaboration and application was continued from 2002 with the appointment of Professor Paul Hunt as UN Special Rapporteur on the Right of Everyone to the Highest Attainable Standard of Health (Commission on Human Rights 2002). Most recently, in December 2008, the UN General Assembly adopted an Optional Protocol to the ICESCR allowing individuals and groups to bring complaints against States for violations of the right to health, among other social and economic rights (UN 2008). The first-hand experiences of the Special Rapporteur are considered in the third chapter of this volume. The Optional Protocol has yet to come into force, so its effects remain to be seen. We turn, therefore, to the path-breaking normative implications of General Comment 14. This develops the specific implications of the right to health as a social and economic right of progressive realization. The latter attribute does not mean that the right is emptied of 'all meaningful content' (CESCR 2000: para 31). On the contrary, it implies a 'specific, continuing obligation to move as expeditiously and effectively as possible towards the full realization of Article 12' (CESCR 2000: para 31). Detailed and regularly monitored targets are essential to this process. Moreover, although it is unfolding over time, the implementation of the right demands that certain essential steps are taken immediately. Most significant of these is the requirement that States adopt and implement a national health strategy addressing the needs of the whole population with regard to health care provision and the underlying determinants of health (CESCR 2000: para 43). A planned, systemic approach to health is thus a requirement of international human rights law. General Comment 14 goes on to state that 'gross inequality in health status, particularly between developed and developing countries, as well as within countries, is politically, socially and economically unacceptable' (CESCR 2000: para 38). No longer a matter of fate, health injustices must be specifically tackled.

The terms of General Comment 14 mean that the right to health cannot be reduced to a bare mechanism for reallocating resources to (or within) the health budget, vitally important as this is. It is not merely a vehicle for individual litigation in pursuit of private advantage (although this is not without significance in its implementation). Rather, as the essays in this collection demonstrate, the right to health has a powerful and wide-ranging contribution to make to law, politics and policy-making. This contribution registers in three important and interrelated ways: cognitive, archaeological and critical. The cognitive gain from the right to health arises from its coupling of law with diverse health knowledges (Bauch 1996; Harrington 1999). As has been suggested above Art 12 ICESCR is an open-textured norm. Its core term ('the highest attainable standard of physical and mental health') cannot be adequately defined within the self-referential terms of legal argument. Rather, the right can only gain significant content through specific standards and measures developed by health practitioners, and with the input of ordinary citizens. It is, of course, true that law and biomedicine have long been linked in this way. The application of coercive mental health legislation, for example, often depends on the opinion of one or more psychiatrists (Keywood 2003). But such cognitive openings of the law to medicine are generally quite narrowly circumscribed. The scope of Art 12 is, by contrast, much greater. As General Comment 14 states, it entails an immediate obligation to commence planning for an integrated health care system and for measures to secure the non-medical, underlying determinants of health (CESCR 2000: para 30). To this extent, the meaning of the core term is produced by the interaction of a variety of disciplines in and around public health.

The coupling of law and public health in Art 12 facilitates a kind of parallel processing, whereby measures and proposals are simultaneously subject to evaluations within each system (Luhmann 1997: 776–788). Thus, data showing health disparities as between men and women, say, register as a matter of concern within public health science. For that reason, they simultaneously constitute evidence of a violation of Art 12 (see CESCR 2000: para 57). The effect is to extend the reach of human rights law: a great deal more of the social world becomes subject to the application of legal standards; many more sources of injustice and inequality are brought to light and condemned. It also provides a normative challenge to health workers and administrators, imbuing much of their work with direct normative significance. Human rights law can thus provide an orientation to values beyond the interests of the profession and the profit-maximizing calculus of the market (Farmer 2005: 234).

The cognitive gain extends beyond the disciplinary symbiosis of law and public health. As several contributors to this volume note, the right to health includes strong obligations on States to ensure transparency, participation and accountability. These requirements, it can be argued, do not merely follow on from a predefined right to health; they are not simply the legal manifestation of a 'top-down' regime of consumer surveys and formulaic consultation procedures.

Rather, by enabling popular participation in the definition of health needs and in the development of health policy, they contribute reflexively to the process of defining the right itself (see Teubner 1990: 27). This process is ongoing. The political opening up through the right to health thus represents a distinctive gain in knowledge and information, as the users and potential users of health services actively participate in shaping their own prospects (CESCR 2000: para 53). In other words, by virtue of its inherent openness, the right to health facilitates its own self-transformation and, thereby, the open-ended transformation of society.

The archaeological potential of the right to health is realized through a retrieval of formerly suppressed knowledges relating to human welfare. Action to improve health has long been dominated by a rigidly biomedical model, which privileges clinical care over more wide-ranging interventions (McKeown 1976). This model strongly promoted the monopolistic ambitions of the medical profession. Alternative therapy and lay healing practices were marginalized and subordinated to medicine by legislative fiat. Curative medicine has also proven to be a fertile sphere of accumulation for commercial interests (Leys 2001). Its key features – drugs, equipment and clinical services – are produced as discrete, saleable commodities. These absorb much the greater part of public and private spending on health across the globe. By contrast, as has been noted, the 'inclusive' right to health requires policy-makers to move beyond narrow vertical interventions aimed at specific diseases and to address the underlying determinants of ill health (CESCR 2000: para 4). This holistic approach revives the nineteenth-century tradition of social medicine associated with Rudolf Virchow, which was directed at the underlying economic and environmental causes of human morbidity (see Göckenjan 1985). It draws equally upon the primary health care movement of the 1970s, associated with the World Health Organization's Declaration of Alma Ata (WHO 1978). The latter also promoted a holistic approach and put community participation, in developing countries and elsewhere, at the heart of health improvement strategies.

The critical potential of the right to health lies in its capacity to open up formerly closed areas of thought and discourse regarding health improvement and access to care. Traditional limits to debate over health are set by common sense assumptions regarding necessary constraints: the finitude of resources for health; the biological origins of disease; the inevitability of tragic choices in allocation and so on. As a result, many obstacles to better health have been naturalized in policy discourse and in law (see Baxi 2002: 24–41) – they are a matter of fate, about which little can be done directly. Vast health inequalities between different parts of the world, or between different groups within the same country, are thus naturalized. The negative health consequences of State policies (e.g. for development and industrialization) and private industry (e.g. by pollution and poor working conditions) are similarly rendered as mere externalities, as matters of fate. This regime of common sense underpins a globally unjust allocation of health benefits and burdens. It effaces individual and institutional responsibility and throws the disadvantaged upon the mercy of public and private philanthropy (see Pogge 2002). Moreover, responses to health problems are contained within a framework of binary oppositions: the market and the State; political freedoms and social entitlements; acts causing ill health and failures to prevent ill health. Health-promoting interventions are relegated to the subordinate pole of each of these binaries. Thus: regulating the marketing of breast milk substitutes amounts to State intervention in the 'normal' workings of the market; democracy requires a free press, but not freedom from hunger; tort law offers redress for positive harm, but not for failure to render aid (see Ruger 2006).

The human right to health challenges the 'taken-for-granted' status of these assumptions and oppositions. It does this through its detailed normative engagement with all areas of social life relevant to health, and in particular its close coupling with lay knowledges and the broad range of health sciences, as discussed above. Full elaboration of the right demands the generation of information regarding the many social causes of ill health (CESCR 2000: paras 13, 30). It presumes that these are susceptible to positive intervention at a collective level and it requires such interventions in discharge of States' human rights obligations. Each increase in knowledge mandated by the right to health, each detailed policy recommendation, each conceptual refinement of the right itself, opens up a space for critical debate over the terms of justice and solidarity. The right thus demystifies the existing rhetorical and practical limits to health improvement. This may surprise hostile commentators who see the right as no more than a slogan, empty and abstract.

These themes are raised in various ways by the different contributions to this book. Some focus on the broad scope of the right to health and its grounding, or lack of grounding, in a shared conception of justice. Others address specific, concrete topics in health policy, unfolding the implications of the right in those areas. Several engage with the historical development and current relevance of the right within the broader political conjuncture. The definition and uses of the right to health in different fora are considered: courts, legislatures, public administration and civil society organizations. Of course, we cannot distil a single substantive message from the rich diversity of thought pursued in these essays. The overriding insight is perhaps more abstract, concerning the increasingly detailed normative understanding of the right to health, its growing prominence within legal and non-legal discourses and its centrality to social and political reform. All chapters show that we have moved beyond the period of defensiveness, when most discussion on the right to health was detained by the existential question of whether it could ever exist in the first place. A beginning has been made.

2 Chapters

In the first chapter **Upendra Baxi** reflects on the relevance of justice to understanding and implementing the human right to health. He highlights the profound importance of health as a prerequisite to the enjoyment of all other rights. The right to health must be conceived in equally wide-ranging terms, as regards both its scope and the addressees of obligations arising under it. However, current debates on global health are constrained by a pragmatic focus on what is feasible within given limits. In the present conjuncture, justice is neither expedient nor fashionable. Consequently, the right has been elaborated in the relatively confined and instrumental terms of international policy discourses, such as the Millennium Development Goals. As exemplified in General Comment 14 and in the reports of the Special Rapporteur, these have certainly helped to fill out the normative content of the right to health. However, Baxi argues, much critical force is lost in the absence of an animating theory (or theories) of health care justice. Health care justice offers a distinctive idiom in which to challenge the accepted limits to the enjoyment of the right to health. Scarcity of resources, civil and international wars, the history of conquest and colonialism and unequal economic development are all 'man-made' causes of ill-health. Relational justice demands that we identify the perpetrators, as well as the victims, in these cases. A parallel conception of reparative justice requires us to trace responsibility for violations over national frontiers and across the generations, beyond the realm of the State and into the private sector. Baxi concedes that languages of justice are commonly indeterminate and subject to contestation. But this represents more of an opportunity than a shortcoming, in so far as it exposes questions of distribution and fairness to the widest possible scrutiny and debate. The ongoing challenge to the World Trade Organization's global patent regime is an outstanding example of the creative potential of justice-based arguments and activism. On the one hand, significant, if incomplete, progress has been made in extending access to essential medicines in the most impoverished nations. On the other hand, the hegemony of trade and profit has been disrupted and the closed fora of international trade diplomacy opened up to non-commercial voices.

In their chapter, **Paul Hunt** and **Sheldon Leader** reflect on the experiences of the former as United Nations Special Rapporteur on the Right of Everyone to the Highest Attainable Standard of Health between 2002 and 2008. Through a wide variety of studies concerning specific health themes, as well as country reports, the Special Rapporteur worked to elaborate the normative content of Art 12 ICESCR and in particular to build upon General Comment 14 of the CESCR. Over the course of the mandate it became clear that, while health workers are central to realizing the right to health, they are often alienated by the abstract and legalistic terms in which the right is framed. The Special Rapporteur's resulting engagement with medical and other professionals needs to be emulated by health lawyers and scholars. The very structure of Art 12 demands a close integration of legal standards and public health knowledge. States are required to formulate national health plans as a matter of immediate obligation. They must act on these plans, taking coordinated, concrete steps toward the progressive realization of the right. Benchmarks and indicators, as well as systems of impact assessment and quality control, are integral to this process. They also provide substance to the concomitant duties of transparency, participation and accountability. Hunt and Leader acknowledge the role of courts in clarifying the right to health and in vindicating individual rights, but they warn of the potential for litigation to skew health care allocations in favour of those with the readiest access to the legal system. They draw on this insight in responding to

Baxi's criticisms of the Special Rapporteur's emphasis on policy and planning. It may in fact be the latter approach that secures the greatest improvement in health for the worst off. Furthermore, they insist that many of the practical recommendations made during the mandate are clearly imbued with a spirit of justice, albeit implicitly. Institutional constraints must be acknowledged, however. The Special Rapporteur was required to build on positive international human rights law, which does not endorse any single theory of justice.

Lisa Forman considers the pioneering right to health jurisprudence of the South African Constitutional Court with reference to the concept of the 'minimum core' elaborated in General Comment 14. It is a chief virtue of the latter that, by developing a detailed taxonomy of normative obligations, it disrupts the reified distinction between positive and negative rights, so often deployed to thwart the legal claims of the poor and needy. Forman shows that there are positive and negative dimensions to both civil–political and social–economic rights. Moreover, State action in each dimension of either type of right may lead to very significant expenditure. In any case, as she notes, several important elements of the minimum core under Art 12 relate to planning, governance and accountability. These engage the democratic and deliberative functions of the State at least as much as the directly allocative tasks. In its well-known Treatment Action Campaign decision, the South African Court refused to test the HIV/AIDS policy of the South African government with reference to the minimum core standard, preferring instead a more 'procedural' reasonableness test. Many commentators were disappointed at this turn. However, Forman questions whether the decision really 'fractures the spirit and intent of international human rights law', particularly when the true import of the Court's reasoning and the practical outcome of the case are considered. For one thing, the refusal of the minimum core concept was strategic to a significant degree – calculated to show due deference to executive competence. In substance, the Court demanded that the government account for the fact that its health policies and resource allocation had been determined in wanton disregard for the most basic needs of the most impoverished and vulnerable in South African society. Viewed in this way, the Court's reasoning was certainly compatible with the internationally defined minimum core. It also kept faith with the transformative purpose of the Constitution in so far as it refused to treat the non-availability of resources for basic needs as a simple matter of fate. Under South African constitutional law, as much as under international human rights law, scarcity is removed from the naturalized realm of necessity and opened up to political, legal and moral debate. At the all-important level of practice, the government was forced to provide antiretroviral therapy for women and infants as well as the necessary facilities across the territory.

The last two decades have seen a huge increase in research outsourcing, with drug trials initiated and approved in developed countries, but conducted in resource-poor settings. To what extent are scientific investigators obliged to provide these low-cost 'bioworkers' with ancillary care (i.e. for conditions identified during the research, but unrelated to the trial itself)? **Roger Brownsword** grounds his response to this question in the notion of a 'shared moral community of rights'. In such a community, agents take the essential interests of others as seriously as their own, and it is recognized that more than an absence of restraint is required for agency to flourish. As he suggests, this ethical standpoint will have purchase in legal regimes founded on human rights principles. He elaborates and applies a four-stage test to determine whether participants can have legitimate expectations of ancillary care, i.e. is the researcher in a position to assist; can she do so; is it reasonable to expect her to do so having regard to her own interests; and would it be fair having regard to the participant's own capacity and conduct. The positive obligation that Brownsword identifies on this basis is not diminished by the fact that foreign researchers and local trial subjects belong to different communities of rights. It is no less than the obligation owed to domestic participants in the UK's Biobank initiative, which he considers in parallel here. The ethical conclusion is unlikely to be reflected in English private law, however. Unlike a shared community of rights, the latter leans rather more towards an ethic of self-reliance, emphasizing negative rather than positive background obligations. Indeed, the prior approval system of ethics committees may prove a more reliable and effective means of securing moral obligations to provide ancillary care than *ex post* litigation.

In her chapter, **Brigit Toebes** demonstrates the power of a human rights framework in identifying and combating the threat to health posed by corruption. The open-textured nature of Art 12 ICESCR facilitates the integration of sociological and activist insights on the nature, causes and effects of corruption into legal analysis of this problem. Defining corruption as 'the misuse of entrusted power for private gain', Toebes illustrates its endemic nature and its pernicious consequences for the functioning of health systems and for human well-being in developing countries. Using the pattern of analysis laid down by the CESCR in General Comment 14, she is able to elaborate specific obligations and corresponding duty-holders. The latter category must be drawn widely given the role of foreign aid in much health care provision, as well as the worldwide commercialisation of medical practice and the central role of health professionals in the delivery of care. Furthermore, as Toebes demonstrates, concrete violations of the right to health can be specifically enumerated in this context, highlighting areas for immediate State action. The practice of medicine is marked by stark asymmetries, and health care systems are highly complex. Acts of corruption, such as bribery, always involve at least two parties, neither of whom will be interested in remedying the wrong. These features heighten the need for systemic measures against corruption, focused on planning, prevention, accountability and responsibility. The potential of the right to health in this area lies precisely in that fact that it provides detailed normative guidance in relation to these systemic issues to at least the same extent as it furnishes the individual citizen with subjective, litigable rights.

A further specific focus is provided by **Aoife Nolan** in her discussion of the right to health care of children as interpreted by domestic and international courts. This right is well anchored in international law, both in the ICESCR and in the Convention on the Rights of the Child. General Comments on both have elaborated its content, emphasizing the special priority that States must give to protecting and promoting the health interests of children. Nolan identifies three underlying justifications for this: the physical susceptibility of children to diseases with drastic long-term consequences; the social vulnerability of children to discrimination that either proceeds from, or increases the risk of ill health; and the political exclusion of children from democratic decision-making on the distribution of resources for health. As Nolan shows, the international law right is increasingly reflected in national constitutional provisions. These vary greatly: some expressly protect the child's right to health, others do so by way of combining generic children's rights with a separate provision on the right to health, others again through the incorporation of the international covenants into domestic law. Some make the right directly justiciable, others include it among 'directive principles of social policy'. Nolan's survey of national case law reveals a similar diversity in judicial approaches to the nature of the State's obligation. This has been construed on the one hand as an immediate duty to meet the essential health needs of children (Argentina, Colombia) or on the other hand as an obligation to decide 'reasonably' on the allocation of resources taking particular account of the special position of children (South Africa). Nolan concludes that the developing child's right to health has promoted access to care, both in individual cases and through improved planning. However, she cautions that its enjoyment will depend, not just on constitutional texts, but also on the effectiveness of the court system, as well as a wide range of non-legal factors.

Benjamin Mason Meier draws on original archive research to chart the history of the World Health Organization's (WHO) involvement with the right to health. This is a tale of unfulfilled promise, as initial enthusiasm for a human rights approach has given way to a narrower, more technically defined mission. The Organization's 1946 Constitution defined 'health' broadly in terms of physical and social well-being, beyond the mere absence of disease. As in the Universal Declaration of Human Rights, enjoyment of the medical and social preconditions for health was characterized in the Constitution as a fundamental human right. A change of leadership in 1953 resulted in WHO abandoning its broad focus in favour of a strongly biomedical orientation to discrete health problems. The aim of this 'medicalization' was to avoid politicizing the work of WHO in the intensely polarized climate of the early Cold War. Its consequence was that WHO played no role in the legal codification of the right to health in Art 12 ICESCR. As a result, the normative content of the latter was vague as to the underlying determinants of health. Moreover, unlike other UN agencies in their respective fields, WHO refused to contribute to the enforcement of Art 12 through monitoring and reporting mechanisms. The lack of a legal basis for comprehensive public health strategies was to prove a significant obstacle to WHO when it resumed its interest in social medicine in the mid-1970s. The 'Health for All' strategy embodied in the 1978 Declaration of Alma-Ata was expressly based on an inclusive understanding of the right to health. Politically controversial and lacking a normative anchor of sufficient weight, however, the strategy foundered. In the 1980s, vertical and targeted programmes returned to favour, seen as more in conformity with WHO's limited mandate in international law, and in consonance with the ascendant neo-liberal economic order. As Meier notes in conclusion, given WHO's historic disengagement, it has fallen to the UN itself, through the CESCR and the Special Rapporteur, to take up again the task of elaborating the normative content of the right to health.

In the final chapter, **Paul O'Connell** takes up the challenge issued by Baxi in the first, specifying the normative content of the right to health against the backdrop of contemporary neo-liberal globalization. He critically examines two prominent manifestations of this regime: the worldwide commercialization of health care delivery and the globalization of patent rights over essential medicines. Each is directly linked to violations of the requirement that the means to the enjoyment of the human right to health are accessible to all sectors of the population, without significant distinction as to economic class, social status, gender and physical location. Privatization of health care services results in a skewing of access, which favours the better-off in society, rather than the less-well-off, who often have more pressing health needs. These needs are systematically neglected when medicine is treated only as a tradeable commodity. Where formerly universal systems are dismantled in favour of differential access, this violation of the core principle of non-discrimination is compounded by a breach of the equally fundamental requirement of non-retrogression. The dramatic intensification of patent protection under the World Trade Organization's Agreement on Trade-Related Aspects of Intellectual Property Rights (TRIPS) is also normatively suspect having regard to Art 12 ICESCR. Ironically, in this case it is the absence of market competition from generics that allows monopoly rents to be extracted, putting essential medicines out of reach of the great majority in developing countries. This discriminatory outcome is again accompanied by strong retrogressive effects where formerly relaxed national patent regimes, embodying a needs-based approach to health, are tightened up to comply with international trade law. O'Connell conceives of the right to health, not just as a juridical standard, but as a political–rhetorical means of resisting the effects of neo-liberalism in this area. The latter is secured (and obscured) by a raft of contradictory assumptions regarding the benefits of idealized free markets and the exclusive property rights of patent holders. This neo-liberal ideology helps to produce, and then to normalize and rationalize, increasing inequality in health care and other sectors. One important value of Art 12 lies in its potential for condensing and relaying a counter-common sense regarding basic human needs and the institutions required to meet them. It offers a ground on which the furtive, cynical reason of neo-liberalism can be met by the work in progress of human rights based on justice.

Notes

1 As of 17 November 2009, 160 States had ratified the ICESCR. It is notable that this does not include South Africa and the Unites States of America which have signed, but not yet ratified the Covenant.

Bibliography

Bauch, J. (1996) *Gesundheit als sozialer Code. Von der Vergesellschaftung des Gesundheitswesens zur Medikalisierung der Gesellschaft [Health as a Social Code. From the Societalization of Health Science to the Medicalization of Society]*, Weinheim, Juventa.

Baxi, U. (2002) *The Future of Human Rights*. Delhi: Oxford University Press.

CESCR (2000) *Substantive Issues Arising in the Implementation of the International Covenant on Economic, Social and Cultural Rights: The Right to the Highest Attainable Standard of Health*. General Comment No. 14, 22nd Sess., Agenda Item 3. UN Doc. E/C.12/2000/4.

Commission on Human Rights (2002) Resolution 2002/31, 22 April 2002.

Evans, T. (2002) 'A Human Right To Health?', *Third World Quarterly*, 23: 197–215.

Farmer, P. (2005) *Pathologies of Power: Health, Human Rights and the New War on the Poor*. London: University of California Press.

Göckenjan, G. (1985) *Kurieren und Staat machen [Curing and State Formation]*, Frankfurt-am-Main: Suhrkamp.

Harrington, J. (1999) 'AIDS, Public Health and the Law. A Case of Structural Coupling?', *European Journal of Health Law*, 6: 211–232.

Keywood, K. (2003) 'Rethinking the Anorexic Body: How English Law and Psychiatry "Think" ', *International Journal of Law and Psychiatry*, 26: 599–616.

Leys, C. (2001) *Market-Driven Politics: Neoliberal Democracy and the Public Interest*. London: Verso.

Luhmann, N. (1997) *Die Gesellschaft der Gesellschaft [The Society of Society] 2 vols*. Frankfurt-am-Main: Suhrkamp.

MacDonald, T. (2005) *Health, Trade and Human Rights*. Oxford: Radcliffe Publishing.

McKeown, T. (1976) *The Role of Medicine: Dream, Mirage, or Nemesis?* London: Nuffield Provincial Hospitals Trust.

Pogge, T. W. (2002) 'Responsibility for Poverty-Related Ill Health', *Ethics and International Affairs*, 16(2) 72–79.

Ruger, J. P. (2006) 'Ethics and Governance of Global Health Inequalities', *Journal Of Epidemiological Community Health*, 60: 998–1002.

Sell, S. K. (2002) 'TRIPs and the Access to Medicines Campaign', *Wisconsin International Law Journal*, 20: 481–522.

Teubner, G. (1990) ' "And God Laughed": Indeterminacy, Self-Reference and Paradox in Law', *Stanford Literature Review*, 7: 15–51.

Thomas, C. and Weber, M. (2004) 'The Politics of Global Health Governance: Whatever Happened to "Health for All by the Year 2000"?', *Global Governance*, 10: 187–205.

UN (2008) General Assembly Resolution A/RES/63/117.

WHO (1978) *Primary Health Care: Report of the International Conference of Primary Health Care Alma-Ata, USSR*, 6–12 September 1978, Geneva: World Health Organization.

2 The place of the human right to health and contemporary approaches to global justice

Some impertinent interrogations

Upendra Baxi

1 Prefatory remarks

All questions about human rights raise the familiar concerns regarding their *origins* (sources, whether human or transhuman), *authorship* (the debate over human rights as gifts of 'West to the Rest'), *reach* (universality *v.* cultural specificity), *nature/type* (in terms of here-and-now enforceability and progressive realisation), *limits* (because no human right can claim any absoluteness, all human rights invite conflicting interpretations), *scope* (what obligation do rights cast and upon whom) and of the *justice* of rights (justification for prioritisation, hierarchies, and distribution of rights.) The human right to health (hereinafter, simply HRTH) talk constitutes no exception.

However, the HRTH talk is not excessively preoccupied with the first two sorts of concerns (*origins* and *authorship*). This may well also be true about kindred social and economic human rights enunciations (e.g. human rights to nutrition, literacy, shelter and housing, access to water as a resource and to water-based resources). In any event, as compared to talk about other kindred rights, HRTH talk seems to more adequately foreground a sustained engagement with the *scope* and *justice* dimensions in the sense explained above. The HRTH emerges primarily in contemporary theory in terms of healthcare justice (hereinafter HCJ). Its *scope* obligations extend, as with all contemporary social and economic human rights values, standards and norms, to State conduct; however, these also extend beyond the State to the realms of medical educational and research establishments, institutions and networks, and especially increasingly to global pharmaceutical industries, and to technologies of self-caring.

This latter deserves a word of explanation. The HCJ notions seek to combine two related but distinct ethical languages – the languages of 'justice' and of 'care' – in a way that the talk about kindred human rights does not. I do not explicitly burden this chapter by revisiting the discourse illustrating the imponderables thus entailed – for example whether the languages of caring constitute, as it were, a world apart from the languages of contemporary human rights, or the ways in which some deep feminist thoughtways – from Carol Gilligan (1993) to Martha Nussbaum (2001) – exemplify the tension between the languages of justice and care. Nor does this chapter directly address aspects of causation of ill-health.

HCJ approaches accentuate the duties of self-care in a way that would seem scarcely appropriate for the related realms of social and economic human rights. It would be simply ethically intolerable to maintain that accessing human rights to nutrition, shelter/housing, literacy or access to water ought to remain predicated on the moral responsibility arising from duties of care to oneself; by contrast, public and institutional healthcare policy regimes that set limits to access to healthcare routinely thrive upon a full acknowledgement of such duties. Even when liable to the indictment of State, market, or legal paternalism, some priorities and limits remain fully set for those who torment their bodies via the ruination of liver through excessive alcoholism, of the lung from excessive smoking, of life-style induced health failures including exposure to communicable diseases, or the human brain via psychotropic and narcotic substances. While such persons may not be justifiably denied HCJ, they remain confronted with a lesser threshold weight for the provision of healthcare services. Further, and in terms of justice obligations, there is an understandable trend towards elevating HRTH as the most basic of all social and economic rights. A minimum of health remains necessary in order to have and enjoy these and other related human rights. Because physical and psychic impairments more deeply affect our right to be and to remain human, our 'right to have rights' (to adapt Hannah Arendt's fecund notion (Arendt 1950)) requires us 'to keep people functioning as closely to normal as possible' (Daniels and Sabin 1997). What this may mean in terms of prioritisation or limit-setting – an institutional feature of most healthcare systems – or by 'fair equality of opportunity,' constitute vexed concerns but perhaps not to the point of denying the implicit ontological elevations of the HRTH discourses. Health (translated here as a modicum of well-being) is a sine qua non for accessibility, exercise and enjoyment of all other human rights. Put another way, one may not have all the human rights without first being *alright*.

The HRTH discourse maintains a rather difficult position between a basic human right to physical survival and the range of quality of life concerns. Conceptions of 'health' oscillate between 'bare life', directed to ensuring physical survival, and the conceptions of 'good life' that accentuate agency and choice. Conditions of bare life remain imposed, almost always violently by social and political structures and events.[1] Impoverishment thus constitutes the regimes of planned global, regional and national policy-making that in the name of 'development' or 'progress' consign vast masses of human beings to forms of living death. Forms of biopower and biopolitics that thus systematically enact impoverishment ordain that the impoverished somehow cheat their ways into survival; here, as it were, 'existence precedes essence'. Bare life is also produced by the insurgent or establishment practices of mass atrocity and politics of cruelty created by war or warlike events, which render entire populations hostages to the practices of 'ethical violence.' Think here of the paradigmatic events in Darfur and Sri Lanka, as well as the 'war on terror' situations. Situations of forced mass migrations, as well as mass disasters caused by multinational capital, archetypically signified by the Bhopal, Agent Orange and Ogoniland catastrophes, further constantly reinvent forms of bare life (Baxi 2004).

In contrast, the HRTH quality of life type discourse continues to invite attention to bare life somewhat differently in the contexts of human well-being that no presently available technology or therapy may ever fully provide. Under these conditions stands articulated a nascent human right to choose termination of an individual life via physician-assisted suicide: the right to a dignified death (Baxi 2009: 123–4). On another register, however, and for those who can afford it, 'good life' considerations emerge in terms of the newly emerging human right to genetic enhancement.[2] All this now furnishes the multiple talks of the town and the gown celebrating new social epistemologies under the banner of bioethics. The HRTH discourse remains shot through with differential access to new technologies, with all their promises and perils (Brownsword 2008; Murphy 2009).[3]

While the extant HRTH and HCJ talkfurnishes some concrete markers for judging the legitimacy of governance decisions, or even structures, legitimacy as such (i.e. belief systems that justify political and legal domination) may still fall short of any adequate HCJ criteria (conceived in terms of fair distribution of healthcare opportunities and facilities). The latter invites consideration of a leading question a long while back in time, enunciated by St. Augustine: 'What is a state without justice but a band of robbers?' This question may further invite a rephrasing: 'What are human rights bereft of justice but playthings of possessive individualism and the producers of designer policy goods in the global marketplace of policy prescriptions?' Or would Augustine have indeed changed his mind, too, and stopped using the 'J' word altogether?

Had he chosen this last option, Augustine would have been in the distinguished company of some HRTH experts, including our eminent friend Professor Paul Hunt who has laboured so hard to produce a remarkable set of human-rights-based indicators for the protection and promotion of HRTH. Professor Hunt invites us to consider HRTH '. . . as a right to an *effective and integrated health system*, encompassing healthcare and the underlying *determinants of health*, which is responsive to national and local priorities, and accessible to all' (UN 2006: 7).[4] An 'effective health system' is now declared as a 'core social institution no less than a court system or a political system' (UN 2006: 7)

This most welcome conceptual reaffirmation of the notion of human right to a '*system*' initially suggests – with John Rawls (1999) – that 'justice' is a virtue of the basic structures of social and political orderings; yet, overall, the Hunt Report remains focused on global social *policy*, rather than global *justice*. The distinction that I thus suggest is by no means an easy one, yet it remains crucial. Public or official policies provide platforms for executive and legislative action; at times, these also provide a basis for informed public criticism and for social action. It may even be agued that public policy regimes are necessary to advance the doing of justice, both in terms of some here-and-now transformations and as a long-run horizon for fashioning just healthcare futures. Yet, at the same moment, it also remains a global social fact that those who seek global healthcare policy may well keep a respectful distance from discourse concerning global health justice. This may be so because: (a) it is no longer globally politically correct to talk about 'justice'; (b) when general theories concerning justice address the tasks of justice (redistribution), they do so on a meta-ethical level that is least apposite to the languages of global social policy; and (c) the languages of justice in any event may often conflict with the HRTH languages. This chapter seeks to offer some partial, and tentative, responses to all these objections.

2 The 'J' word as politically incorrect

There is ample evidence, and not just in relation to HRTH, that it seems no longer politically correct to speak of 'justice' in the context of the normative/institutional United Nations 'system' and related hegemonic 'development' discourses. Every effort is continually at play in avoiding the now dreaded 'J' word. This avoidance is marked by a diasporic dispersal of notions of justice via myriad phrase regimes such as: 'sustainable development,' 'fair globalisation,' 'poverty alleviation,' 'the right to development,' and now even the global social policy statements so insincere as the Millennial Development Goals and Strategies (Baxi 2006).[5] I believe that recourse to the method of 'content analysis' (so often deployed in literature and media studies) will fully demonstrate the several ways in which the UN system hegemonic policy languages, authorise a full ouster of the 'J' word by non-governmental experts (whether in the UN human rights treaty-bodies or the guest artists who feature as Special Rapporteurs or even *ad hoc* independent experts).

Of course all the various ensembles of the United Nations beings speak about the issues of intra-, and inter- national inequity, structural exploitation, impoverishment and unequivocal duties of reasonable help to those who suffer. Yet, it remains true that neither the assemblages of governmental policy actors, nor the variously named independent experts, may afford the reflexive luxury of speaking to the tasks of justice. How may we understand this expulsion of the languages of justice?

Several explanations suggest themselves. First, 'justice' languages remain fraught with indeterminacy compared with policy and rights languages; second, some contemporary acts of justice-theorising do not yield any easy translation into acts of policy; third, and more crucial, because 'justice is conflict' (Hampshire 2000) – the 'J' word summons politics of passion and insurgent political action not always conducive to reasoned deliberation in aid of advancing the consensus on HRTH specific norms and standards; fourth, if alternate languages (such as those mentioned earlier) do equally well the task of exposing structural political injustices and ways of moving ahead, why should there be recourse to 'justice' notions?; and fifth, there is pragmatic value in relegating the uses of the 'J' word, which is then confined to the corridors of subaltern human rights discourses.

The dominant practitioners of subaltern HRTH discourses (those at least speaking on *behalf* of the worst-off humans, if not always *at their behest*) of course contest this indictment of relinquishment and relegation. Yet, it is scarcely the case that justice languages remain any the more 'indeterminate' compared with rights and policy languages. It remains also the case that justice languages often creatively prise open the mystifications produced by global policy languages, as indeed came to pass in the Doha Declaration (WTO 2001) that caveated the 'hard' patent regime for the intellectual/industrial property rights that functioned to protect multinational corporation (MNC) outpricing of access to antiretroviral drugs necessary to combat the HIV/AIDS pandemic. The Doha Declaration[6] thus creatively disrupts via displays of some 'fuzzy' and 'deviant' logics (to here adapt Susan Haack's 'Phrase Regimes')[7] in ways that call the UN–WTO-constituted bluff. Sixth, subaltern critique also frequently suggests that the UN beings – these new epistemic HRTH communities – err egregiously when they feel constrained to *celebrate* some enormous systemic constraints that block action on behalf of the diseased and variously injured, unhealthy, starving and powerless peoples. Rather, it demonstrates that the languages of constraint are carefully crafted to avoid the justice–obligations owed to these peoples. Further, we now know (if any such demonstration were necessary in the first place) that 'scarcity' is a multiple function of misallocation of resources, the combined and uneven acts of a corrupt sovereign, and 'developmental' mal-governance.

True, the divide is now diminishing in a hyper-globalising posthuman era to a point when both sides practice some new incarnations of global practical reason, which enact the pragmatic motif of not making the 'best' the enemy of the 'good.' Subaltern HRTH activists seem to have little choice than to invoke fully the interpretive wonders ushered in by the relevant United Nations Human Rights Treaty Bodies exemplified by the normative regimes of the Committee on Economic and Social Rights General Comment 14 in relation to 'the right to highest attainable standard of health' (CESCR 2000).

The subaltern HRTH talk thus remains always an act of global political hope aimed at providing some secure niches for HRTH, by seeking to recast the conventional recourse to, and inflections arising from, the Kantian and post-Kantian theory of 'imperfect obligations' (Rainbolt 2000: 243). Positivist activist loyalties towards the excessively familiar affirmation of the State obligations to 'respect, protect and fulfil', and in turn of obligations to 'facilitate, provide and promote', the HRTH (CESCR 2000: Para 30) now remain fully offered to view indeed as the best 'weapon for the weak' and vulnerable. Even so, and with sincerest apologies for this heavy remark, the thus fully made available enunciative *embarras de riches* postpones the gains of learning immanent in metaphysical or post-metaphysical theories *of*, and *about*, justice that contest structurally imposed healthcare injustices.

3 The poverty of meta-justice theorising?

Much here depends on how one may privilege/de-privilege 'meta-theory.' Almost by definition, most general theories about 'justice' do not specifically engage all human rights norms and standards as we (meaning here international human rights lawpersons) know these. Meta-theory as, for example, ardent students of John Rawls (1999) and Jürgen Habermas (1990) know well, conceptualises basic liberties and human freedoms distinctively in terms of a thin, and parsimonious, listing of 'primary' moral 'goods'. Neither, to the best of my knowledge and belief, remains fully concerned with HRTH as such. Nor do these have any specifically located range of concerns for the problem of healthcare inequalities and inequities, or the rights to water, food, shelter, housing and livelihood. Rather, they address some key conceptions such as 'liberty,' 'equality' and 'fairness' as the virtues, and 'basic structure of a just society' (to have recourse to the Rawlsian notion). The task is therefore one of translating meta-theory into specifically human rights *regional* approaches to justice, as providing a versatile range of conceptual frameworks and normative tools of immense help towards the realisation of some social and economic human rights. The superbly gifted corpus of Norman Daniels pursues this task of seeking to resituate John Rawls' *A Theory of Justice* (1999), in the field of healthcare. Not many United Nations beings, however, remain persuaded by the demonstration of the truth of Daniels' saying: 'Justice is good for our health' (Daniels *et al.* 1999).[8]

This worthwhile maxim, however, directs attention to HCJ as an affair of intranation HCJ tasks. The nascent approaches to global justice address, on the other hand, the justice-responsibilities of State and State-like actors (the international financial institutions, UN agencies, intergovernmental aid and development networks and the world economic regimes, such as the WTO). This chapter partially unfolds the importance of some of these new approaches to global justice, with the caveat that much considered work remains still needed. It is perhaps time to begin to pursue a rather difficult task concerning the clarification of relationships between justice theories and HRTH discourse. Of course, *theory-aversion* (the synergies of social movement and human rights activisms) that insists on the *irrelevance* of ethical and philosophical inquiry may not serve full well the tasks of HCJ, if only because the anti-theory view almost always contains a series of implicit positionalities collectively fashioned by theory. More pertinent remain acts/performances of *resistance to theory* that incarnate the specificity of the exigent political as a universal norm (Baxi 2008).[9] This problem emerges in terms of the disregard by acts of global social policies that devalue, and indeed thrive upon, some orders of non-, or even anti-human-rights values and considerations.

I believe that understanding justice theories remains both *desirable* and *necessary* for the development of HRTH: desirable because the entire so-called global policy framework concerning the HRTH carries already some *implicit* perspectives or theoretical outlooks regarding HCJ, and necessary at least because HRTH entails a prioritisation of healthcare justice over other related, but also autonomous, human needs/rights regimes. Already active in both are the habits of thought that posit a distinction between a universal *human right to health* and the *specific modelling* of *programs for an affordable human right to healthcare.* It has been well argued that the former remains less ethically coherent and viable than the latter (Buchanan 1984). This sort of anti-theory perspective entirely overlooks the tasks of understanding an ethic of human rights. On another register, we stand confronted with a realm of indistinction between everyone's right to HCJ and health*care policy beneficence-based modelling.* To illustrate, the 'special attention to disadvantaged persons and communities' as a marker of the rights-based approach to health rights reaches nowhere near the dynamic proportion of healthcare justice. I could do no better here than fully quote Daniels:

> Rawls's 'Difference Principle' permits inequalities in income only if they work . . . to make those who are worst off as well off as possible. This principle is not a simple trickle down principle that tolerates any inequality so long as there is some benefit that flows down the economic ladder; it requires a maximal flow downward. It would therefore flatten socioeconomic inequalities in a robust way, assuring far more than a 'decent minimum . . .'
>
> (Daniels 2001: 8)

Let us also look at, in this context, the second component of the Hunt Report which speaks in the highly ritualised United Nations rhetoric of the requirements of a human-rights-based approach for 'the active and informed participation of individuals and communities in policy decisions that affect them' and of 'effective, transparent and accessible monitoring and accounting mechanisms' (UN 2006: 8). Clearly excluded from the range of 'participation' are those who remain inherently incapable of this, such as those exposed to severe psychical impairment, the violated populaces of the variously constituted practices of genocidal governance and politics, and the victims of the MNC-induced archetypal mass disasters, signified by Bhopal, Agent Orange and Ogoniland.

This ritualistic invocation of the mantra of 'participation' simply bypasses some further hard problems. An intransigent threshold question is raised by Norman Daniels and James Sabin (1997). How may any addressal of a general theory of 'elements' of a deliberative democratic accountability extend to 'non-public institutions'? Put another way, how may we proceed to extend to the latter formations the range of requirements of procedural decision-making fairness considerations?

Daniels and Sabin fully pose the difficulties involved in extending this due process paradigm to non-State healthcare providers (managed care organisations (MCOs)). The ways in which State actors/agencies need to resolve the problems of 'distrust, legitimacy, and fairness' (Daniels and Sabin 1997: 305) in proceeding towards some 'limit-setting' decisions manifestly differ with the MCOs (or healthcare organisations (HCOs)). Within the latter zone of what has recently been named as 'pharmacopolitics' (Rawlins 2005), what 'due process' requirements may best be addressed to their 'priority-stetting' agendum?[10] For example, how may we conceive of due process (whether procedural or substantive) in relation to private, industrial, and increasingly global health providers, as yet fully unbound by any specific human rights obligations? Daniels and Sabin (1997) remind us that any mimetic extension of State due process standards may remain entirely unproductive in at least two respects: (a) how may either genre of HRTH or HCJ best proceed to strike a 'fair' balance of the articulate individualised needs for patient-care with the aggregative concerns regarding healthcare needs'; and (b) how may competitive non-State healthcare provision afford the 'best last chance' type access to as yet unproven therapies for a willing populace?

4 Moving from the realm of distribution to production decisions

The rather cruelly expressed global social fact is just this: HRTH, as with other human rights discursive frames, produces a rich range of normative referents, yet the material production servicing the HRTH and HCJ talk lies almost always in so many MNC, global capital and trade-related aspects of intellectual property rights (TRIPS)-intoxicated 'heads' and 'hands'! Global production decisions often determine the contours of any future-based realisation of the HRTH and HCJ. As remains well known, global pharmaceutical corporate governance regime decisions do not address cures or remedies for the deadly diseases in the global South. Its research, drug safety, pricing and marketing policies, and aggressive pursuit of 'evergreen' patenting, continue to mock not just the HRTH/HCJ talk; more poignantly, these also continue to produce the vast masses of suffering and human-rightless third-world humanity.[11]

'Uncle' Marx reminded us a long while ago that one may not justifiably divorce the realms of 'production' and 'distribution'. The ways in which production decisions are made do not merely *condition*, but even *determine* the range of distribution decisions, effects and affects. As such, production relations determine the magnitudes of human and social immiseration. In Volume 1 of *Capital* (1976), Marx painstakingly and poignantly described what may in a later idiom best be described as the human right-to-health costs of the early industrial 'revolution' mode of production. Despite some long and valiant histories of efforts by the ILO, the International Red Cross, and the WHO, the rather exponentially growing global industries and markets (these assortments of non-public institutions, arrangements and networks) still continue to affirm and celebrate the divorce between 'production' and 'distribution' decisions and outcomes.

Further, in the era of a dramatic paradigm shift, from the universal human rights of all human beings towards trade-friendly, market-related human rights of global capital,[12] all this policy talk about 'participation', 'transparency', 'accountability' and 'monitoring' comes to possess a hollow ring! The impunity and immunity that multinational pharmaceutical corporations presently enjoy needs to be fully perforated by the invention of a normative human rights category that instantiates crimes against human health as furnishing the constitutive element of crimes against humanity. This is precisely what I suggested as a maverick *ad hoc* expert responding to a request of the United Nations Secretary General in 1983. My first draft was reproduced verbatim in the first draft of the report to the General Assembly by the Secretary General, but was fully excised in the final report![13]

The general point I wish to make here is not that such attempts at fostering these human-rights-based HRTH approaches are unimportant; rather, the point is to suggest the elements of a critique of expedient, rather than principled, smooth global social policy prose. Once again I revert specifically here to Norman Daniels, for whom, adapting Rawls, '*effective* rights of political participation' entail the working out of the 'fair opportunity principle' that 'assures access to high quality public education, early childhood interventions (including day care) aimed at eliminating class or race [as well one may add gender] disadvantages, and universal coverage for appropriate healthcare' (Daniels 2001: 2). A deeper reason for participatory rationality worthy of full note here is also offered by Daniels. Because consensus on 'distribution principles' is notoriously hard to arrive at, 'fair process' for arriving at 'critical resource allocation decisions' must attend to what he fascinatingly names as 'accountability for reasonableness' (Daniels 2001: 2). This, I believe, suggests more effectively than the Hunt Report phrase-regime an 'attempt to connect views about deliberative democracy to decision-making at various levels, whether *public* or *private*, in our complex health systems' (Daniels 2001: 3).

5 The scope of healthcare justice

There has been considerable discussion with, and since, Norman Daniels' inaugural work concerning the scope of healthcare justice (Daniels 1985). I do not here intend to provide a full review of all this, which remains a task of a future monographic work; but I do wish to highlight some interlocutions that may have pertinence for the further development of HRTH.

First, the notion that healthcare constitutes a '*special* social good' (Daniels 1985: 56) remains attractive because it fully justifies the case for prioritising HCJ needs over other needs, and may thus provide a firm basis for the HRTH talk. It is true, as Daniels and some others maintain, that healthcare needs are distinctive, not just because these present questions of life and death for masses of unfortunately placed humanity, but because various health impairments entail 'greater curtailment of an individual's share of the normal opportunity range' (Daniels 1985: 43). Clearly, staggeringly high rates of mortality and morbidity, often reproduced along class, caste, race and gender axes, constitute a 'global disease burden' which summon howsoever 'imperfect duties' for concerted social action in way that other related, but distinct, basic human needs type discourses do not.

Via all its talk about impoverishment[14] as a 'social determinant' of violations of HRTH, the Hunt Report (UN 2006: 5) highlights the need to take a fuller account of the task of conversion of insistent basic healthcare needs into global human-rights-based social policy languages that also speak to other relatively '*non-health-based*', although no less *significant*, human needs such as shelter/housing, literacy, education and employment. Crucial as this narrative shift remains, it also blurs some bright lines between the relatively autonomous, even if somewhat hegemonic, HRTH frameworks. I revert soon enough, in this context, to some exemplary thinking offered by Thomas Pogge.

The Hunt Report insists, as already noted, on the identity of a healthcare system as 'core social institution no less than a court system or a political system' (UN 2006: 7). A major difficulty here arises in terms of some autopoiesis frameworks offered initially by Niklas Luhmann and developed since then by the gifted reworking of Gunther Teubner (Přibán and Nelken 2001; Teubner 1988). Were we to deploy the languages of systems analysis, how may the much-vaunted assertions of HRTH proceed to demarcate the relations between a system and its environments? Is it the case after all that the other systems (such as the rights to food and water, livelihood and shelter, literacy and education) merely furnish 'environments' for the HCJ system? Using the Hunt metaphor of the 'core institution,' it is I hope not too unfriendly to ask: which here is the 'core' and which the 'periphery' or (to evoke Derrida) the 'dangerous supplement'?

Second, Daniels' view that healthcare needs should be ordered in terms of individuals and peoples having healthcare rights and entitlements defined within a set of basic 'institutions regulated by fair equality of opportunity principles' (Daniels 2008: 57) does not go so far as to affirm each individual human being's coequal human right to health. What stands rather fully affirmed here is a close cousin of the shorthand that Paul Hunt after all offers by way of a universal human 'right to an *effective and integrated health system*, encompassing healthcare and the underlying *determinants of health*, which is responsive to national and local priorities, and accessible to all' (UN 2006: 5). It still remains important to recall the discussion in the preceding section of the many ways in which this offering constitutes a 'poor cousin' to what Daniels has in full view. What then may follow in terms of the development of the HRTH (Cust 1993)? Put another way, the duties of beneficence here constantly seem to collide with those arising from the notion of healthcare *justice*.

Third, some thinkers insist on a broader scope for justice theorising that warrants some further inclusion in terms of translating constraints into opportunities for doing better by the diseased and variously injured, unhealthy, starving and powerless peoples. On this view, the development of HRTH ought to fully recognise and combine further diverse concerns, such as ways of financing/resourcing healthcare systems, cost-containment, healthcare technologies and the range of self-inflicted health problems.[15]

To aggravate further: the scope problem surely suggests a crucial move from theories of justice to those of bioethics. These at least invite engagement from HCJ theorists with the posthuman condition constituted by new genetics, nanotech and robotic (GNR) technologies of disembodiment, as signified by the continuing diminishment of clear lines between human, animal and machine, especially via artificial intelligence, bio- and nano- and *Star Wars*-type developments in military technologies. In part, I have addressed the concerns thus arising elsewhere (Baxi 2007). The Hunt Report fails to engage this discourse of the posthuman in all its varied implications for HRTH.

6 Circumstances of healthcare justice and approaches to global justice

We also need to attend to the scope of HCJ theorising in terms of what Rawls named as 'circumstances of justice' (1999: 11). True, as Rawls insists, and as Daniels fully concedes, considerations of, and for, HCJ arise only in an economy of *scarcity*, rather than, of super-*abundance*. If so, two basic concerns arise (Rawls 1999: 14; Daniels 2008: 24): first, how may we proceed to construct regimes of 'scarcity' within national political economy; and second, what causal connections may be said to exist between globally constituted and locally produced regimes of 'scarcity'?

Given space, as well as my own competence constraints, I may not here fully dwell on these concerns. Even so, it remains intolerably clear that the circumstance of HCJ remains more, rather than less, fully designed by the acts and performances of the political production of scarcity. These are fully uninformed by concerns about redistributive HCJ for the worst-off within nations, and among globally constituted HRTH worst-off peoples, as cruelly depicted by the multiple-Oscar-winning performances of the Bollywood film *Slumdog Millionaire*. The much-vaunted HRTH discourse here reaches its manifold terminal limits. Much the same may affect our otherwise gifted HRTH narratives, which fail to register, or even fully elide the distinction between war and 'civil' strife-torn circumstances of HCJ and the relatively stable contexts of peaceful (or pacified) rights-based development policy regimes. This peacetime concern for circumstances of justice furnishes little or no warrant for un-mindfulness about, in the superbly enchanting, and cruellest, United Nations phrase-regime, 'human rights in difficult situations'.

The notion of 'difficult situations' remains almost entirely devoid of the various contexts of organised collective political violence. First, in 'severely divided societies', to here invoke a gifted and poignant phrase of Donald Horowitz (1985), both incumbent governmental regimes and insurgent ones engage in violence that creates conditions destructive of the culture of HRTH, as well the institutional availability of healthcare systems. The so-called 'civil' wars vary in intensity, duration, and immediate and long-term effects. Second, the histories of the early, middle and late phases of the Cold War need to be fully acknowledged in any global social policy for healthcare, and the approaches to global justice as well as theories of HCJ must take account of some duties of reparative health justice. Third, a programme of economic sanctions pursued unilaterally or within some international legal framework that imposes intergenerational health costs invites again some serious engagement with the notion of reparative health justice. Fourth, the stated objectives and conduct of the ongoing two 'terror' wars – the 'war *on* terror' and also the 'war *of* terror' (Baxi 2005) – deserve close scrutiny on the HCJ platforms. Fifth, so do mass disasters caused by multinational corporations mentioned above. Sixth, nor may the producers of HRTH, and HCJ theories, be altogether be left of the hook, as it were, as and when their narratives remain rather ambivalent concerning the near-absolute disregard, and violation, of HCJ rights of undocumented aliens, migrant workers, persons caught in the vicious webs of human sexual trafficking, and many others equally subject to a denial in the retail and also wholesale of social, economic and cultural human rights.

It is also clear that HCJ theorising needs to approach the tasks of justice outside territorially organised States, societies and peoples, because stopping at national frontiers impoverishes HRTH approaches. Transboundary health risks continue to grow apace, the most recent being the instances provided by 'mad cow disease,'

SARS and avian flu, and some industrial mass disasters like oil spills or nuclear meltdowns. These create adverse health consequences that respect no territorial or ideological frontiers; they affect the human health of us all in various ways. All this leads us towards understanding what implications the emergence of some nascent approaches to global or, as some would designate this, planetary justice,[16] may have on the art of HCJ theorising.

There is unfortunately no theoretical agreement concerning how the tasks of fashioning a theory of justice across borders may be fully addressed. Yet, we ought at least to note the fact that the great Rawls in his *Law of Peoples* (2001) declined to extend the difference principle to global justice theorising on the grounds of respect for the moral autonomy of communities of rational, reasonable and decent, if not fully liberal, peoples. This further animated his rather spartan conception of duties of assistance, beyond the situations of natural disasters and some obligations of mitigating societies burdened with unfavourable natural circumstances (for example, landlocked societies). In contrast, both Charles Beitz and Thomas Pogge, in particular, have consistently questioned this approach and in its place have offered normative approaches that fully sustain alternate visions of global justice (Beitz 1979, 1981; Pogge 2002b; Baxi 2001).

In this context, I particularly invite your attention to two articles by Thomas Pogge: 'Human Rights and Global Health: A Research Programme' (2005) and 'Responsibility for Poverty-Related Ill Health' (2002a). I will not dwell at very great length on what I believe to be its many-splendoured contribution, in particular toward a theory of global justice in relation to healthcare. A couple of general remarks will have to perforce suffice as I draw this chapter to a conclusion. In the later article, Pogge (2005) actually says, or comes very close to saying, that contemporary human rights values, norms and standards, especially the Universal Declaration of Human Rights, provide standards of critical morality and an ethic of understanding for a theory of, or about, global justice. In the earlier article, Pogge (2002a) maintains the familiar cosmopolitan position that argues against forms of compatriotism (the notion that we owe moral obligations to co-nationals and few, if any, to non-nationals).[17] Specifically, he develops a HRTH stance here in which he problematises this distinction to the point of asserting that the medical conditions of 'foreigners', in whose incidence we are materially involved, have greater moral weight for us than compatriots' medical conditions, in whose incidence we are not materially involved (Pogge 2002a). He further distinguishes between a 'passive concept of justice' which defines healthcare justice solely in terms of on the distribution of relevant goods and ills it brings about and an 'active concept of justice' which 'diverts some attention from those who *experience* justice and injustice' and directs it towards to 'those who *produce* them' (Pogge 2002a: 77).[18] The consequent elaboration of 'relational responsibilities' thus places the burden of proof, as it were, on the producers, rather than the victims, or otherwise consumers of healthcare justice. The further suggestion that there are simply no bright lines here, is a cogent ethical call for 'shared' as against 'distributed' political responsibility, echoing that made in a different context by the late lamented Iris Marion Young (2004).[19]

To be sure, Pogge anticipates fully further theory-contentions and remains philosophically vigilant about these. Speaking entirely for myself, I need to say two things, First, I remain anxious about the identification of contemporary human rights values, standards, and norms with a theory of, or about, global justice, while not questioning at all the use of practical reason for healthcare justice in the contemporary circumstance of justice-theorising. My reason for saying this is my belief that human rights languages remain very diverse and signify, among other things, the fact that the languages of human rights remain also the languages of governance and the syndrome of shared sovereignty (Baxi 2008). Second, I would have further appreciated, in the light of delineation of circumstances of justice, a more adequate elaboration of what I have already named as an approach to global health *reparative justice*. These need to go beyond forms of contemporary implicatedness of the present duties owed by co-nationals to non-nationals, to include the burdens of inter-generational justice obligations owed by those said to have benefited from such 'ancient wrongs' such as slavery and colonisation, the Cold War, and some contemporary wars against human rights and world pluralisms constituted by diverse assemblages of neoliberal and globalising practices of global governance. However, I believe that the research agendum that Pogge offers in his 2005 article has the potential of addressing further these additional theoretical burdens, especially by way of a *Programschrift* for reconciling the market-friendly and trade-related human rights paradigm with the paradigm of the universal human rights of all human beings.

All this goes much beyond (to invoke *Hamlet*) the 'stale, weary, and unprofitable uses' of the global social policy discourse that all too often masquerades as HRTH talk.[20] I wonder what *more* may we ask, or expect from, a theory of global HCJ?

Notes

1 Some religiously mandated practices justify the taming or disciplining the body as necessary for the pursuit of the life of the Spirit. Though I do not here pursue any spiritual conceptions of health as well-being, all these matter decisively for the pious.
2 For a recent analysis, see Savulescu (2006).
3 For example, see the sustained, precious provocation offered by Nussbaum (2006).
4 Emphasis added. The following discussion draws on the Special Rapporteur's Report to the UN Commission on Human Rights (UN 2006). The latter is referred to hereinafter as 'the Hunt Report'.
5 For more charitable, but no less exasperated analysis, see Alston (2005).
6 See further the precious analysis by Aginam (2005).
7 See Haack (1993, 2001).
8 See also Daniels (2001).
9 See, further, chapter 1 in Baxi (2007).
10 See Buchanan (1984: 311–35).
11 The contemporary tasks of global HCJ thus entail further conversation with the socialist-type HRTH protection best offered in health studies, for example, by a constant reference to the salience of the Cuban healthcare system. At the very least, it needs saying, even in the post-Marxian world, that some 'socialist' HCJ still may command the merit of anxious deliberative attention.
12 On this contrast, see chapter 8 in Baxi (2008).

13 I have produced the full text of my report in Baxi (1994).

14 I have forlornly maintained the need to speak of 'impoverishment' rather than 'poverty'. 'Impoverishment' directs attention to the fact that people are constantly made 'poor' by willed performances of public policy measures and choice. See, for some further elaboration, my Introduction to Baxi (1989).

15 See Fleck (1989). Incidentally, this call for a 'constitutional model for healthcare justice', while no doubt important, remains undeveloped. The HRTH indicators contained in the Hunt Report may contribute to remedying this.

16 See Lohmann (2006).

17 Unusually enough, I have addressed some of these concerns in as arcane a sphere as private international law or the conflict of laws, see Baxi (1999).

18 Emphasis added.

19 See also, the literature cited in Baxi (2008).

20 For example, consider the politics of naming the Commission on Intellectual Property Rights, Innovation and Public Health (2006) and the not too strange inversion in the order of words registered by the final title of the Report.

Bibliography

Aginam, O. (2005) *Global Health Governance: International Law and Public Health in a Divided World.* Toronto: University of Toronto Press.

Alston, P. (2005) 'Ships Passing by in the Night: The Current State of Human Rights and Development Discourse Seen through the Lens of Millennial Development Goals', *Human Rights Quarterly*, 27: 755–829.

Arendt, H. (1950) *The Origins of Totalitarianism.* New York: Harcourt Brace.

Baxi, U. (2009) 'Judging Emmanuel Levinas? Some Reflections on Reading Levinas: Law, Politics, Justice', *Modern Law Review*, 72: 116–29.

Baxi, U. (2008) *The Future of Human Rights.* 3rd ed. Delhi: Oxford University Press.

Baxi, U. (2007) *Human Rights in a Posthuman World.* Delhi and Oxford: Oxford University Press.

Baxi, U. (2006) 'Human Rights and Development: Law, Policy and Governance', in Kumar, C. R. and Srivastava, D.K. (eds.) *A Report for all Seasons? Small Notes on Reading in Larger Freedom.* Hong Kong: Butterworth Lexis/Nexis, pp. 415–514.

Baxi, U. (2005) 'The "War on Terror" and the "War of Terror": Nomadic Multitudes, Aggressive Incumbents, and the "New International Law"', *Osgoode Hall Law Journal*, 43: 7–43.

Baxi, U. (2004) 'The "Just War" for Profit and Power: The Bhopal Catastrophe and the Principle of Double Effect', in Bomann-Larsen, L. and Wiggen, O. (eds.) *Responsibility in World Business: Managing Harmful Side-effects of Corporate Activity.* Tokyo: United Nations University Press, pp. 175–201.

Baxi, U. (2001) 'The Failure of Deliberative Democracy and Global Justice', in Enwezor O. *et al.* (eds.) *Democracy Unrealized: Document 11_Platform 1* Ostfildren-Ruit, Hatje Cantz Publishers, pp. 113–32.

Baxi, U. (1999) 'Mass Torts, Multinational Enterprise Liability, and Private International Law', *Recueil des Cours*, 276: 297–428.

Baxi, U. (1994) *Mambrino's Helmet? Human Rights for a Changing World.* Delhi: Har-Anand Publishers.

Baxi, U. (ed.) (1989) *Law and Poverty: Critical Essays.* Bombay: N.M. Tripathi.

Beitz, C. R. (1981) 'Economic Rights and Distributive Justice in Developing Societies', *World Politics* 33: 321–46.

Beitz, C. R. (1979) *Political Theory and International Relations*. Princeton, NJ: Princeton University Press.

Brownsword, R. (2008) 'Regulating Nanomedicine – The Smallest of Our Concerns?', *NanoEthics* 2: 73–86.

Buchanan, A. E. (1984) 'The Right to a Decent Minimum of a Health Care', *Philosophy and Public Affairs*, 13: 55–78.

CESCR (2000) *Substantive Issues Arising in the Implementation of the International Covenant on Economic, Social and Cultural Rights: The Right to the Highest Attainable Standard of Health.* General Comment No. 14, 22nd Sess., Agenda Item 3. UN Doc. E/C.12/2000/4.

Commission on Intellectual Property Rights, Innovation and Public Health (2006) *Public Health, Innovation and Intellectual Property*. Geneva: WHO.

Cust, K. F. T. (1993) 'Justice and Rights to Health Care', *Reason Papers*, 18:153–68.

Daniels, N. (2008) *Just Health. Meeting Health Needs Fairly*. Cambridge: Cambridge University Press.

Daniels, N. (2001) 'Justice, Health, and Healthcare', *American Journal of Bioethics* 1: 1–16.

Daniels, N., Kennedy, B. and Kawachi, I. (1999) 'Why Justice is Good for Our Health: The Social Determinants of Health Inequalities', *Daedalus*, 128: 215–51.

Daniels, N. and Sabin, J. (1997) 'Limits to Heath Care: Fair Procedures, Democratic Deliberation and the Legitimacy Problem for Insurers', *Philosophy and Public Affairs*, 26: 303–50.

Daniels, N. (1985) *Just Health Care*. Cambridge: Cambridge University Press.

Fleck, F.M. (1989) 'Just Health Care (II): Is Equality Too Much?', *Theoretical Medicine and Bioethics*, 10: 301–10.

Gilligan, C. (1993) *In a Different Voice. Psychological Theory and Women's Development*. Cambridge, MA: Harvard University Press.

Haack, S. (2001) 'An Epistemologist in the Bramble-Bush: At the Supreme Court with Mr. Joiner', *Journal of Health Politics, Policy and Law*, 26: 217–48.

Haack, S. (1993) *Evidence and Inquiry: Towards Reconstruction in Epistemology*. Oxford: Blackwell.

Habermas, J. (1990) *Moral Consciousness and Communicative Action*. Cambridge: Polity.

Hampshire, S. (2000) *Justice is Conflict*. Princeton, NJ: Princeton University Press.

Horowitz, D. (1985) *Ethnic Groups in Conflict*. Berkeley, CA: University of California Press.

Lohmann, L. (2006) 'Carbon Trading: A Critical Conversation on Climate Change, Privatization, and Power', *Developmental Dialogue*, 48: 1–360.

Marx, K. (1976) *Capital. A Critique of Political Economy vol. 1*, London: Penguin.

Murphy, T. (2009) 'The Texture of Reproductive Choice: Law, Ethnography, and Reproductive Technologies', in Murphy, T. (ed.) *New Technologies and Human Rights*. Oxford: Oxford University Press, pp 222–45.

Nussbaum, M. C. (2006) *Frontiers of Justice: Disability, Nationality, Species Membership*. Cambridge, MA: Harvard University Press.

Nussbaum, M. C. (2001) *Women and Human Development. The Capabilities Approach*. Cambridge: Cambridge University Press.

Pogge, T. W. (2005) 'Human Rights and Global Health: A Research Programme', *Metaphilosophy*, 36: 182–209.

Pogge, T. W. (2002a) 'Responsibility for Poverty-Related Ill Health,' *Ethics & International Affairs*, 16: 72–9.

Pogge, T. W. (2002b) *World Poverty and Human Rights: Cosmopolitan Responsibilities and Reforms*. Cambridge: Polity Press.

Přibán, J. and Nelken, D. (eds.) (2001) *Law's New Boundaries: The Consequences of Legal Autopoiesis*. Dartmouth: Ashgate.

Rainbolt, G. (2000) 'Perfect and Imperfect Obligations', *Philosophical Studies*, 98: 233–56.

Rawlins, M. D. (2005) 'Pharmacopolitics and Deliberative Democracy', *Clinical Medicine*, 5: 471–5.

Rawls, J. (2001) *The Law of Peoples*. Cambridge, MA: Harvard University Press.

Rawls, J. (1999) *A Theory of Justice*. Cambridge, MA: Harvard University Press.

Savulescu, J. (2006) 'Justice, Fairness, and Enhancement', *Annals of the New York Academy of Sciences*, 1093: 321–38.

Teubner, G. (ed.) (1988) *Autopoietic Law: A New Approach to Law and Society*. Florence: European University Institute.

UN (2006) *The Right of Everyone to the Enjoyment of the Highest Attainable Standard of Physical and Mental Health: Report of the Special Rapporteur, Paul Hunt. UN ESCOR, Commission on Human Rights, 62nd Sess., Agenda Item 10*. UN Doc. E/CN.4/2006/48.

WTO (2001) *Doha Ministerial Declaration*. 20 November. WT/MIN(01)/DEC/1.

Young, I. M. (2004) 'Responsibility and Global Labour Justice', *Journal of Political Philosophy*, 12: 365–88.

3 Developing and applying the right to the highest attainable standard of health

The role of the UN Special Rapporteur (2002–2008)

Paul Hunt and Sheldon Leader [1]

1 Introduction

In 2002, the United Nations established the position of Special Rapporteur on the right of everyone to the enjoyment of the highest attainable standard of physical and mental health ('right to the highest attainable standard of health' or 'right to health'). Between 2002–2008, the first appointee, Paul Hunt, submitted some 30 reports on a wide range of right-to-health issues, as well as reports on several States, and GlaxoSmithKline, the major pharmaceutical company (Freeman 2009).

We aim to provide a brief introduction to a few elements of Hunt's work and also a preliminary response to the critique developed in Upendra Baxi's contribution to this book. Our aim is both constructive and defensive. Constructively, we signal some of the innovations in thinking about the right to health that have been, and remain, necessary in order to bring the general phrases and principles enunciated in legal instruments into contact with the real world of strategic decision-making and practical implementation. Defensively, we aim to show how Hunt's approach to the mandate withstands Baxi's critique.

The first section outlines the evolution of Hunt's approach to the mandate. The second summarises the framework that he uses to analyse or 'unpack' the right to the highest attainable standard of health. The third explores one critical element of this framework: accountability. The fourth introduces the right-to-health features of a health system. Finally, the fifth provides a brief response to Baxi's critique.

2 Evolving approaches to the UN mandate, 2002–2008

In 2002, the UN Commission on Human Rights adopted a resolution establishing a new 'special procedure': the Special Rapporteur on the right of everyone to the enjoyment of the highest attainable standard of physical and mental health (Commission on Human Rights 2002). Although the Commission had been establishing 'special procedures' in relation to civil and political rights for some decades, it was not until the late 1990s that it turned its attention to economic, social and cultural rights. The Government of Brazil, supported by other developing countries, drove the initiative to establish a 'special procedure' on the right to health. Developed countries, on the other hand, were circumspect. Indeed, two – USA and Australia – voted against the resolution when it came before the UN Economic and Social Council.

The Special Rapporteur is not a member of the UN secretariat, but independent, reporting directly to the General Assembly and Human Rights Council (which recently replaced the Commission). Although supported by the UN secretariat, the position of Rapporteur is unpaid. During his tenure, Hunt raised funds to enable the appointment of a few researchers to assist with the discharge of the mandate.

The Special Rapporteur's mandate is set out in the founding UN resolution of 2002, as well as some later resolutions (Commission on Human Rights 2002). These long resolutions may be very briefly summarised as requiring the Special Rapporteur to help States better promote and protect the right to the highest attainable standard of health.

After lengthy consultations, especially with civil society and UN bodies, Hunt set out in 2003 his broad approach to the mandate (UN 2003). In brief, he identified three main objectives: to raise the profile of the right to health as a fundamental human right; to clarify the contours and content of the right to health; and to find practical ways of operationalising the right to health. He recognised that these objectives could only be realised with the advice and assistance of a wide range of allies. Crucially, he identified two interrelated themes that would recur throughout his reports: (a) poverty and the right to health (b) discrimination and the right to health.

Like other Special Rapporteurs, his output had three official forms: thematic reports, country reports, and 'communications', i.e. letters of complaint. Over six years, he wrote some 30 reports, including annual reports on 'communications'; all of these are in the public domain. The thematic reports look at issues such as sexual and reproductive health rights, access to medicines (including the duties of States and pharmaceutical companies), mental disability, water and sanitation, maternal mortality, the skills drain, the health-related Millennium Development Goals, and indicators and benchmarks (UN 2004a, 2006a, 2007a, UN 2005c, UN 2004b, UN 2006b). One thematic report publishes Human Rights Guidelines for Pharmaceutical Companies in relation to Access to Medicines (UN 2008c). The country reports are on Mozambique, Peru, Romania, Uganda, Lebanon/Israel (following the war of mid-2006) and Sweden (UN 2005a, 2005d, 2005e, 2006c, 2006d, 2007d). Reports on India and Colombia/Ecuador (regarding the aerial spraying of glyphosate along their common border) are forthcoming. An additional country report looks at donors' human rights responsibilities of international assistance and cooperation in health by exploring Sweden's role in relation to (a) Uganda's health sector and (b) the health-related activities of the World Bank and International Monetary Fund (UN 2008a). Under the rubric of country reports, he also reported on the World Trade Organization, Guantánamo Bay and the pharmaceutical company GlaxoSmithKline (GSK) (UN 2004c, 2006e, 2009). Two of these reports (Guantánamo Bay and Lebanon/Israel) were co-authored with other 'special procedures'. All of these country reports were preceded by visits to the place or institution in question, except Guantánamo Bay, where the USA imposed unacceptable conditions on the visit (specifically, the authorities refused to allow private interviews with the detainees). All the thematic and country reports were presented, in writing and orally, to either the General Assembly or Human Rights Council/Commission, where they were discussed. When country reports are presented, the relevant Governments have a right of reply. Unfortunately, this facility was not extended to GSK, although the company wished to address the Council after the presentation of the Special Rapporteur's report. Instead, GSK's written response to the report was distributed in the Council.

It is not possible here to review the Special Rapporteur's methods of work, although it should be emphasised that he and his colleagues consulted very widely before preparing either thematic or country reports. These consultations were not only with Ministers, public officials, civil society groups and academics. They also included listening to the most disadvantaged, such as internally displaced people living in the conflict zone of northern Uganda, the inhabitants of remote villages in Peru's sierra and the bombed-out inhabitants of south Beirut and southern Lebanon.

When reviewing these reports, it is possible to identify some trends and phases in the Special Rapporteur's approach to the mandate.

Promulgated by the UN Committee on Economic, Social and Cultural Rights (CESCR) in 2000, General Comment 14 represents a critically important stage in the evolution of our understanding of the right to the highest attainable standard of health (CESCR 2000). The General Comment shaped much of the Special Rapporteur's work. However, as its name suggests, it provides a general analysis of the right to health. Building on this analysis, the Special Rapporteur's reports endeavour to make the right to health more specific and accessible. Thus, some reports take the analysis provided by General Comment 14 and apply it to specific elements of the right to health, such as access to medicines (UN 2006a). Others apply the General Comment to specific right-to-health issues, such as the skills drain, and specific groups of people, such as those with mental disabilities (UN 2005c, 2005b). Also, country reports apply the Comment's general analysis to the right to health in specific jurisdictions. It is one thing to talk generally about how health-related facilities and services must be available, accessible, acceptable and of good quality; it is something else to specifically apply that analysis to access to medicines, sanitation, indigenous peoples, and so on.

This specific application of General Comment 14 enabled the Special Rapporteur to develop and refine elements of the analysis set out in general terms in the Comment. For example, while the Comment briefly addresses the controversial issue of international assistance and cooperation, several reports of the Special Rapporteur develop the idea of donors' human rights responsibilities of international assistance and cooperation in health (UN 2008). The Comment briefly underscores the crucial importance of accountability, while most of the

Special Rapporteur's reports insist upon, consider and apply this vital human rights concept, sometimes in considerable detail, as discussed in Section 4. The Comment devotes two important paragraphs to indicators and benchmarks, and, as we will see, the Special Rapporteur wrote three reports on this issue, the last of which sets out a methodology for a human-rights-based approach to health indicators (UN 2006b). This process of applying General Comment 14 to specific contexts helped to refine the analytical framework for 'unpacking' the right to health, which we briefly summarise in Section 3.

The application and refinement of this analytical framework was necessary but not sufficient. Experience showed that some health workers were understandably uncomfortable with the legal and abstract nature of the framework. For example, some did not readily grasp all of the framework's elements, such as the idea that States have duties to respect, protect and fulfil the right to health. Some found the concept of accountability elusive. For many health workers, the framework remained conceptual, legal and divorced from the realities of public health and medicine. This is a powerful indictment because, without the active engagement and support of many health professionals, the right to health will never realise its potential to reduce suffering and save lives.

This led to closer cooperation with health workers and a revised approach typified, for example, by the reports on Peru and Uganda (UN 2005d, 2006c). The Ugandan report focuses on a single issue: neglected diseases, i.e. those diseases mainly afflicting the poorest people in the poorest communities. The analytical framework set out in General Comment 14, and subsequently refined, informs the Ugandan report, but the report endeavours to be more operational in its discussion about, for example, incentives to encourage health professionals to work in Uganda's underserved areas; participation and Uganda's village health teams; the burden placed on the Ugandan authorities by the uncoordinated health interventions of the international community; the need to enhance research and development for neglected diseases; the importance of an integrated health system; accountability and an enhanced role for the Ugandan Human Rights Commission; and so on. As in the Peru report, the framework's elements are still there – access, accountability and others – but they are applied in a more practical, operational manner. The Ugandan report is also important because it is the first country report to focus on a single issue (neglected diseases), and therefore enables more detailed discussion and recommendations.

Around this time there were other shifts in emphasis in the Special Rapporteur's approach to his mandate. For example, he began repeatedly to emphasise the common ground between medicine, public health and the right to health; the indispensable role of health workers in the delivery of the right to health; and how the right to health can help health workers deliver their professional objectives. All these arguments are found in the earliest work of the Special Rapporteur but, as the mandate unfolded, they began to have greater prominence (Hunt 2006). If they are to succeed, however, such arguments cannot rely upon excessively legal phrases and abstract analysis that risk alienating many health workers whose primary interest is the formulation and practical implementation of health policies, programmes and projects. At the same time, the empowering, transformative message of human rights must not be sacrificed.

Discussions with health workers revealed another problem. The thematic reports were focusing on specific issues, specific groups of people, and so on. Moreover, some of the country visits were now single issue, such as Uganda (neglected diseases) and India (maternal mortality). While this focused approach brings major advantages, it has a serious drawback: it can lead to a fractured consideration of the right to the highest attainable standard of health, making it more difficult to look at larger, systemic issues upon which the right to health depends. This focused approach was the mandate's equivalent of narrow vertical health interventions that, without care, can undermine the wider health system. Interestingly, General Comment 14 does not clearly provide a systemic approach to the right to health.

This legitimate criticism of the Special Rapporteur's approach was one of the factors that led to an examination of health systems from the right-to-health perspective. Also, at last the international community was beginning to recognise that many health systems were failing and collapsing. After years of neglect, the clarion cry was to strengthen health systems. For these and other reasons, the Human Rights Council passed a resolution in 2006 asking the Special Rapporteur to prepare a report on health systems and the right to health (Human Rights Council 2006). Because of its importance, we explore this issue in Section 5.

Throughout his tenure, the Special Rapporteur distinguished between judicially and policy-oriented processes. Although the two approaches are closely related and mutually reinforcing, the former aims to promote and protect the right to health via the elaboration of rules and principles derived from case law, building up general guidance from the lessons learned via the resolution of particular disputes. Judicial and quasi-judicial forms of accountability exemplify this approach. In his reports, the Special Rapporteur frequently insists that the judicial contribution to the right to health should be deepened and become more widespread. We introduce some of the relevant case law in Section 4.

Policy-oriented processes have a different focus: the right to health is brought to bear upon, and integrated into, all relevant local, national and international policy-making initiatives. Whereas the judicial approach is aimed at remedying the existing defective implementation of human rights and rules, the policy approach is more forward-looking. It takes the initiative and helps to build appropriate health policies and programmes, without waiting to see if a court or quasi-judicial body declares that the existing arrangements are deficient. Satisfying the demands of the right to health is still the target, as it is in the judicial approach, but the solution sought by the policy approach comes from developing appropriate health initiatives, not from the resolution of cases brought by victims in vindication of their entitlements. Policies must have the operational procedures and features, as well as health outcomes, arising from the legally binding right to health and subject to judicial and quasi-judicial supervision and enforcement. The policy approach, which led the Special Rapporteur to consider the integration of the right to health into Poverty Reduction Strategy Papers, the health-related Millennium Goals, trade policies, health system strengthening, and so on (UN 2004a, 2004b, 2004c, 2008b), depends upon techniques and tools – indicators, benchmarks, impact assessments, and others – that demand close cooperation across a range of disciplines. Critically, medicine and public health have an indispensable contribution to make to the policy approach. By way of illustration, in Section 5 we signal what happens when the right to health is brought to bear upon policies that aim to strengthen health systems.

The policy approach is not a soft option. For example, as we show in Section 5, it places a legal obligation on policymakers to ensure that health systems include a comprehensive health plan that encompasses the public and private sectors, outreach programmes for the disadvantaged, and so on. The policy approach is not without accountability: it includes a requirement that policymakers are subject to judicial and non-judicial forms of review.

The right to health requires both approaches, and if this fundamental human right is not brought to bear upon local, national and international policymaking, it runs the risk of marginal relevance, surfacing only when, as a last resort, it is argued in courts – institutions that are often inaccessible to the disadvantaged and impoverished.

3 The right-to-health analytical framework

3.1 Overview

As signalled in Section 2, the UNCESCR, Special Rapporteur and many others have developed a way of 'unpacking' or analysing the right to health with a view to making it easier for interested parties, such as adjudicators, policymakers and civil society groups, to understand and apply. The analytical framework is made up of ten key elements and has general application to all aspects of the right to health, including underlying determinants of health such as access to water and sanitation. We briefly summarise the framework here, elements of which are used by other contributors to this volume. Nobody suggests that the framework provides answers to some of the complex, critical issues raised by health, such as how to deal with competing health priorities within a finite budget. It addresses a prior, and more elementary, problem: how to move beyond the one-line right-to-health formulations found in legal texts and towards a more detailed understanding of the key components of the right to the highest attainable standard of health. As signalled in Section 2, the framework has to be applied to specific elements of the right to health (e.g. access to medicines); issues (e.g. the skills drain); groups of people (e.g. those with mental disabilities); and those with right-to-health duties, such as States and pharmaceutical companies.

3.2 National and international human rights laws, norms and standards

The relevant laws, norms and standards relevant to the particular issue, programme or policy must be identified. These will include both general provisions and standards relating to the right to health, in addition to international instruments that relate to specific groups and contexts (UN 2003: Annex 1).

3.3 Resource constraints and progressive realisation

International human rights law recognises that the realisation of the right to health is subject to resource availability. Thus, what is required of a developed State today is of a higher standard than what is required of a developing State. However, a State is obliged – whatever its resource constraints and level of economic development – to realise progressively the right to the highest attainable standard of health (UN 1966). In essence, this means that a State is required to be doing better in, say, two years time than it is doing today. The principle of non-retrogression means that there is a (rebuttable) presumption that a State may not backslide. In order to measure progress (or the lack of it) over time, indicators and benchmarks must be identified; for this reason, one of Hunt's reports provides a human-rights-based approach to health indicators (UN 2006b).

3.4 Obligations of immediate effect

Despite resource constraints and progressive realisation, the right to health also gives rise to some obligations of immediate effect. Sometimes known as core obligations, these include the duty to avoid discrimination, provide essential drugs as defined by WHO, and adopt a comprehensive national health plan of action (CESCR 2000). These are obligations without which the right would be deprived of its raison d'être and as such they are not subject to progressive realisation, even in the presence of resource constraints. The precise scope of these immediate obligations has not yet been clearly defined; for the health and human rights communities, this remains important work-in-progress.

3.5 Freedoms and entitlements

The right to health includes both freedoms (for example, the freedom from discrimination or non-consensual medical treatment and experimentation) and entitlements (for example, the provision of a system of health protection that includes minimum essential levels of water and sanitation). For the most part, freedoms do not have budgetary implications, while entitlements do.

3.6 Available, accessible, acceptable and good quality

All health services, goods and facilities should comply with each of these four requirements (CESCR 2000). An essential medicine, for example, should be available within the country. Additionally, the medicine should be accessible. Accessibility has four dimensions: accessible without discrimination, physically accessible, economically accessible (i.e. affordable), and accessible health-related information. As well as being available and accessible, health services should be provided in a culturally acceptable manner. This requires, for example, effective coordination and referral with traditional health systems. Lastly, all health services, goods and services should be of good quality; a medicine, for example, must not be beyond its expiry date.

There is a similarity between these requirements and the four 'As' of public healthcare envisaged by the Declaration of Alma-Ata in 1978: geographical accessibility; financial accessibility; cultural accessibility; and functional accessibility (WHO 1978).

3.7 Respect, protect, fulfil

This subsidiary framework relates to the tripartite obligations of States to respect, protect and fulfil the right to the highest attainable standard of health, as explained and used by CESCR, the Committee on the Elimination of Discrimination Against Women (CEDAW) and the Sub-Commission on the Promotion and Protection of Human Rights (CESCR 2000). A version of this subsidiary framework is also enshrined in the Constitution of South Africa.

The obligation to respect, for example, places a duty on States to refrain from interfering directly or indirectly with the enjoyment of the right to health. The obligation to protect means that States must prevent third parties from interfering with the enjoyment of the right to health. The obligation to fulfil requires States to go beyond the requirement of non-interference by placing a positive requirement on them to adopt the necessary measures, including legislative, administrative and budgetary, to ensure the full realisation of the right to the highest attainable standard of health.

3.8 Non-discrimination, equality and vulnerability

Because of their crucial importance, the analytical framework demands that special attention be given to issues of non-discrimination, equality and vulnerability in relation to all elements of the right to the highest attainable standard of health (CESCR 2000). This might mean, for example, that extra resources are directed to ensure that health-related services are accessible, at a higher cost per head to the state, to both, for example, an ethnic minority living in a remote region and those living closer to metropolitan areas. As we observe in Section 5, equality and non-discrimination are akin to the health concept of equity, and all three components have a social justice component.

3.9 Active and informed participation

Participation is grounded in internationally recognised human rights, such as the rights to participate in the formulation and implementation of government policy, to take part in the conduct of public affairs, and to freedom of expression and association. In the specific context of the right to health, this requires that there be an opportunity for individuals and groups to participate actively and in an informed manner in health-related planning, policymaking, implementation, monitoring and accountability processes that affect them (CESCR 2000). Community participation is one of the themes recurring throughout the Declaration of Alma-Ata. Of course, some traditional elites are likely to resist the active and informed participation of the disadvantaged. Those working on health and human rights have given insufficient attention to participation, which is why a recent monograph by Helen Potts, *Participation and the Right to the Highest Attainable Standard of Health*, is especially timely (Potts 2009).

3.10 International assistance and cooperation

In line with obligations envisaged in the UN Charter and some human rights treaties, developing countries have a responsibility to seek international assistance and cooperation, while developed States have some responsibilities towards the realisation of the right to health in developing countries (Mesquita 2008). Donors' human rights responsibilities of international assistance and cooperation in health are explored in several of Hunt's reports, including the examination of Sweden's role in relation to (a) Uganda's health sector and (b) the health-related activities of the World Bank and International Monetary Fund (UN 2008a).

3.11 Monitoring and accountability

The right to health introduces globally legitimised norms or standards from which obligations or responsibilities arise. These obligations have to be monitored, and those responsible have to be held to account. Transparent, effective and accessible accountability mechanisms are among the most crucial characteristics of the right to the highest attainable standard of health. Because of their importance, we devote Section 4 to the critical issue of monitoring and accountability.

3.12 Summary

These ten key elements of the right-to-health analytical framework underscore what the right to health contributes to medicine and public health. For example, the preoccupation with non-discrimination, equality and vulnerability requires a State to take effective measures to address the health inequities that characterise some populations. The focus on active and informed participation requires a State to adopt, so far as possible, a 'bottom-up' participatory approach in health-related sectors. The requirement of monitoring and accountability can help to ensure that health policies, programmes and practices are meaningful to those living in poverty.

Crucially, the key elements of the framework are not merely to be followed because they accord with sound management, ethics, social justice or humanitarianism. States are required to conform to the key features as a matter of binding law. Moreover, they are to be held accountable for the discharge of their right-to-health responsibilities arising from these legal obligations.

We will now introduce accountability, one element of the right-to-health framework, and also explore the practical application of the framework to health systems (Section 5). In this way, we endeavour to show the potential of the right to the highest attainable standard of health to empower the disadvantaged and strengthen health systems.

4 Monitoring and accountability

4.1 Overview

Accountability is one of the central features of human rights. Without accountability, human rights can become no more than window-dressing. Whether human rights are applied to development, poverty reduction, trade, health systems, neglected diseases, maternal mortality, HIV/AIDS or anything else, they require that accessible, transparent and effective mechanisms of accountability be established.

Accountability provides individuals and communities with an opportunity to understand how those with human rights responsibilities have discharged their duties. Equally, it provides those with human rights responsibilities the opportunity to explain what they have done and why. Where mistakes have been made, accountability requires redress. In the context of the right to health, redress has many forms, including compensation, restitution, rehabilitation (e.g. the provision of medical or public health services), full and public disclosure, public apology, new legislation, revised policies and programmes, and so on. However, accountability is not necessarily a matter of blame and punishment. Sometimes called 'constructive accountability', it may be a process that helps to identify what works, so it can be repeated, and what does not, so it can be revised (Freedman 2003). Effective monitoring is an essential precondition of accountability.

In the context of the right to the highest attainable standard of health, there are many different types of monitoring and accountability mechanisms, including national human rights institutions, Health Commissioners, democratically elected local health councils, public hearings, patients' committees, impact assessments, judicial proceedings, and so on. A human right as complex and extensive as the right to the highest attainable standard of health requires a range of effective, transparent, accessible, independent accountability mechanisms. The media and civil society organisations have a crucial role to play (Potts 2008; Yamin 2008).

In some States, the private health sector, while playing a dominant role, is largely unregulated. Crucially, the requirement of human rights accountability extends to both the public and private health sectors. Additionally, it is not confined to national bodies; it also extends to international actors working on health-related issues. Accountability mechanisms are urgently needed for all those – public, private, national and international – working on health-related issues.

Although human rights demand accountability, this does not mean that everybody working in health and human rights – all health professionals and specialised agencies – have the task of holding duty-bearers to account. The health and human rights movement needs human rights advisers, implementers and enablers, as well as those whose job it is to hold duty-bearers to account. All these functions will rarely reside in one organisation or individual. For example, while the WHO, UNICEF and UNFPA should be human rights advisers, implementers and enablers, it is not their primary task to hold States to account. The accountability function must be provided by some organisation or person, but probably not by a specialised UN agency, unless the agency decides to establish a discreet independent procedure and body for this purpose.

As already observed, monitoring and accountability is an integral feature of the right-to-health analytical framework that the Special Rapporteur has applied and refined since 2002. Repeatedly, his reports have sought to enhance monitoring and accountability in relation to the right to the highest attainable standard of health. Here, we signal three illustrative components of the Special Rapporteur's work on monitoring and accountability.

First, the international right to health, and some national right-to-health provisions, are subject to progressive realisation. Thus, it is essential to devise a methodology for measuring and monitoring progressive realisation, otherwise States may use this concept as a way of delaying, or altogether avoiding, their human rights obligations. Accordingly, the Special Rapporteur devotes three reports to the problem of how to measure and monitor progressive realisation, the third of which sets out a human-rights-based approach to health indicators (UN 2006b). No doubt this methodology can be improved, but it is no longer possible for a State to say that it awaits a way of measuring and monitoring the progressive realisation of the right to health. The human-rights-based approach to health indicators helps to deepen the accountability of States, as well as others with health and human rights responsibilities.

Second, national human rights institutions are among the non-judicial mechanisms that have an important role to play in enhancing the accountability of States and others in relation to the right to the highest attainable standard of health. For many years, national human rights commissions, ombudsmen and similar institutions have held authorities accountable in relation to civil and political rights, and they can play a comparable role in relation to economic, social and cultural rights, including the right to health. With an appropriate mandate, as well as the necessary functions, powers, capacity and independence, an ombudsmen-type institution can adjudicate on complaints, conduct public enquiries, promulgate standards, make recommendations and hold accountable those with right-to-health responsibilities. Moreover, national human rights institutions can be more accessible to the disadvantaged than national courts of law.

The Special Rapporteur recommended, for example, that an independent mental health commissioner be established as a matter of urgency to address the widespread problems concerning mental healthcare in Romania (UN 2005e). Sweden is rightly famous for, and proud of, the ombudsman institution. While it has a number of ombudsmen undertaking important human rights work, the right to health is not fully encompassed within their various mandates. Thus, the Special Rapporteur recommended that a Swedish national human rights institution be established to address the right to health and other human rights issues (UN 2007b). He recommended that the Ugandan Human Rights Commission establish a unit to monitor and hold accountable all actors – public, private, national and international – in relation to neglected diseases and the right to health (UN 2006c). His report on the skills drain – the migration of health professionals from developing to developed countries – observes that this is a perverse subsidy by the poor to the rich, which undermines health systems and the right to health in migrants' countries of origin. This, he argues, is inconsistent with donors' human rights responsibilities of international assistance and cooperation in health, and he recommends that donors establish independent national offices to monitor the impact of governments' policies on the right to health in developing countries, and hold the authorities accountable (UN 2005c). In both his Human Rights Guidelines for Pharmaceutical Companies in Relation to Access to Medicines and report on GlaxoSmithKline, the Special Rapporteur recommends that an independent mechanism be established to monitor and hold accountable pharmaceutical companies in relation to their right-to-health responsibilities to enhance access to medicines (UN 2008c, 2009). In some cases, these recommendations have been acted upon. The Ugandan Human Rights Commission, for example, has established a specialist unit to focus on monitoring and accountability in relation to the right to health. Of course, these non-judicial mechanisms of monitoring and accountability are not enough, but, like courts, they have a role to play. Judicial accountability is the third approach to monitoring and accountability that the Special Rapporteur has repeatedly advocated. We will briefly introduce this in the following section.

4.2 *Judicial accountability: a selection of health and health-related cases*

4.2.1 *Overview*

The limitations of judicial processes are well known. However, as the following cases illustrate, courts can clarify the meaning of the right to health, as well as other health-related rights, and also secure better health-related services for individuals and communities. While some of the cases rely upon the right to health, focusing on either heathcare (e.g. access to emergency medical treatment) or the underlying determinants of health (e.g. access to uncontaminated food), other decisions rely upon health-related rights, such as the right to life, where interpreted by the courts to mean protecting health. Some of the cases rely upon both the right to health and other health-related rights. The cases are broadly grouped under some of the overlapping, interrelated key elements of the right-to-health analytical framework outlined in Section 3.

4.2.2 *Progressive realisation, resource availability and immediate obligations*

The Constitution of South Africa includes a Bill of Rights, which, under section 27, recognises the right of access to healthcare services. According to the Bill of Rights, the State is required to take reasonable measures, within its available resources, to achieve the progressive realisation of this human right. The case of *Minister of Health v. Treatment Action Campaign* concerned State provision of Nevirapine, an antiretroviral drug used to prevent mother-to-child-transmission (MTCT) of HIV.[2] Applying the concepts of progressive realisation and resource availability, the Constitutional Court confirmed that the Government must 'act reasonably to provide access to the socio-economic rights identified in the Constitution on a progressive basis' and it ordered the authorities to 'devise and implement, within its available resources, a comprehensive and co-ordinated programme to recognise progressively the rights of pregnant women and their new-born children to have access to health services to combat MTCT of HIV'.

As already observed, while many elements of the right to the highest attainable standard of health are subject to progressive realisation and resource availability, the right also gives rise to some obligations of immediate effect that are subject to neither. Equal treatment between women and men, for example, is not subject to progressive realisation and resource availability. A State may not argue that it does not currently have sufficient resources to provide equal services for women and men, and so, for the time being, it is going to focus on services for men, but it will progressively make available the same services for women over the next few years just as soon as the necessary funds become available. As the next case shows, some Courts have held that other elements of the right to health also give rise to immediate obligations that are subject to neither progressive realisation nor resource availability.

In *Paschim Banga Khet Mazdoor Samity v. State of West Bengal*, the Supreme Court of India held that the Government could not escape its responsibility, on account of financial constraints, to provide emergency treatment. In this case, a man fell from a train and suffered serious head trauma.[3] He was taken to a number of State hospitals, but none were able to provide him with emergency treatment: they lacked bed space, as well as trauma and neurological services. The issue before the Court was whether inadequate medical facilities for emergency treatment constituted a denial of the right to life.

The Court found that it was the duty of a State to ensure that medical facilities for emergency treatment are adequately available. It required the State to ensure that primary health centres are equipped to provide immediate stabilising treatment for serious injuries and emergencies. In addition, the Court ordered the State to increase the number of specialist and regional clinics around the country available to treat serious injuries, and to create a centralised communication system among State hospitals, so that patients could be transported immediately to the facilities where space is available. The Court recognised that substantial expenditure was needed to ensure that medical facilities were adequate. However, it held that 'a State could not avoid this constitutional obligation on account of financial constraints'.

4.2.3 Available, accessible, acceptable and good quality

As signalled in Section 3, and illustrated by the following cases, health facilities, goods and services must be available, accessible, acceptable and of good quality. The precise practical application of these requirements – available, accessible and so on – may vary from one country to another depending upon, for example, resource availability.

a) *Available*: The right to health requires functioning health facilities, goods and services to be available in sufficient quantity throughout a State. In the case of *Mariela Viceconte v. Ministry of Health and Social Welfare*, Mariela Viceconte, and the National Ombudsman, asked the Court to order the Argentine Government to take protective measures against haemorrhagic fever that threatened 3.5 million (COHRE 2003).[1] More specifically, they asked the Court to order the Government to produce a WHO-certified vaccine (Candid–1) for Argentine haemorrhagic fever. According to the Court, it was the Government's responsibility to make healthcare available in a situation where the existing healthcare system, including the private sector, was not protecting individuals' health. In light of the Constitution's incorporation of international treaties that recognise the right to health, the Court found that the Government had not 'fulfilled its obligations to make available the Candid–1 vaccine'. Because the private sector saw the production of the vaccine as unprofitable, the Court ordered the State to produce Candid–1.

b) *Accessible*: The right to health imposes an obligation on a State to ensure that health facilities, goods and services are accessible to everyone within its jurisdiction. In this context, access has four main dimensions. The facilities, goods and services must be: physically accessible; economically accessible (i.e. affordable); and accessible without discrimination. Also, subject to confidentiality of personal data, health information must be accessible.

In *Minister of Health v. Treatment Action Campaign*, as well as considering the issue of resource availability and progressive realisation, the South African Constitutional Court also considered whether or not Nevirapine was accessible. The Government provided Nevirapine at only two research and training sites per province. The drug could also be obtained from private medical providers. As a result, mothers and their babies who did not have access to the research and training sites, and who could not afford access to private healthcare, were unable to gain access to Nevirapine. The Government argued that 'until the best programme has been formulated and the necessary funds and infrastructure provided . . . the drug must be withheld from mothers and children who do not have access to the research and training sites'. However, the Court held that the State's limited provision of Nevirapine was unreasonable. It ordered that the Government act without delay to provide, inter alia, the drug in public hospitals and clinics when medically indicated.

c) *Acceptable*: The right to health requires that all health facilities, goods and services must be respectful of medical ethics, such as the requirements of informed consent, and culturally appropriate. In *Andrea Szijjarto v. Hungary*, a Hungarian woman of Roma origin alleged that she had been coercively sterilised.[5] In 2000, she went into labour and was taken to hospital. Upon examination, it was found that the foetus had died and a Caesarean section was urgently needed. On the operating table, she was asked to sign a form consenting to the Caesarean section, as well as a 'barely legible note' handwritten by the doctor, giving permission for sterilisation. The reference to sterilisation was in a language that she did not understand. In her application to the Committee on the Elimination of Discrimination against Women, she alleged that this conduct constituted a violation of her right to appropriate healthcare services, as well as her right to decide freely and responsibly on the number and spacing of her children. The Committee decided that Hungary had 'failed to provide Andrea with appropriate information and advice on family planning, and ensure that Andrea had given her fully informed consent to the operation' and recommended that the Government provide the applicant with appropriate compensation.

d) *Good quality*: Health facilities, goods and services must be scientifically and medically appropriate, and of good quality. The Bangladeshi Supreme Court considered this requirement in *Dr. Mohiuddin Farooque v. Bangladesh*.[6] Dr. Farooque challenged the failure of the authorities to take effective measures to deal with a large consignment of imported skimmed milk powder that contained radioactive material. The Court found that the contaminated powder was a threat to health and thereby gave rise to a breach of the right to life under Article 32 of the Bangladeshi Constitution. Through an interpretation of Article 18 of the Constitution, which requires the State to improve the quality of health and nutrition, the Court interpreted the right to life to include, among others, the 'protection of health and normal longevity of an ordinary human being'. The Court ordered the Government to test the consignment's radiation level.

4.2.4 Duties to respect, protect and fulfil

As outlined in Section 3, States have duties to respect, protect and fulfil the right to the highest attainable standard of health.

a) *Respect*: The duty to respect requires the State to refrain from denying or limiting equal access for all persons, including prisoners, minorities, asylum seekers and illegal immigrants, to preventive, curative and palliative health services.

K.L. v. Peru concerned a 17-year-old Peruvian who was denied a therapeutic abortion.[7] When K.L. was 14 weeks pregnant, doctors at a public hospital in Lima diagnosed the foetus with anencephaly, a foetal abnormality that would endanger K.L.'s health if pregnancy continued. Under Peru's Criminal Code, therapeutic abortion is permissible when necessary to safeguard the life or health of the woman. However, K.L. was denied a therapeutic abortion by the director of the hospital. She was compelled to carry the foetus to term and forced to feed the baby until his inevitable death, several days after birth. According to K.L., Peru's failure to respond to the reluctance of some of the medical community to comply with the legal provision authorising therapeutic abortion violated the International Covenant on Civil and Political Rights (ICCPR). The Human Rights Committee held that, by denying the complainant's request to undergo an abortion in accordance with the Peruvian Criminal Code, the Government was in breach of its obligations under Article 7 and other provisions of ICCPR. The Committee decided, inter alia, that the Government must take steps to prevent the future occurrence of similar violations. One way for the Government to conform to its existing obligations under the Criminal Code is to provide clear, appropriate guidance to health professionals about when a therapeutic abortion is lawful and should be available.

b) *Protect*: The duty to protect requires States to take measures that prevent third parties (e.g. private companies) from interfering with the right to the highest attainable standard of health.

In *Social and Economic Rights Action Center and Center for Economic and Social Rights v. Nigeria*, members of the Ogoni community in Nigeria alleged that the military Government had violated their rights to health and a clean environment, as well as several other human rights, by facilitating the operations of oil companies in Ogoniland.[8] The applicants alleged that the operations of an oil consortium, comprising the Nigerian National Petroleum Company and Shell Petroleum Development Corporation, contaminated the environment, which led to serious and widespread health problems among the Ogoni people. The African Commission on Human and Peoples' Rights held that the Ogoni had suffered violations of a number of their human rights, including their rights to health and a clean environment, as a result of the Government's failure to prevent pollution and ecological degradation. It found that the Government had failed to adequately regulate and monitor the oil consortium. The Commission issued a number of orders; for example, environmental and social impact assessments should be prepared in the future, and health and environmental information should be made available.

c) *Fulfil*: The duty to fulfil requires States to adopt appropriate legislative, administrative, budgetary, judicial and other measures towards the full realisation of the right to health.

In *Purohit and Moore v. Gambia*, mental health advocates witnessed the inhuman treatment of mental health patients in the psychiatric unit of the Royal Victoria Hospital in Gambia.[9] They submitted a complaint to the African Commission on Human and Peoples' Rights on behalf of the mental health patients detained in the unit. The principal legislation governing mental health in Gambia was the Lunatics Detention Act (1917). The complaint pointed out that, from the human rights perspective, this colonial legislation was seriously deficient in numerous respects. The Commission held that the legislation was 'lacking in terms of therapeutic objectives'; 'matching resources and programmes' for the treatment of persons with mental disabilities were also inadequate. The Commission ordered the Government to replace, as soon as possible, the Lunatics Detention Act with a new legislative scheme for mental health that was compatible with the African

Charter on Human and Peoples' Rights, as well as more specific international standards for the protection of persons with disabilities.

4.3 Summary

Without accountability, a State can use progressive realisation and the scarcity of resources as an excuse to do virtually nothing – or to respond to whichever interest group has the loudest voice. Independent, effective and accessible mechanisms of accountability compel a State to explain what it is doing, and why, and how it is moving, as expeditiously and effectively as possible, towards the realisation of the right to health for all. Supported by appropriate legislation, courts can ensure that the interests of the poor and disadvantaged – so often overlooked – are given due weight. Of course, courts are not a panacea; for example, sometimes authorities are slow to comply with court orders. Also, in some circumstances, the right to health may be used by the better-off and privately insured to extract from the State expensive medicines and other treatments that are unavailable on private insurance – thereby removing resources from publicly funded programmes that are designed to address the health of disadvantaged individuals, communities and populations. At first sight, this is a powerful complaint, but it can be addressed readily by appropriate legislative drafting that requires adjudicators to take into account the social justice implications of those decisions that come before them (Ferraz and Vieira 2008).

As one form of accountability, courts have a significant role to play in the promotion and protection of health-related rights. Non-judicial accountability mechanisms are also needed. The design of appropriate, independent accountability mechanisms demands creativity and imagination. Often associated with accountability, lawyers must be willing to understand the distinctive characteristics and challenges of the right to the highest attainable standard of health, and to learn from the rich experience of medicine and public health. For example, the health community is accustomed to maternal death audits or reviews. Might these audits or reviews provide a vehicle for enhancing human rights accountability in relation to maternal mortality?

Based upon a detailed understanding of the right to health, the Colombian Constitutional Court recently issued a 400-page landmark judgment, which effectively ordered a phased restructuring of the country's health system, by way of a participatory and transparent process, based upon current epidemiological information (Yamin and Parra-Vera 2009). We now turn to the key features of a health system that are demanded by the right to the highest attainable standard of health.

5 Right-to-health features of health systems

5.1 Overview

In his contribution to this volume, Baxi considers one of Hunt's reports that is mainly devoted to a methodology that sets out a way of measuring and monitoring the progressive realisation of the right to the highest attainable standard of health (UN2006b). In seven short paragraphs, however, the report also briefly introduces the idea that the right to health depends upon having in place 'an effective, integrated, responsive health system, encompassing healthcare and the underlying determinants of health, accessible to all'. This was written and presented to the United Nations in 2006, and the Human Rights Council responded by adopting a resolution that asks the Special Rapporteur to identify and explore 'the key features of an effective, integrated and accessible health system' (Human Rights Council 2006). He was asked to undertake this task 'bearing in mind the level of development of countries and from the perspective of the right to the highest attainable standard of physical and mental health'. Two years later, the Special Rapporteur presented to the Council his 25-page discussion on the right-to-health features of a health system (UN 2008b). This report includes a passage (which space does not permit us to summarise here) that draws an analogy between the rights to health and a fair trial: it suggests that the right to health can help to establish a health system in much the same way that the right to a fair trial helps to establish a court system. In turn, this 2008 report generated a number of other publications, most especially a 38-page co-authored article called 'Health systems and the right to health: an assessment of 194 countries', published by *The Lancet* (Backman *et al.* 2008). While the original handful of paragraphs that attracted the attention of Baxi has grown considerably, certainly the ideas and their application remain works-in-progress.

In the following paragraphs, we do not attempt to provide a list of essential services and facilities that are needed for a well-functioning health system. Rather, we identify a number of additional, and frequently neglected, features arising from the right to the highest attainable standard of health that are informed by health good practices and required of all health systems.

5.2 WHO's health system building blocks

The Declaration of Alma-Ata identifies some vital components of an effective health system. The Declaration is especially instructive because of its public health, medicine and human-rights aspects, and it provides compelling guidance on the core obligations of the right to health (WHO 1978).

Other attempts have been made to identify what constitutes a functioning health system (WHO 2000). WHO identifies six essential building blocks that make up health systems: health services (medical and public health); health workforce; health information system; medical products, vaccines and technologies; health financing; and leadership, governance and stewardship (WHO 2007a). Although debatable, these building blocks provide a useful way of looking at health systems, and can be thought of as building blocks for the realisation of the right to health. However, a health system might have all these building blocks but still not serve human rights. For example, the system might include both medical care and public health, but not secure fair access, or there might be a health information system, but key data might not be suitably disaggregated.

A major challenge for human rights is to apply or integrate the right to health across the six building blocks. The right-to-health analytical framework set out in Section 3 has to be systematically and consistently applied to health services, health workforce, health information, medical products, financing and stewardship – that is, all the elements that together constitute a functioning health system. The right-to-health analysis of availability, accessibility, cultural acceptability, quality, participation, international assistance and cooperation, monitoring and accountability, etc. can be applied to health systems to identify some of the right-to-health features of health systems, encompassing what health systems do (for example, providing access to essential medicines and safe drinking water) and the way in which they function (for example, transparently, in a participatory process and without discrimination). Health systems run the risk of being impersonal, top-down and dominated by experts, but the right to health places the well-being of individuals, communities and populations at the centre. Irrespective of which of the many definitions of a health system is used, all the following features should be part of any health system.

5.3 Legal recognition

Countries should give recognition to the right to health in national law and by ratifying relevant human-rights treaties. In some countries, legal provisions on the right to the highest attainable standard of health are generating significant case law (Singh *et al.* 2007). For example, Hogerzeil and colleagues analysed 71 court cases from 12 countries, and concluded that in 59 cases access to essential medicines was enforced through the courts as part of the right to health (Hogerzeil *et al.* 2006). However, legal recognition is just one of the first steps on a long and difficult journey to realising the right to health. Without follow-up from social movements, health workers, progressive government ministers and public officials, activist courts and international support, in addition to governmental respect for the rule of law, legal recognition is likely to be an empty promise (Palmer *et al.* 2009).

5.4 Standards

Although important, legal recognition of the right to health is usually confined to a general formulation that does not set out in any detail what is required of those with responsibilities for health. For this reason, countries must not only recognise the right to health in national law, but also ensure that there are more detailed provisions clarifying what society can expect by way of health-related services and facilities. For example, provisions are needed for quality and quantity of drinking water, blood safety, essential medicines, the quality of medical care, etc. Such clarifications may be provided by laws, regulations, protocols, guidelines and codes of conduct. The WHO has published important standards on various health issues (WHO 2008).

Many others have also contributed; for example, the Sphere Project provides minimum standards for responses to disasters (Sphere Project 2004). Clarification is important for providers, so that they know what is expected of them, and also for those for whom the service or facility is intended, so they know what they can legitimately expect.

5.5 Participation

Health systems must also include institutional arrangements for active and informed participation in strategy development, policymaking, implementation and accountability by all relevant stakeholders, including disadvantaged individuals, communities and populations. Examples of such participation include conferences to develop national health plans in Brazil and Peru; a legislative requirement of Maori participation in New Zealand's District Health Boards; village health teams in Uganda; and the participatory transfer of an HIV/AIDS clinic from Médecins Sans Frontières to the Guatemalan Ministry of Health (Potts 2009). Participation improves health outcomes (Manandhar 2004).

5.6 Transparency

Tempered by the confidentiality of personal data, this requirement applies to all those working in health-related sectors, including countries, international organisations, public–private partnerships, business enterprises and civil-society organisations (CESCR 2000). The Medicines Transparency Alliance, funded by the UK Government, is an alliance of governments, international agencies, pharmaceutical companies and civil-society organisations, committed to increasing transparency of information on the quality, availability and pricing of essential medicines in the public, private and non-profit sectors.

5.7 Equity, equality and non-discrimination

Health systems must be accessible to all, including those living in poverty, minority groups, indigenous people, women, children, people living in slums and rural areas, people with disabilities, and other disadvantaged individuals, communities and populations. Additionally, health systems must be responsive to the particular health needs of women, children, adolescents, elderly people, and so on (CESCR 2000). Outreach programmes are needed to ensure that disadvantaged people have the same access as more privileged people. Several European governments, for example, have established Roma health mediator programmes. As members of the Romany community themselves, the mediators aim to improve community health by mediating between patients and health workers during consultations, and communicating with Romany communities on behalf of the public health system. Although the programmes have limitations, mediators have greatly assisted some Romany (Open Society Institute 2005).

The right-to-health principles of equality and non-discrimination are akin to the health concept of equity. All three concepts have a social justice component. In some respects, equality and non-discrimination, reinforced by law, are more powerful than equity (Braveman and Gruskin 2003). For example, if a Government or other body does not take effective steps to tackle discrimination, it can be held to account and required to take remedial measures.

5.8 Respect for cultural difference

From the right-to-health perspective, health systems must be respectful of cultural difference (CESCR 2000; UNFPA 2004). Health workers must be sensitive to issues of culture, ethnicity and sex; strategies must be in place to enable indigenous people to study medicine and public health, and so on (UN 2005d).

5.9 Quality

All health-related services and facilities must be of good quality (CESCR 2000). For example, water quality regulations and standards consistent with the WHO guidelines for the quality of drinking water should be in place. The good quality requirement also extends to the way patients and others are treated: health workers must treat patients and others politely, with respect. Because medicines may be counterfeited, States must establish appropriate regulatory systems (Hunt and Khosla 2008). In Nigeria, for example, there is evidence that the National Agency for Food and Drug Administration and Control's dual strategy of strengthening the regulatory environment, while encouraging intolerance of counterfeit drugs through public enlightenment campaigns, is improving medicine safety and quality (Akunyili 2006).

5.10 Planning

Some important implications arise from the right to health being subject to progressive realisation and resource availability. The crucial importance of planning is recognised in the Declaration of Alma-Ata, General Comment 14, and elsewhere (WHO 1978; CESCR 2000; Green 2007). States must have comprehensive national health plans, encompassing both the public and private sectors, for the development of health systems; because the plans have to be evidence-based, a situational analysis with disaggregated data is needed before the plan is drafted. Health research and development should also inform the planning process (Hunt *et al.* 2007).

The plan must include certain features, such as clear objectives (and how these are to be achieved), timeframes, effective coordination mechanisms, reporting procedures, a detailed budget, financing arrangements (national and international), indicators and benchmarks to measure achievement, and accountability devices. Indicators and benchmarks are already commonplace features of many health systems, but they rarely have all the elements that are important from a human-rights perspective, such as appropriate disaggregation (CESCR 2000).

The identification of indicators and benchmarks to measure the progressive realisation of the right to health is a national and international process that involves countries, international organisations, the UNCESCR, and others. A wealth of data is available at the global level, some of which is highly relevant to the right to health. But are international bodies making other data important to the right-to-health perspective available? If not, countries may wrongly assume that these other data, and the issues to which they relate, are less important. Many countries look to UN bodies for technical assistance, ideas and leadership. Whether or not UN bodies are providing data that are highly relevant to the right to health available at a global level is an important issue. According to *The Lancet* report of 2008 on health systems and the right to health, much of the data that is important from the right-to-health perspective is not yet being collected at the international level (Backman *et al.* 2008).

A fair, transparent, participatory, and inclusive process for prioritising competing health needs is required, one that takes into account explicit criteria, such as the well-being of those living in poverty, and not just the claims of powerful groups with vested interests (UN 2007a). The process of prioritisation should give particular attention to the core obligations identified in General Comment 14 because they are required of all countries, whatever their stage of economic development. As we observed in Section 3, one of the core obligations is to adopt and implement a national public health strategy and plan of action, on the basis of epidemiological evidence, which addresses the health concerns of the whole population (CESCR 2000).

Before the finalisation of the plan, key elements must undergo impact assessment to ensure that they are likely to be consistent with national and international legal obligations, including those relating to the right to the highest attainable standard of health (MacNaughton 2009). In addition, the present realisation of the right to health must be maintained, although this might be waived in exceptional circumstances.

Progressive realisation does not mean that a government is free to choose whatever measures it wishes to take so long as they reflect some degree of progress. General Comment 14 requires that governments take deliberate, concrete and targeted steps to ensure progressive realisation as quickly and effectively as possible (CESCR 2000).

Progressive realisation, maximum available resources and core obligations need closer conceptual and operational attention. Some courts (as in *Minister of Health v. Treatment Action Campaign*) have rejected the idea of core obligations, and required that government policies are reasonable. Other courts have taken the same position as the UNCESCR in General Comment 14, finding that some health-related responsibilities are so fundamental that they are subject to neither progressive realisation nor resource availability (Yamin and Parra-Vera 2009). This position most closely matches the right to health: progressive realisation is an important concept with a crucial role, but only up to the boundaries of core obligations.

5.11 Referral systems

Health systems should have a mix of primary (community-based), secondary (district-based) and tertiary (specialised) facilities and services, providing a continuum of prevention and care (WHO 2000). The system also needs an effective process by which health workers assess whether patients will benefit from additional services and refer patients from one facility or department to another. Referrals are needed between alternative health systems (e.g. traditional health practitioners) and mainstream health systems. The absence of an effective referral system is inconsistent with the right to health.

5.12 Coordination

Health systems and the right to health depend on effective coordination across a range of public and private stakeholders (including non-governmental organisations) at the national and international levels. Effective coordination between various sectors and departments, such as health, environment, water, sanitation, education, food, shelter, finance and transport is important for health systems, which also require coordination within sectors and departments, such as ministries of health. The need for coordination extends to policymaking and delivery of services (WHO 2000). Uganda has recently added several interventions, such as de-worming of children, supplementation with vitamin A and health promotion information, to its Child Health Days. Now known as Child Health Days Plus, these days depend on, and reinforce, improved coordination between and within sectors and national and international partners, including civil society (WHO 2007b).

5.13 International cooperation

Health systems have international dimensions, including the control of infectious diseases, the dissemination of health research and regulatory initiatives, such as the revised International Health Regulations (WHO 2008). The international dimension of health systems is reflected in countries' human rights responsibilities of international assistance and cooperation, which can be traced through the Charter of the UN, the Universal Declaration of Human Rights, and some more-recent international human-rights declarations and binding treaties (Mesquita 2008; UN 2008a). At the least, all countries have a human rights responsibility to cooperate on trans-boundary health issues and to do no harm to their neighbours. High-income countries have an additional responsibility to provide appropriate international assistance and cooperation in health for low-income countries. High-income countries should especially help others fulfil their core obligations. The Swedish International Development Cooperation Agency, for example, supports several stakeholders with crucial roles in relation to the right to health in Uganda. The Agency has given funds to various organisations: the Ugandan Government; WHO for its human rights work in Uganda; the Uganda Human

Rights Commission; and civil society organisations, including Straight Talk, which aims to increase understanding of adolescence, sexuality and reproductive health (UN 2008a). For their part, low-income countries have a responsibility to seek appropriate international assistance and cooperation to help them strengthen their health systems.

General Comment 14 confirms that the human-rights responsibility of international assistance and cooperation in health extends to countries' actions as members of international organisations (CESCR 2000). Scandinavian countries, for example, have proposed a trust fund for justice and human rights in the World Bank (UN 2008a).

5.14 Legal obligation

Crucially, the right to the highest attainable standard of health gives rise to legally binding obligations. Health systems must have, for example, a comprehensive national health plan, outreach programmes for the disadvantaged, a minimum package of health-related services and facilities, effective referral systems, arrangements to ensure the participation of those affected by decision making in health, respect for cultural difference, and so on. One of the distinctive contributions of the right to the highest attainable standard of health is that it reinforces good health practices with legal obligation and accountability. States are legally obliged to take all appropriate steps to implement the right-to-health features of health systems. Of course, some governments implement these features without reference to the right to health. But many governments do not ensure that these features are in place, and, in these cases, the right to health has an especially important role.

5.15 Monitoring and accountability

We have already emphasised that accountability is among the essential features of the right to the highest attainable standard of health (Section 3) and later we explored this feature in more depth (Section 4), so we will not repeat this discussion, but rather emphasise that accountability in respect of health systems is often extremely weak. Sometimes the same body provides health services, regulates and also holds to account. In some countries, the private health sector is largely unregulated and unaccountable. Accountability is often little more than a device to check that public funds for a health system were spent as they should have been. Of course, that is important, but human rights accountability is much broader: it is also concerned with ensuring that health systems are improving, and the right to the highest attainable standard of health is being progressively realised, for all, including disadvantaged individuals, communities and populations. As observed in Section 4, something as complex and important as a health system needs a range of effective, transparent, accessible and independent mechanisms, which hold accountable the public and private sectors, as well as international bodies that affect the ability of the health system to deliver for all.

Moreover, as already discussed, accountability depends upon monitoring and demands redress, such as full disclosure, public apology, and changes in law and policy.

In summary, when a State is bound by the international or national right-to-health, and its health system does not have the features arising from the right to health, some of which we have signalled in this Section, the government is in breach of its legally binding human rights obligations. Accordingly, the authorities can and should be held accountable and subject to effective remedies ranging from a public apology to compensation.

6 A response to Upendra Baxi

6.1 Overview

In his contribution to the present collection, Professor Upendra Baxi considers some paragraphs from one of the Special Rapporteur's reports of 2006, and argues that Hunt's overall approach is weakened by the absence of a background theory of justice. By that, Baxi means a theory that does not just assert the existence of basic rights, but also gives them a sufficiently specific content, scope and weight, allowing the parties to grapple with a sufficient range of issues. Without such a vision of justice, he argues, the arguments advanced by the Special Rapporteur are faulty. Before responding to Baxi's points, it is useful to summarise the main ones he makes.

Baxi suggests that the analysis and proposals in the reports are recommendations of policy, but do not reach into the domain of justice. That is, they 'provide platforms for executive and legislative action', but these platforms will (the critique suggests) fail to address concerns that cut across and constrain policymakers. A particular set of recommendations about provision of adequate access to healthcare might make sense as a good compromise between goals of quality, cost and political acceptability, but may nevertheless be distinctly unfair: excluding those on the margins – those who are exploited or otherwise oppressed in a way that renders them unable to participate in the terms of this legislative or executive adjustment.

Not only is the weight of a basic right ignored, the argument continues, but so is its content. Whereas the reports call for 'special attention' to be given to disadvantaged persons and communities, this 'reaches nowhere near the dynamic proportion of healthcare justice'. This more dynamic demand is illustrated, for Baxi, by the principle made famous by John Rawls, according to which scarce resources, including those for healthcare, must be distributed from the better-off to the least-well-off, until any further distribution downwards would make the least-well-off yet worse off.

Finally, one of the faults alleged is that of narrowness of scope. For example, the reports are said to fail to engage the challenges posed by private actors. It is alleged that the reports do not address abuses of private power, such as corporate negligence or worse, which can have severe impacts on health.

6.2 The limitations of the argument

In part, Baxi is taking positions no different from many of those advanced in the reports, even if the terminology is different. As we consider these points at which Baxi is pushing at an open door, however, we will also indicate other parts of his argument with which we disagree.

By warning against policy directed primarily at legislatures and executives, Baxi risks falling into another trap: over-reliance on the judiciary as the appropriate body on which to rely for delivery of healthcare justice (HCJ); this would be a big mistake. Health professionals, and those they serve, need to see the law neither as the last, nor the first, port of call. Legal procedures in most parts of the world are lengthy, expensive, and often offer much less in solving an immediate problem than other avenues of action. However, that does not drive out the notion of HCJ as an important, and independent, element in the system. Indeed, it is – contrary to Baxi's assertions – a key concern of the reports, as signalled in this chapter, especially Sections 2 and 5. The special demands of HCJ are apparent where the Special Rapporteur calls for e.g. active and informed participation in health-related planning, policymaking, implementation, monitoring and accountability; equitable access to health facilities and services; more resources for people with mental disabilities; enhanced health programmes for neglected communities suffering from neglected diseases; states and pharmaceutical companies to improve access to medicines for those living in poverty; and states to protect communities' environmental health from the damaging impact of mining and other industries. Moreover, the reports argue that these and other measures are required as a matter of legal obligation in relation to which those responsible should be held accountable.

To the charge of ignoring the special impact of private companies in provoking violations of the right to health, the reports contain the response: for example, a report of 2006 looks at the human rights responsibilities of States and pharmaceutical companies in relation to access to medicines, concluding 'it is inconceivable that some human rights do not place legal responsibilities on business enterprises' (UN 2006a). Another sets out detailed Human Rights Guidelines for Pharmaceutical Companies in relation to Access to Medicines (UN 2008c; Khosla 2009). In 2009, the UN published the Special Rapporteur's report on one of the world's leading pharmaceutical companies, GlaxoSmithKline (UN 2009). Throughout, the Special Rapporteur argues that pharmaceutical companies should be held accountable, by independent mechanisms, in relation to their human rights responsibilities regarding access to medicines.

Returning to Baxi's claim that the reports neglect the demands of HCJ, there is a further important distinction to draw. While we warn against over-reliance on courts and the law for delivery of an adequate healthcare system, the reports are careful to signal the important contributions that a judiciary can make when called on. Key legal cases can clarify elements of the ethics of HCJ that might not otherwise be apparent. For example, the courts in the jurisdictions referred to in Section 4, which draws on one of the Special Rapporteur's reports from 2007, have looked closely at the competition between the demands of urgent care and the demands of financial efficiency, showing on several occasions the reasons for preferring the former over the latter, but also indicating other situations in which healthcare demands need to cede to longer-range planning choices taken by governments. These are simultaneously moral and legal issues, where both find their forum for clarification in the courtroom. So, in so far as Baxi wants the ethical details of an HCJ demand to be made clear – in a way that broad policy recommendations might not – it is a demand that is respected and illustrated in the reports.

It is important, however, to see the wider importance of the law in this domain, beyond the refining of general rules that courts can sometimes deliver about the right to health. When a State comes to see that, arising from the right to health, it has a legal obligation to establish an effective and responsive health system that is accessible to all, an important message is sent to the executive and legislative branches as they formulate the details of such a system. A national judiciary that takes seriously its obligations under the International Covenant on Economic, Social and Cultural Rights (ICESCR) might annul a budget that failed to provide for the special treatment of vulnerable groups or fell down on other dimensions of the Covenant's demands. The courts might equally annul the executive's projects for the location of hospitals, finding that they do not provide adequate access for the less well-off; for the provision of emergency services, which might manifest the same fault; or for the overall failure to integrate planning in a way that provides for an equitable health system. Some of these issues are canvassed in this chapter, especially in Sections 4 and 5, as well as in some of the reports. Without needing to go to court, health workers may nevertheless find that they have an arsenal of arguments that can be deployed to alter the course of a national policy – in the name of both HCJ and the right to health.

6.3 Justice and the uncertainties of international law

There is an important blind spot in Baxi's approach. A theory of justice, including one that applies to issues in healthcare, is not only a set of principles guiding the scope and relative priorities among human rights. It must also contain a view about which roles and institutions in society are appropriate for the deployment of different parts of those principles. Consider the conflict between the following three views of what counts as a just distribution of healthcare resources between the better-off and the least-well-off:

(a) When allocating scarce resources for healthcare, they must be distributed to the least-well-off and away from the better-off. The limit to this requirement is reached only when any further distribution downwards would make the least well-off yet worse-off because of the particular impact on incentives for wealth creation.

(b) Healthcare resources may be legitimately taken from the better-off to help the worse-off, but it is not necessary to go to the length of position (a). It is right to impose some burden on the better-off, but not to the point of maximising benefits to the worse-off.

(c) While it is legitimate to improve the position of the least-well-off if you can, position (b) goes too far: this improvement should never be at the price of taking away health resources from the better-off.

Of course, it is possible to choose between these three positions on their intrinsic merits – asking, for example, which best meets the tests of a social contract, utilitarian or some other foundation. That is a set of theoretical deliberations that can contribute to public debate as informed individuals decide, for example, on how to cast their votes in a referendum on the issue. Baxi offers position (a) as a good way in which to understand the special attention to the disadvantaged persons and communities that HCJ requires.

However, this recommendation fails to address the mandate of the Special Rapporteur, which required him to interpret and apply the existing international right to the highest attainable standard of health. So far as this right is clear, a Special Rapporteur must apply it without fear or favour. This frequently led Hunt into deeply controversial areas. Take, for example, the human rights responsibilities of pharmaceutical companies in relation to access to medicines. In his view, many of the requirements of the right to health are reasonably clear when applied to pharmaceutical companies and medicines. Thus, he devoted three substantive reports to these contested issues (UN 2006a, 2008c, 2009). He did not make up the relevant law but sought to apply his understanding of existing right-to-health law, policy and practice to pharmaceutical companies and medicines. However, where he found the international right to health genuinely unclear and uncertain, it was not within his mandate to determine otherwise. As we understand it, the international right to health does not clearly favour distributive principle (a), (b) or (c). So far as we are aware, there has been no compelling general position taken by international human rights law on them. In these circumstances, Hunt did not – as Special Rapporteur – favour one principle over another. Of course, national jurisdictions will adopt positions regarding (a), (b) and (c), and one of the Special Rapporteur's roles is to provide some of the tools that will help to make this national choice an informed one. Like other human rights, the right to health is a site of conflict and it is a Special Rapporteur's responsibility to take sides – not on the basis of his or her personal convictions about redistribution or any other issue, but on the basis of a principled understanding of existing international human rights law.

While the international right to health does not clearly favour any of the three positions, it is not silent on the hotly contested question of the distribution of health resources. As signalled throughout this chapter, the international right to health places obligations on States to take positive measures against discrimination and disadvantage. Here we confine ourselves to two situations where the redistribution of resources is required by the international right to health.

First, as discussed in Sections 3–5, the right to health places some immediate, or core, obligations on all States, whatever their stage of economic development.

These obligations, which are not subject to progressive realisation, include the duty to avoid discrimination, provide essential drugs as defined by WHO, and adopt a comprehensive national health plan of action. If a given distribution is responsible for non-compliance with a State's immediate obligations, the State has a duty to redistribute resources to ensure compliance with these core duties. Second, even if a State has met its core obligations, it continues to have a legally binding responsibility progressively to realise the right to health for all. If, however, progressive realisation is confined to the better-off, while the health situation of the disadvantaged stagnates or deteriorates, the State has a duty to redistribute resources to ensure progressive realisation for all. We derive these positions from our understanding of the international right to health, supported by analogous human rights law, such as the decision of the European Court of Human Rights in *James v. UK*, that 'The taking of property in pursuance of a policy calculated to enhance social justice within the community can properly be described as being 'in the public interest'.[10]

In conclusion, while the international right to health places positive obligations on States to address discrimination and disadvantage, it is not clear which distributive principle it prefers. Certainly, the relationship between international human rights law and these distributive principles needs to be scrutinised and should be made clearer, and we welcome and appreciate Baxi's insights into these important issues. In the meantime, however, it is more appropriate for a Special Rapporteur to insist on the States' positive obligations to address discrimination and disadvantage, rather than distributive principles in relation to which international law remains opaque.

6.4 Omissions or exclusions?

Do the Special Rapporteur's reports provide fresh tools for entering into debate and policy choices about health, or do they block that entrance? Baxi points to several areas in which he feels that not enough is said. We agree that the reports might have said more about one of the important phrases in Article 2(1) of the ICESCR: 'maximum available resources'. While a great deal was said in the reports about two other phrases from Article 2(1), progressive realisation and international assistance and cooperation, it proved impossible to devote the same time and space to the concept of resource availability, although this was examined in some reports for example in the context of the imposition of budget ceilings and also the prioritisation of health interventions (UN 2006a, 2007a). More work was also called for regarding participation, although it was considered, for example, in the reports on mental disability, Uganda and Peru (UN 2005b, 2005d, 2006a). Baxi has not shown, nor do we believe, that these issues are now more difficult to entertain because of the Special Rapporteur's work. On the contrary, the reports have highlighted the critical importance of addressing these and other issues, and have offered a framework and tools by which they can be addressed. In the six years of his mandate, the Special Rapporteur could not address all right-to-health issues – that would be the work of a lifetime.

7 Conclusion

Like other human rights, the right to the highest attainable standard of health is a site of struggle (Yamin 2004; Hunt 1996). In recent years, the contours and content of the right have become clearer, making it possible to tease out its practical implications for health policies, programmes and projects. The right brings with it a set of analytical, policy and programmatic tools. As always, the right also retains its powerful rhetorical, campaigning qualities. It should be seen as one important element in a strategy for progressive social change.

The operational impact of the right to health depends upon multiple variables. Progressive governments must be persuaded to integrate the right across their policymaking processes, in accordance with their legal obligations. The WHO and other international organisations must be prevailed upon to champion the right. Civil society organisations must campaign around health and human rights. Activist judges and lawyers must be willing to learn from health workers and find innovative ways to vindicate the right. Health workers must grasp the potential of the right to help them achieve their professional objectives. Human rights mechanisms must take this fundamental human right seriously, and its meaning must be further clarified. More right-to-health tools must be fashioned. Disadvantaged individuals, communities and populations must apprehend that the right empowers them by granting entitlements, placing legal and moral obligations on others. This in turn calls for greater imagination in fashioning accountability mechanisms that are accessible and responsive to all.

Today, there are numerous health movements and approaches, including health equity, primary healthcare, health promotion, social determinants, health security, continuum of care, biomedical, macroeconomics, and so on – all are very important. It is misconceived, however, to regard human rights as yet another approach with the same status as the others. Like ethics, the right to the highest attainable standard of health is not optional – and, like ethics, it recurs throughout all other approaches. The right provides the only perspective that is both underpinned by universally recognised moral values and reinforced by legal obligations. Of course, it does not provide neat answers to numerous complex health issues, any more than does any other single approach. Nonetheless, properly understood, the right to the highest attainable standard of health has a profound contribution to make towards building healthy societies and equitable health systems.

Notes

1 We have a number of acknowledgements and thanks to convey. The right-to-health analytical framework summarised in Section 3 is found in several places e.g. Hunt and Mesquita (2006) (*Human Rights Quarterly*); however, Section 3 draws in particular from Hunt, Backman, Mesquita *et al.* (2009) (OUP). Section 4 draws from Potts 2008 (Essex), Hunt and Khosla 2009 (Foundation of Law, Justice and Society), UN (2007c) and UN (2008c). Sections 5 and 6 draw from several publications, especially Backman, *et al.* (2008, *The Lancet*), but also Hunt and Backman (2008, *Health and Human Rights Journal*) and UN (2008b). We are extremely grateful to all concerned.

2 [2002] (5) SA 721, CC.
3 [1996] SCJ 25.
4 [1998] Case No 31.777/96.
5 CEDAW, Communication No. 4/2004.
6 [1996] 48 DLR, HCD 438.
7 Human Rights Committee, Communication No. 1153/2003.
8 African Commission on Human and Peoples' Rights, Communication No. 155/96.
9 African Commission on Human and Peoples' Rights, Communication No. 241/2001.
10 [1986] 8EHRR 123 (at para 41).

Bibliography

Abramovich, V. (2003) 'Argentina: the right to medicines', in COHRE, *Litigating Economic, Social and Cultural Rights: Achievements, Challenges and Strategies* Geneva: COHRE.

Akunyili, D. (2006) 'The fight against counterfeit drugs in Nigeria', in *Transparency International – Global Corruption Report 2006: Corruption and Health.* Berlin: Transparency International, 96–100.

Backman, G., Hunt, P., Khosla R., Jaramillo-Strouss, C., Fikre, B., Rumble, C., Pevalin, D., Paez, D., Pineda, M., Frisancho, A., Tarco, D., Motlagh, M., Farcasanu, D. and Vladescu, C. (2008) 'Health systems and the right to health: an assessment of 194 countries', *The Lancet*, 372, 13 December 2047–85.

Braveman, P. and Gruskin, S. (2003) 'Defining equity in health', *Journal of Epidemiology and Community Health*, 57: 254–58.

CESCR (2000) *Substantive Issues Arising in the Implementation of the International Covenant on Economic, Social and Cultural Rights: The Right to the Highest Attainable Standard of Health.* General Comment No. 14, 22nd Sess., Agenda Item 3. U.N. Doc. E/C.12/2000/4.

Commission on Human Rights (2002) Resolution 2002/31, 22 April 2002.

Ferraz, O. and Vieira, F. (2008) *Public Policies and Inequalities in Brazil: Equity as the Fundamental Principle, Working Paper*, http://ssrn.com/abstract=1137872.

Freedman, L. (2003) 'Human rights, constructive accountability and maternal mortality in the Dominican Republic: a commentary', *International Journal of Gynaecology and Obstetrics*, 82: 111–114.

Freeman, M. (2009) 'The right to health', in Morgan, R. and Turner, B. (eds), *Interpreting Human Rights: Social Science Perspectives*, London: Routledge.

Green, A. (2007) *An Introduction to Health Planning for Developing Health Systems.* Oxford: Oxford University Press.

Hogerzeil H. V., Samson, M., Vidal Casanovas, J. and Rahmani, L. (2006) 'Access to essential medicines as part of the fulfilment of the right to health – is it enforceable through the courts?' *The Lancet*, 22 July: 368 305–11.

Human Rights Council resolution (2006) A/HRC/2/L.9, 2 October 2006.

Hunt, P. (1996) *Reclaiming Social Rights: International and Comparative Perspectives.* Aldershot: Dartmouth Publishing Company.

—— (2006) 'Public health and human rights: at the crossroads', presentation to the American Public Health Association, Annual Meeting, Boston, USA, 9 November 2006, see http://www2.essex.ac.uk/human_rights_centre/rth.

Hunt, P. and Khosla, R. (2008) 'The human right to medicines', 5 SUR *Revista Internacional de Direitos Humanos* 99–116.

—— (2009) *The Role of Courts in the Implementation of Economic, Social and Cultural Rights: A Right to Health Case Study*. Oxford: The Foundation of Law, Justice and Society.

Hunt, P. and Backman, G. (2008) 'Health systems and the right to the highest attainable standard of health', *Health and Human Rights Journal*, 10(1): 81–92.

Hunt, P. and Mesquita, J. (2006) 'Mental disabilities and the human right to the highest attainable standard of health', *Human Rights Quarterly*, 28: 332–56.

Hunt, P., Stewart, R., Mesquita, J. and Oldring L. (2007) *Neglected Diseases: A Human Rights Analysis*. Geneva: Special Programme for Research and Training in Tropical Diseases.

Hunt, P., Backman, G., Bueno de Mesquita, J., Finer, F., Khosla, R., Korljan, D. and Oldring, L. (2009) 'The right to the highest attainable standard of health', in Detels, R., Beaglehole, R., Lansang, M. A. and Gulliford, M. (eds.) *Oxford Textbook of Public Health* 5th ed., Oxford: Oxford University Press, pp. 335–50.

Khosla, R. and Hunt, P. (2009) *Human Rights Guidelines for Pharmaceutical Companies in Relation to Access to Medicines: The Sexual and Reproductive Health Context*, University of Essex: Human Rights Centre.

MacNaughton, G. and Hunt, P. (2009) 'Health impact assessment: the contribution of the right to the highest attainable standard of health', *Public Health*, 123: 302–5.

Manandhar, D., Osrin, D., Shrestha, B., Mesko, N., Morrison, J., Tumbahangphe, K., Tamang, S., Thapa, S., Shrestha, D. and Thapa, B. (2004) 'Effect of a participatory intervention with women's groups on birth outcomes in Nepal: cluster-randomised controlled trial', *The Lancet*, 364, 11 September, 970–9.

Mesquita, J. and Hunt, P (2008) *International Assistance and Cooperation in Sexual and Reproductive Health: A Human Rights Responsibility for Donors*, University of Essex: Human Rights Centre.

Open Society Institute (2005). *Mediating Romani Health: Policy and Programme Opportunities*. New York: Open Society Institute.

Palmer, A., Tomkinson, J., Phung, C., Ford, N., Joffres, M., Fernandes, K., Zeng, L., Lima, V., Montaner, J., Guyatt, G. and Mills, E. (2009) 'Does ratification of human-rights treaties have effects on population health?' *The Lancet*, 6 June, 373: 1987–92.

Potts, H. (2008) *Accountability and the Right to the Highest Attainable Standard of Health*. University of Essex: Human Rights Centre.

—— (2009) *Participation and the Right to the Highest Attainable Standard of Health*. University of Essex: Human Rights Centre.

Singh, A., Govender, M. and Mills, E. (2007) 'Do human rights matter to health?', *The Lancet*, 11 August, 370: 521–7.

Sphere Project (2004) *Humanitarian Charter and Minimum Standards in Disaster Response*. Geneva: Sphere Project.

UN (1966), International Covenant on Economic, Social, and Cultural Rights, 16 December 1966, 993 U.N.T.S. 3.

—— (2003) *The Right of Everyone to the Enjoyment of the Highest Attainable Standard of Physical and Mental Health: Report of the Special Rapporteur, Paul Hunt. U.N. ESCOR, Commission on Human Rights, 59th Sess., Agenda Item 10*. U.N. Doc. E/CN.4/2003/58. 13 February 2003.

—— (2004a) *The Right of Everyone to the Enjoyment of the Highest Attainable Standard of Physical and Mental Health: Report of the Special Rapporteur, Paul Hunt. U.N. ESCOR, Commission on Human Rights, 60th Sess., Agenda Item 10*. U.N. Doc. E/CN.4/2004/49. 16 February 2004. (Sexual and reproductive health rights; Niger's Poverty Reduction Strategy)

—— (2004b) *The Right of Everyone to the Enjoyment of the Highest Attainable Standard of Physical and Mental Health: Report of the Special Rapporteur, Paul Hunt. U.N. General Assembly, 59th Sess., Agenda Item 105(b)*. U.N. Doc. A/59/422. 8 October 2004. (Millennium Development Goals)

—— (2004c) *The Right of Everyone to the Enjoyment of the Highest Attainable Standard of Physical and Mental Health: Report of the Special Rapporteur, Paul Hunt. U.N. ESCOR, Commission on Human Rights, 60th Sess., Agenda Item 10.* U.N. Doc. E/CN.4/2004/49/Add.1. 1 March 2004. (World Trade Organization)

—— (2006a) *The Right of Everyone to the Enjoyment of the Highest Attainable Standard of Physical and Mental Health: Report of the Special Rapporteur, Paul Hunt. U.N. General Assembly, 61st Sess., Agenda Item 66(b).* U.N. Doc. A/61/338. 13 September 2006. (Access to medicines; maternal mortality)

—— (2006b) *The Right of Everyone to the Enjoyment of the Highest Attainable Standard of Physical and Mental Health: Report of the Special Rapporteur, Paul Hunt. U.N. ESCOR, Commission on Human Rights, 62nd Sess., Agenda Item 10.* U.N. Doc. E/CN.4/2006/48. 3 March 2006. (Indicators and benchmarks)

—— (2006c) *The Right of Everyone to the Enjoyment of the Highest Attainable Standard of Physical and Mental Health: Report of the Special Rapporteur, Paul Hunt. U.N. ESCOR, Commission on Human Rights, 62nd Sess., Agenda Item 10.* U.N. Doc. E/CN.4/2006/48/Add.2. 3 March 2006. (Uganda)

—— (2006d) *Report of the Special Rapporteur on Extrajudicial, Summary or Arbitrary Executions, Philip Alston; the Special Rapporteur on the Right of Everyone to the Enjoyment of the Highest Attainable Standard of Physical and Mental Health, Paul Hunt; the Representative of the Secretary-General on Human Rights of Internally Displaced Persons, Walter Kälin; and the Special Rapporteur on Adequate Housing as a Component of the Right to an Adequate Standard of Living, Miloon Kothari. U.N. Human Rights Council, 2nd Sess., Agenda Item 2.* U.N. Doc. A/HRC/2/7. 2 October 2006. (Lebanon and Israel)

—— (2006e) *Report of the Chairperson-Rapporteur of the Working Group on Arbitrary Detention, Leila Zerrougui; the Special Rapporteur on the Independence of Judges and Lawyers, Leandro Despouy; the Special Rapporteur on Torture and other Cruel, Inhuman or Degrading Treatment or Punishment, Manfred Nowak; the Special Rapporteur on Freedom of Religion or Belief, Asma Jahangir; and the Special Rapporteur on the Right of Everyone to the Enjoyment of the Highest Attainable Standard of Physical and Mental Health, Paul Hunt. U.N. ESCOR, Commission on Human Rights, 62nd Sess., Agenda Items 10 and 11.* U.N. Doc. E/CN.4/2006/120. 27 February 2006. (Guantánamo Bay)

—— (2005a) *The Right of Everyone to the Enjoyment of the Highest Attainable Standard of Physical and Mental Health: Report of the Special Rapporteur, Paul Hunt. U.N. ESCOR, Commission on Human Rights, 61st Sess., Agenda Item 10.* U.N. Doc. E/CN.4/2005/51/Add.2 4 January 2005. (Mozambique)

—— (2005b) *The Right of Everyone to the Enjoyment of the Highest Attainable Standard of Physical and Mental Health: Report of the Special Rapporteur, Paul Hunt. U.N. ESCOR, Commission on Human Rights, 61st Sess., Agenda Item 10.* U.N. Doc. E/CN.4/2005/51. 11 February 2005. (Mental disability)

—— (2005c) *The Right of Everyone to the Enjoyment of the Highest Attainable Standard of Physical and Mental Health: Report of the Special Rapporteur, Paul Hunt. U.N. General Assembly, 60th Sess., Agenda Item 73(b).* U.N. Doc. A/60/348. 12 September 2005. (Skills drain)

—— (2005d) *The Right of Everyone to the Enjoyment of the Highest Attainable Standard of Physical and Mental Health: Report of the Special Rapporteur, Paul Hunt. U.N. ESCOR, Commission on Human Rights, 61st Sess., Agenda Item 10.* U.N. Doc. E/CN.4/2005/51/Add.3. 4 February 2005. (Peru)

—— (2005e) *The Right of Everyone to the Enjoyment of the Highest Attainable Standard of Physical and Mental Health: Report of the Special Rapporteur, Paul Hunt. U.N. ESCOR, Commission on Human Rights, 61st Sess., Agenda Item 10.* U.N. Doc. E/CN.4/2005/51/Add.4. 21 February 2005. (Romania)

—— (2007a) *The Right of Everyone to the Enjoyment of the Highest Attainable Standard of Physical and Mental Health: Report of the Special Rapporteur, Paul Hunt. U.N. General Assembly, 62nd Sess., Agenda Item 72(b).* U.N. Doc. A/62/214. 8 August 2007. (Water and sanitation; prioritisation)

—— (2007b) *The Right of Everyone to the Enjoyment of the Highest Attainable Standard of Physical and Mental Health: Report of the Special Rapporteur, Paul Hunt. U.N. Human Rights Council, 4th Sess., Agenda Item 2.* U.N. Doc. A/HRC/4/28/Add.2. 28 February 2007. (Sweden)

—— (2007c) *The Right of Everyone to the Enjoyment of the Highest Attainable Standard of Physical and Mental Health: Report of the Special Rapporteur, Paul Hunt. U.N. Human Rights Council, 4th Sess., Agenda Item 2.* U.N. Doc. A/HRC/4/28. 17 January 2007. (The health and human rights movement: progress and obstacles; cases on the right to health and other health-related rights)

—— (2008a) *The Right of Everyone to the Enjoyment of the Highest Attainable Standard of Physical and Mental Health: Report of the Special Rapporteur, Paul Hunt. U.N. Human Rights Council, 7th Sess., Agenda Item 3.* U.N. Doc. A/HRC/7/11/Add.2. 5 March 2008. (Sweden in relation to Uganda, the World Bank and IMF)

—— (2008b) *The Right of Everyone to the Enjoyment of the Highest Attainable Standard of Physical and Mental Health: Report of the Special Rapporteur, Paul Hunt. U.N. Human Rights Council, 7th Sess., Agenda Item 3.* U.N. Doc. A/HRC/7/11. 31 January 2008. (Health systems)

—— (2008c) *The Right of Everyone to the Enjoyment of the Highest Attainable Standard of Physical and Mental Health: Report of the Special Rapporteur, Paul Hunt. U.N. General Assembly, 63rd Sess., Agenda Item 67(b).* U.N. Doc. A/63/263. 11 August 2008. (Accountability; Human Rights Guidelines for Pharmaceutical Companies in relation to Access to Medicines)

—— (2009) *The Right of Everyone to the Enjoyment of the Highest Attainable Standard of Physical and Mental Health: Report of the Special Rapporteur, Paul Hunt. U.N. Human Rights Council, 11th Sess., Agenda Item 3.* U.N. Doc. A/HRC/11/12/Add.2. 5 May 2009. (GlaxoSmithKline)

UNFPA (2004) *Culture Matters – Working with Communities and Faith-Based Organisations: Case Studies from Country Programs.* New York: UNFPA.

WHO (1978) *Primary Health Care: Report of the International Conference of Primary Health Care Alma-Ata, USSR, September 6–12 1978*, Geneva: World Health Organization.

—— (2000) *World Health Report 2000, Health Systems: Improving Performance.* Geneva: World Health Organization.

—— (2007a) *Everybody's Business: Strengthening Health Systems to Improve Health Outcomes: WHO's Framework for Action.* Geneva: World Health Organization.

—— (2007b) *Report of the Global Partners' Meeting on Neglected Tropical Diseases: A Turning Point.* Geneva: World Health Organization.

—— (2008) *International Health Regulations (2005)*, 2nd edn, Geneva: World Health Organization.

Yamin, A. (2004) 'Journeys towards the Splendid City', *Human Rights Quarterly*, 26: 519–38.

—— (2008) 'Beyond compassion: the central role of accountability in applying a human rights framework to health', *Health and Human Rights Journal*, 10(2): 1–20.

Yamin, A. and Parra-Vera, O. (2009), 'How do courts set health policy? The case of the Colombian Constitutional Court', *PLoS Med*, 6(2): e1000032.

4 What future for the minimum core?

Contextualising the implications of South African socioeconomic rights jurisprudence for the international human right to health

Lisa Forman

1 Introduction

The South African Constitutional Court's emerging jurisprudence on the right to health has provided a ground-breaking and often controversial illustration of this right's justiciability. The Court's enforcement of South Africa's constitutional right to access healthcare services has served considerably to erode traditional objections to social rights, illustrating that judicial enforcement of these rights is not only feasible in developing countries, but also may effectively challenge the irrational and uncaring governance that so often perpetuates and exacerbates gross health inequalities. The Court's approach nonetheless poses challenging theoretical questions, given its adoption of a standard of reasonableness to adjudicate potential social rights violations, and its consequent rejection of an enforceable minimum core to these rights. The minimum core concept reflects the fundamental human rights idea that certain individual interests, including the basic health needs of the poor, should be prioritised at any cost. The core suggests that social rights, and the interests they reflect, should place reasonable limits on political and economic actions that intrude so far into basic needs as to render human dignity and equal worth meaningless. The Court's rejection of this idea, and the apparent rupture of the Court's approach from human rights law, begs to be reconciled with international legal theory and practice, so that the validity of international human rights law as an authoritative and indeed realistic guide for State action and judicial review is not diminished, and so that the innovative work of the South African Constitutional Court is not seen to reinforce indefensible objections to social rights.

My chapter explores this apparent disjuncture between international and South African law, by surveying persistent objections to social rights and the right to health, as well as advances made against these objections through the interpretation of international human rights law. I then turn to evaluate in this light relevant South African jurisprudence related to health, and close by analysing the implications of this jurisprudence for international human-rights law theory and practice associated with the right to health.

2 Exploring objections to the right to health

Broad domestic legal recognition and enforcement of the right to health has often been constrained by a range of theoretical and practical objections: that the right is not universal, and so conceptually amorphous as to be meaningless, and allied to this that a right to any level of healthcare would make zero-sum claims on budgets that would irrationally distort resource allocations to the detriment of the public good (Harvard Human Rights Program, Harvard Law School, and the Francois-Xavier Bagnoud Center for Health and Human Rights, Harvard School of Public Health 1995). Central to these objections is the characterisation of social and civil rights as positive and negative rights, respectively. In this view, positive rights are seen as requiring extensive State action and resources to be realised, in contrast to negative rights, which are seen as simply requiring inaction and limited resources to be realised. Thus, it is argued that legal enforcement of positive rights would require courts without institutional competence to make budgetary allocations and social policy, which would breach the democratic separation of powers. These logics have long motivated academics, governments and courts to refute the appropriately legal nature of economic and social rights, and to suggest that they are rather political, aspirational or programmatic rights more appropriately claimed through the ballot box (Cranston 1973; Steiner and Alston 2000: 267). As a result, domestic adjudicators are often overly deferential to social and economic policy, and reluctant to recognise and enforce positive obligations pertaining to social welfare.[1]

While the positive–negative distinction has philosophical roots in the moral philosophy of Immanuel Kant and Isaiah Berlin (Berlin 1969), it has effectively become shorthand for action–inaction and resource-intensive–resource-free, respectively. This contraction is a considerably inaccurate description of both the activity and resources that social and civil rights may in fact impose on governments, since government inaction alone may not secure people's freedoms, and achieving this goal may require an active legal and policy process. Realising ostensibly negative rights may therefore require extensive government action and resources.

These ideas effectively illustrated in social-rights commentary, demonstrating the considerable and often greater costs of realising civil as compared to social rights. For example, in the US context, Stephen Holmes and Cass Sunstein draw figures from the 1996 US Budget, which show considerably greater state expenditure on realising property rights than education rights [US$ 6.6 billion against US$2.1 billion, respectively (Holmes and Sunstein 2000: 233)]. Similarly, Jeremy Waldron argues that a range of civil and political rights, seen as requiring only that the State desist from action in their fulfillment, are in fact extremely resource-demanding, requiring the establishment and maintenance of frameworks that make costly claims on scarce police and forensic resources

(Waldron 1993: 24). Indeed, the inaccuracy of the positive and negative distinction when it comes to describing the broad range of action necessary to realise rights is reflected in evolving human rights doctrine. These ideas have been promoted most persuasively by Henry Shue, who suggests that since fulfilling rights may require multiple kinds of actions, the useful distinction is not between rights, but between duties (Shue 1980: 52–3). Shue argues that the fulfilment of each kind of right requires the performance of multiple kinds of duties, and that we should understand each right as imposing three kinds of duties – namely, to avoid depriving, to protect from deprivation and to aid the deprived (Shue 1980: 52).

This idea of a typology of duties was further developed in human rights scholarship by Asborjn Eide during his tenure as UN Special Rapporteur on the Right to Food (Eide *et al.* 1995). The concept formally entered into international human rights law doctrine in the early 1990s, as the tripartite typology of duties to respect, protect and fulfil that all rights are said to impose (United Nations 1991). Thus, the duty to respect imposes a negative obligation to desist from interfering with people's enjoyment of rights; the duty to protect requires the State to prevent third-party interference with people's rights; and the duty to promote and fulfil describes the State's positive obligation to realise access.

While this typology effectively illustrates that all rights impose both positive and negative duties, the positive–negative conception of social and civil rights persists in legal cultures globally, particularly among lawyers educated with this idea as doctrine. However, even where the newer paradigm of duties is recognised, the typology itself may nonetheless simply internalise the old paradigm that assumes duties to fulfil are resource-heavy and duties to respect are not. Moreover the typology may reinforce perceptions that social rights tend heavily towards the fulfil duty, while civil rights are more often fulfilled through realisation of the respect duty. As Shue indicates, realising social rights does not necessarily require that the State provide goods (although it may), but may instead require that State actors prevent people from being deprived of commodities or the means to grow, make or buy them, including through addressing the institutional and systemic causes of deprivation (Shue 1980: 41). Shue argues that achieving these goals need not be any more positive, unrealistic or unaffordable than designing programmes to control violent crime. Indeed he argues, 'neither looks simple, cheap or "negative" ' (Shue 1980: 45).

In this light, the persistence of the positive–negative distinction between social and civil rights, despite its obvious inaccuracy, is perhaps explained more by ideology than a lack of knowledge. Indeed, post-Second World War schisms between social and civil rights are deeply rooted in Cold War geopolitical tensions, where economic, social and cultural rights came to be associated with socialism, and civil and political rights with Western capitalism. As a result, civil and political rights have often been prioritised over economic and social rights in Western countries, reflected in the notionally temporal but in fact hierarchical categorisation of civil and social rights as first and second generation rights, respectively.

The ideological roots of the distinction between social and civil rights are reified in the positive–negative distinction between these two sets of rights. In this regard, it is notable that this distinction fits neatly into the liberal conception of a non-interventionist State that protects individual freedoms and private property, in contrast to a redistributive State that regulates individual freedom and economic action (Forman 2008a). Similar conceptions of appropriate State action are reflected in liberalism's variants: from the libertarian notion that only a minimal State enforcing contracts and protecting against force, theft and fraud is justified (Nozick 1974: ix), to the core principles of neoliberalism, which hold that government should shrink itself through fiscal austerity, privatisation and deregulation, in order to enable free markets (Williamson 2002). The paradox is that if civil freedoms and property protection actually require extensive resources and State action to be realised, then even a minimal, night-watchman-type State may be interventionist and redistributive, albeit that it may favour the interests of private property and not the poor. In any event, meeting subsistence needs cannot be inconsistent with philosophies focusing on individual autonomy, given how extensively autonomy depends on adequate food, shelter and healthcare (see for example, Sen 2000). In this light, it is likely fair to say that one cannot be concerned with freedom without being concerned with subsistence, unless one is only concerned with the freedom of those who do not lack subsistence. Nonetheless, the ascendance of liberal-oriented constitutional democracy and neoliberal-oriented global economic laws pose conceptual and strategic challenges to advancing the right to health, given the reluctance of courts and governments to interfere with individual or corporate freedom and markets. The challenge therefore is to counter both practical and ideological objections to recognising and enforcing the right to health, and to recognise that, for policymakers and judges, the distinctions between pragmatism and ideology may have become considerably blurred (Forman 2008a).

3 Developing the right to health in international law

Objections to the universality and appropriate legality of the right to health are contradicted by the extensive entrenchment of this right in international and regional human rights treaties, illustrated in Box 1 below. Many of these treaties now hold almost universal ratification. For example, 193 States, an effective universality, are party to the Children's Rights Convention (CRC); 185 States have ratified the Convention on the Elimination of Discrimination Against Women (CEDAW); 173 have ratified the Convention on the Elimination of Racial Discrimination (CERD); and 157 have ratified the International Covenant on Economic, Social, and Cultural Rights (ICESCR) (United Nations Office of the High Commissioner for Human Rights 2008). All of these treaties contain rights related to the non-discriminatory provision of healthcare services.

Box 1: International and regional treaties containing rights to health

United Nations, International Covenant on Economic, Social, and Cultural Rights, 16 December 1966, 993 U.N.T.S. 3, Art 12.1

United Nations, International Convention on the Rights of the Child, 20 November 1989, U.K.T.S. 1992 No. 44, 28 I.L.M. 1448 1989, Art 24.1

United Nations, International Convention on the Elimination of Racial Discrimination, 21 December 1965, 660 U.N.T.S. 195, 5 I.L.M. 352 1966, Art 5.e.iv

United Nations, Convention on the Elimination of All Forms of Discrimination Against Women, 18 December 1979, U.K.T.S. 1989 No. 2, 19 I.L.M. 33 1980, Arts 11.1.f and 12

Council of Europe, The European Social Charter, 18 October 1961, 529 U.N.T.S. 89, Art 11

African Charter on Human and People's Rights, 27 June 1981, O.A.U. Doc. CAB/LEG/67/3 rev. 5, 21 I.L.M. 58, 1982, Art 16

Additional Protocol to the American Convention on Human Rights in the Area of Economic, Social, and Cultural Rights (Protocol of San Salvador), 1988, Art 10.

Moreover, objections to the indeterminacy of the entitlements and duties that this right imposes hold considerably less validity given conceptual advances in the interpretation of social rights, and the right to health in particular. International legal expert principles, guidelines and UN Committee on Economic Social and Cultural Rights (CESCR) General Comments have significantly expanded the specificity of the general scope of social rights, and the entitlements and duties they create (See for example, Limburg 1986; Maastricht 1997; UN 1991). International human rights law commentaries have moved in particular to define the scope of the entitlement under the right to the highest attainable standard of health in Article 12 of the ICESCR, and the duties that progressive realisation within available resources places on States (UN 2000). This interpretive process has been necessary since, beyond identifying a limited number of explicit obligations, Art 12 provides little clarity about the scope of the right to the highest attainable standard of health and the nature of State obligations to progressively realise this right to the maximum of available resources. Since the highest attainable standard of health will vary between countries, depending on available resources and health needs, and since progressive realisation to the maximum of resources seems to imply a highly relative standard of fulfilment, Art 12 has often been misconstrued as an aspirational rather than enforceable individual right (see e.g. Cranston 1973; Goodman 2005).

In contrast, the Committee's interpretation of this right in General Comment 14 indicates that the right to health is an inclusive right, which includes the right to healthcare and the underlying determinants of health, such as food, housing, access to water and adequate sanitation, safe working conditions and a healthy environment (UN 2000: para 4). The right is not a right to be healthy, but rather an entitlement to a system of health protection that provides equal opportunity for people to enjoy the highest attainable standard of health, and which includes a variety of facilities, goods, services and conditions necessary to realise this standard (UN 2000: paras 8, 9). The Committee interprets progressive realisation as requiring States to take immediate action and effective movement towards realising this right, which includes guaranteeing the non-discriminatory exercise of rights, and taking steps towards full realisation, which are deliberate, concrete and targeted as clearly as possible towards meeting treaty obligations (UN 2000: para 31). This means that while States can justify some healthcare deficiencies, they cannot justify the failure to work towards rectifying them. Further guidance on State obligations is provided by the tripartite framework of duties to respect, protect and fulfil rights (UN 2000: para. 33), which as indicated above, impose a range of positive and negative duties on States to realise rights in various contexts.

An important component of this interpretive framework is the notion that social rights contain minimum essential levels – an idea suggested in the ICESCR – which indicates that the rights contained within it can only be limited in so far as is compatible with their nature (UN 1966: Art 4, see Box 1). The ICESCR also specifies that acts aimed at destroying these rights are not permitted (UN 1966: Art 5.1), an idea inherent to the human rights priority placed on human dignity, equal worth and life. This suggests, in the context of the right to health, that acts conducted with the specific intent (rather than simply having the effect) of destroying realisation of the right to health are impermissible.

Following on this idea of a floor for restrictions on social rights, the non-binding 1986 Limburg Principles on the Implementation of the International Covenant on Economic, Social and Cultural Rights proposed that State Parties be obligated to ensure respect for minimum subsistence rights for all regardless of their level of economic development (paras 25, 28). This idea was expanded in the non-binding 1997 Maastricht Guidelines on Violations of Economic, Social and Cultural Rights, which suggested that failures to satisfy minimum core obligations violated the Covenant, and that States had minimum core obligations irrespective of the national availability of resources or other factors or difficulties (para 9).

The CESCR first incorporated minimum core obligations into its interpretations of the ICESCR in General Comment 3, which holds core obligations to be a right's minimum essential levels; in relation to health, this would include 'essential primary healthcare' (UN 1966: para 10). The Committee applies the core concept to health in General Comment 14 in the context of a broader conceptual framework for this right. The Committee's notion of the core includes the related idea that, irrespective of development levels, the right to health contains essential elements such as public health and healthcare facilities, goods and services, including hospitals, clinics, personnel and essential drugs, which are available in sufficient quantity and standards, accessible to all physically, economically and without distinction and of good quality (UN 2000: para 12). Allied to this idea, States are held to have core obligations that include at least: ensuring non-discriminatory access to health facilities, goods and services, especially for vulnerable or marginalised people; access to food, basic shelter, housing, sanitation and water; providing essential drugs as defined by WHO; ensuring equitable distribution of all health facilities, goods and services and adopting a national public health strategy and plan of action addressing the concerns of all (UN 2000: para 43).

One of the most legally significant developments in General Comment 14 is its shift in the standard of compliance required for core obligations. In General Comment 3, a State could justify non-compliance with minimum core obligations by demonstrating every effort to use all resources available to satisfy these obligations as a matter of priority. However, in General Comment 14, the Committee instead asserts that 'a State Party cannot, under any circumstances whatsoever, justify its non-compliance with the core obligations . . . which are non-derogable' (UN 2000: para 47).

This latter formulation poses obvious pragmatic problems: the suggestion that a country where many lack adequate healthcare, running water, food or shelter is a prima facie violator of social rights sounds like nothing more than an admonishment to the country not to be poor. Given this potentially irreconcilable disjuncture between theory and reality, the Committee's move towards viewing the core as non-derogable may reflect a doctrinal overreach. Yet, whatever the extent of derogability permitted in relation to the core, the primary significance of the concept should not be overlooked. The core concept provides what can be seen as a rights-based approach to systemic deprivation, suggesting that where large numbers of people lack realisation of their basic needs, this should not be viewed from a human rights perspective as an irremediable misfortune. Instead, the core concept suggests that such deprivations should instead be seen as a potential violation of the right to health.

The core concept therefore suggests that meeting basic needs must take temporal and resource priority in the State's realisation of rights, and that governmental failures to remedy these deprivations and assist those without access to the basic necessities required to live autonomous and dignified lives should be held to the highest levels of scrutiny. If governments simply lack resources to meet basic needs, they must prove incapacity and not just unwillingness. This distinction between willingness and ability is emphasised in the CESCR's General Comment on health, and provides a commonsense framework for assessing the rights-violations potentially inherent within gross health inequities (UN 2000: para 47).

The core is therefore not intended to inappropriately label genuinely incapable countries as violators, but rather to promote basic needs as placing irreducible claims on resources and governance that cannot be restricted by competing political or economic priorities. The core is intended to indicate that denying basic health needs where there is no scarcity – but rather uncaring, corrupt or neglectful governance – is a human rights violation of the highest order. These are not unreasonable duties to place on poor countries if we are to take social rights seriously. Nor are these the duties of poor countries alone, but should apply equally to what rich countries do both at home and internationally, given the impact that foreign policy imperatives can have on countries' abilities to meet core duties. These duties are specifically recognised in ICESCR, where State Parties undertake to take steps individually and through 'international assistance and cooperation, especially economic and technical' to realise Covenant rights (UN 1966: Art 2). In General Comment 14, the Committee identifies duties with specific relevance to the present inquiry, and emphasises that, given international law on this topic, and the common concern to all countries of remedying gross health inequalities, that States Parties should comply with their commitments to take joint and separate action to fully realise the right to health (UN 2000: para 38).

The Committee's definition of the core indicates that States should provide the basics of a functional public health and healthcare system, and that this should include essential drugs, hospitals, clinics and personnel. The core is not actually defined in terms of specific healthcare services, but rather provides guideposts for policy (Toebes 1999: 288). While the content of the core may vary from country to country, its more normative intent is to protect social rights from resource constraints that eviscerate them to the point that they become meaningless. The core is intended to ensure, as Albie Sachs suggests, that States prioritise the 'minimum decencies of citizenship in the modern world' for the poor, particularly in light of the human impacts of a globalised market system (Harvard Human Rights Program Harvard Law School, and the Francois-Xavier Bagnoud Center for Health and Human Rights, Harvard School of Public Health 1995:12).

The core potentially has other, more practical legal implications, including through advancing a normative hierarchy, which may significantly increase the weight of core claims when judicially balanced against governmental claims of scarcity or competing private interests. The core could, for example, influence the extent to which judges are willing to accept State allegations of resource constraints without rigorous evidential support. The core also may suggest important guidelines for policies outside of health that cause deprivation. For example, viewing essential medicines as a minimum core entitlement should influence how pharmaceutical patents under the World Trade Organisation's Agreement on Trade-Related Aspects of Intellectual Property Rights (TRIPS) are formulated, implemented and interpreted, given how extensively TRIPS may limit medicines access for the poor (Forman 2008b). This impact is exacerbated by the growing proliferation of bilateral and regional free trade agreements (FTAs) where countries are adopting intellectual property rights that are even stronger than TRIPS. These rules tend to make TRIPS even more restrictive, and generally make it more difficult for generic medicines to enter the market (Smith *et al.* 2009).

The core is therefore not a technocratic exercise in policy formation, nor an intellectual whim coming down from on-high in Geneva, but an idea integral to the very core of human rights itself. In this light, the South African Constitutional Court's rejection of the core presents conceptual challenges and pragmatic concerns, particularly given South Africa's importance as a leading human rights jurisdiction, and the global significance of its enforcement of social rights.

4 The right to health in the South African Constitution

South Africa's final Constitution, adopted in 1996, entrenches health rights as part of a bundle of socioeconomic rights, including to food, water, social security, housing and education, as well as children's rights to basic amenities (Constitution 1996: ss 26–29). These rights are located within an explicitly transformative Constitution, with a pervasive foundational commitment to creating a responsive, accountable and open democratic State based on equality, dignity and freedom (Constitution 1996: preamble, ss 1.a, d, 7.1, 36.1, 39.1.a, 41.c, 195.1.f, g). Notably, the Constitution also entrenches a typology of duties similar to that in international human rights law and the State is required to 'respect, protect, promote and fulfil all rights' (s 7.1).

The Constitution entrenches a number of health-related rights, including children's rights to basic healthcare services in section 28.1.c and prisoner's rights to adequate medical treatment in section 35.2.e. The universal health right in section 27 states that everyone has the right to have access to healthcare services, including reproductive healthcare, and that no one may be refused emergency medical treatment (Constitution 1996: ss 27.1.a, 27.3). Section 27 goes on to specify that State duties under this right are to take reasonable legislative and other measures, within available resources, to achieve progressive realisation of the right (Constitution 1996: s 27.2). These formulations provide little indication of the nature or scope of the entitlement that the right to access healthcare services confers, nor of the extent to which resource limitations and progressive realisation could permissibly limit the State's duty to ensure access. Indeed, objections within South Africa to the constitutional entrenchment of social rights explicitly focused on the vagueness of these terms, and the potential legal and political harms that the constitutional entrenchment of an unspecified social right could cause (Davis 1992).

It is notable therefore that when the final Constitution was certified in *Ex Parte Chairperson of the Constitutional Assembly: in re Certification of the Constitution of the Republic of South Africa*, (1993) the Constitutional Court explicitly rejected objections to the democratic legitimacy and competence of the judicial enforcement of social rights, arguing that all judicial review carries budgetary implications, that much of it makes social policy, and that enforcing social and economic rights was certainly not so different a task that it would breach the separation of powers.[2] The Court indicated that socioeconomic rights were 'at least to some extent, justiciable', and '[a]t the very minimum . . . can be negatively protected from improper invasion'.[3] While the Court's decision is certainly an endorsement of the justiciability of social rights, its qualifications in this regard nonetheless reflect a tentative approach to enforcement, which essentially characterised social rights as primarily positive.

Indeed, the first case that the Constitutional Court decided on this right seemed to suggest both that the right was of limited justiciability, and also seemed to indicate a corresponding judicial unwillingness to enforce its positive duties. In *Soobramoney v. Minister of Health (Kwa-Zulu Natal)*, the Constitutional Court held that a provincial hospital's rationing of access to renal dialysis did not breach section 27, and that since social rights depended on resources, an unqualified obligation to meet even basic needs could not be fulfilled.[4] Mr. Soobramoney approached the Constitutional Court after being refused renal dialysis by a State hospital that rationed treatment for patients with chronic renal failure unless they were also eligible for a kidney transplant. The Court dismissed Soobramoney's claim, finding that the provincial hospital's failure to provide renal dialysis facilities for all people with chronic renal failure did not breach the State's obligations under section 27. The Court considered that permitting claims for these and similarly expensive treatments could prejudice all other health needs, and indeed the government's ability to meet broader social and economic needs.[5] The Court recognised that difficult decisions about healthcare allocations and priorities would have to be made and that it would be slow to interfere with rational decisions taken in good faith.[6] It reasoned that in this case, there had been no suggestion that the guidelines were either unreasonable or applied unfairly or irrationally. In these circumstances, the Court found the guidelines to be a rational response to scarce resources which maximised the number of people who could access dialysis.[7] It is significant, however, that the Court made no real inquiry into the evidentiary basis of the resource question, essentially accepting the State's argument of scarcity. The decision seemed to indicate that the constitutional right to health held little real force as against political policy-making or resource allocations, and the decision was largely taken to illustrate that the Constitution's social rights were not justiciable (Moellendorf 1998: 327; Ngwenya 2000: 33). Nonetheless, the implication that the Court would be willing to interfere in policy when rationality was in question was borne out in the seminal *Grootboom* case on housing that followed, which dealt with squatters who were evicted from government-owned land without alternative shelter.

In *Government of the Republic of South Africa and Others v. Irene Grootboom and Others*,[8] the Court enforced the right to housing against the State, finding that its policy fell short of constitutional standards by failing to provide for the shelter needs of those in crisis situations. The Court rejected arguments by *amicus curiae* that it should recognise a minimum core, noting that the UN Social Rights Committee had not defined the core for housing, and arguing that it lacked the competence or information necessary to do so. Instead, the Court indicated that it would enforce social rights according to a constitutional standard of reasonableness, given the country's overwhelming poverty and the constitutional commitment to equality, dignity and freedom. The Court argued in accordance with this standard, that the State had a negative duty not to prevent the right of access to adequate housing. The State, it held, also had a qualified positive duty to act reasonably to provide basic necessities of life to those who lacked them, given how effectively and thoroughly those without food, clothing and shelter were denied dignity and freedom.[9]

The Court indicated that reasonableness required comprehensive programs aimed at meeting short-, medium- and long-term needs.[10] Excluding a significant segment of society would be unreasonable, as would excluding the needs of the poor given their reliance on the State for the basic necessities of life.[11] The Court was emphatic that social rights were entrenched because 'we value human beings and want to ensure that they are afforded their basic human needs', and that this meant that measures aimed at broader realisation could not ignore those whose needs were most urgent and whose ability to enjoy all rights was most in peril.[12] At the same time, the Court recognised that the State could not be required to do more than available resources permitted, and that while resources would determine the content and pace of realisation, government nonetheless should give adequate budgetary support to social rights and plan and monitor efforts to meet all needs.[13]

While *Grootboom* was hailed as a seminal socioeconomic rights case, illustrating the feasibility of enforcing social rights, the Court's rejection of the minimum core was criticised inside the country for short-changing the transformative potential of the social rights provisions of the Constitution (Roux 2002; Bilchitz 2002), Indeed, both admirers and critics of the Court's approach suggest that the reasonableness standard, read in concert with the rejection of the minimum core, raised questions as to whether the entitlement was in fact an individual right that guaranteed particular services, rather than an administrative law model of socioeconomic rights that required sensible priority setting (Sunstein 2000: 123, 131; Bilchitz 2002). Certainly, the case raised questions as to whether the reasonableness standard could offer tangible relief from deprivation and adequately substitute for the minimum core (Fitzpatrick and Slye 2003).

Partial answers to these questions came in *Minister of Health and Another v. Treatment Action Campaign and Others* in 2002.[14] The case took place amidst a tremendous social battle with the executive over government's refusal to provide any forms of AIDS treatment in the public sector. This refusal was significantly based on President Mbeki's support for 'AIDS denialism', which not only disputes that HIV causes AIDS, but views antiretroviral drugs as fatally toxic (Harvey 2000; Cohen 2001; Cameron 2003). To put this decision in context, South Africa has one of the world's largest AIDS pandemics, with an estimated 5.27 million people infected in 2007, approximately 17.64 per cent of adults in the 15–49 year old age group (South African Department of Health 2007). AIDS has become the single largest cause of death in the country, with over 300,000 people dying per year (Dorrington *et al.* 2001), and an estimated 1.2 million deaths from HIV/AIDS to date (Dorrington *et al.* 2004). One-and-a-half million children are estimated to have been orphaned as a result (Dorrington *et al.* 2006: i), and around 80–90,000 infants were being maternally infected every year.

Social contestation over the government's resolute refusal to provide treatment coalesced around its delays and active obstruction of public sector use of Nevirapine, an antiretroviral drug with growing efficacy in preventing mother-to-child transmission (MTCT) of AIDS (Guay 1999; Moodley 2001). The drug had been offered to the government at no cost for five years by Boehringer Ingelheim, the manufacturer and patent holder. Despite government refusals, the expansion of a national MTCT program was well supported among the media, public and medical communities (The Mercury 2002; Abdool Karim 2002), motivated in part by national legal and political advocacy, and the growing protests of health-care workers themselves that government policy interfered with their ethical duties towards patients.

In August 2001, the Treatment Action Campaign (TAC), a national treatment advocacy group, together with doctors working in the public sector and a children's rights non-governmental organisation, instituted legal action against the Minister of Health and Provincial Health departments, arguing that the State's delays and refusal to make Nevirapine available in the public sector breached section 27, as well as children's right to basic health services. The government strongly defended the reasonableness of its approach, citing concerns about the drug in question and the cost of a comprehensive program. It also vigorously contested the democratic legitimacy of judicial review of health policy, or the constitutionality of it making anything more than declaratory orders that simply declare the unconstitutionality of the policy in question (as compared to mandatory orders which specify action to be taken). The *TAC* case therefore required the Constitutional Court to weigh in on a deeply divisive and politically momentous issue. In this light, the case became a test of the Court's willingness to meaningfully enforce the State's duties under section 27, given both the political implications of a judicial decision that challenged State decision-making, and the human implications for millions of HIV-infected or affected South Africans whose lives would be powerfully impacted by the availability of the medicines in question.

Read in this light, the judgment can be seen to illustrate the Court's effort to guard a strong judicial role in enforcing the right to health, while at the same time signalling its self-restraint to government. The Court found State policy to be unreasonable, and held that excluding the drug in question in public healthcare facilities pending study results unreasonably denied a potentially lifesaving drug to children born to mostly indigent mothers who were dependent on the State for their healthcare.[15] The Court firmly rejected the government's arguments that judicial review of health policy breached separation of powers, or that it was confined to making declaratory orders, and asserted its constitutional authority to order injunctive relief and supervisory orders.[16] At the same time, the Court emphatically rejected the direct enforceability of the minimum core, citing institutional incapacity and democratic considerations. The Court argued that it was 'impossible to give everyone access even to a "core" service immediately' and that '[a]ll that is possible, and all that can expected of the State, is that it act reasonably to provide access to the [Constitution's socioeconomic rights] on a progressive basis'.[17] The Court argued that doing more than this would breach the appropriate separation of powers and extend beyond the 'restrained and focused' judicial role contemplated by the Constitution.[18]

Perhaps in order to be seen to be engaging in uncontroversial legal practice, the Court intimated that the case dealt with the State's negative obligation to desist from impairing section 27, rather than with the positive duty to provide healthcare services.[19] Yet, the suggestion that this case dealt with negative duties alone is belied by the Court's declaratory and mandatory order, which not only declared government's responsibility to devise and implement a comprehensive MTCT program within its available resources, but ordered the government to remove restrictions on the drug without delay and make the drug in question available in the public sector, provide for training of counsellors and take reasonable measures to extend testing and counselling facilities throughout the public health sector.

5 Implications of the South African jurisprudence for theory and practice on right to health

The South African jurisprudence raises a range of questions about enforcing social rights and the Court's interpretation of this right. In the remainder of this chapter, I will focus on three key questions in this regard: the theoretical implications and practical adequacy of the reasonableness standard as a substitute for the minimum core; the strengths and pitfalls of the Court's approach to enforcing social rights and positive duties; and the implications of the reasonableness standard for the positive–negative distinction between civil and social rights.

5.1 The theoretical implications of the reasonableness standard versus the minimum core

A primary concern about the reasonableness standard as a substitute for the minimum core is the indeterminacy of its standards, since the reasonableness standard fails to identify specific temporal priorities to guide timely realisation (Roux 2002: 46–47), or to define urgency, desperation, and the key populations of the poor and vulnerable (Liebenberg 2002: 159). Certainly the indeterminacy of the reasonableness standard is exacerbated by the Court's failure to interpret any substantive content into section 27 in the *TAC* decision. I want to suggest, however, that the reasonableness standard is not theoretically inconsistent with the minimum core. While the standard is amorphous, it nevertheless gives important guidance on health policy, by requiring comprehensive policies focused on basic needs of the poor and vulnerable, and on urgent and desperate needs. There is a natural overlap between the reasonableness standard's focus on meeting the needs of the poor and vulnerable, and the focus in health equity on addressing systematic health differences between social groups with varying disadvantage (Braveman and Gruskin 2003: 254). This constitutional imperative is not inconsequential, and requiring State policy to focus on the needs of the poor is largely consistent with the core's emphasis on basic needs. For example, the minimum core focuses on State obligations to ensure equitable distribution of healthcare facilities, goods and services, essential drugs, non-discriminatory access to healthcare, access to food, water, housing and sanitation, and a comprehensive plan to provide healthcare for all (UN 2000: para 43). However, the reasonableness standard would certainly fail to substitute for the core if bald scarcity arguments were allowed to limit State actions designed to meet the basic needs and priority health interests of the poor, so that their social rights, and human rights more generally, were denuded of any content or meaning. The Court's socioeconomic jurisprudence suggests that this is not the case. What we see in *TAC* and *Grootboom*, is a willingness to find unreasonable policies that negatively impact on people's dignity irrespective of the government's allegations of resource scarcity or of their resource implications. This approach is similarly reflected in the 2003 case of *Khosa and Others v. Minister of Social Development and Others; Mahlaule and Another v. Minister of Social Development and Others*, where the Court found that excluding permanent residents from receiving social grants violated the State's obligations to provide access to social security for everyone in section 27.1.c.[20] The Court found that despite the government's averment of constrained resources, financial considerations were far outweighed by 'the importance of providing access to social assistance to all who live permanently in South Africa and the impact upon life and dignity that a denial of such access has'.[21] To this extent, a judicial focus on people's equal dignity and freedom, and the extent of human suffering caused by government policies, may provide an effectively comparable standard to the core. In this light, I would suggest that the Court's rejection of the core should not be seen to fracture the spirit and intent of international human rights law, but rather to be substantially in harmony with it.

5.2 Practical outcomes of the jurisprudence

Ultimately, however, the Court's jurisprudence must be judged on its efficacy in addressing the deprivation in question. In this regard, both *Grootboom* and *TAC* appeared to have significant policy implications: the *Grootboom* decision forced national policy on housing to address the housing needs of people in crisis; while the *TAC* decision significantly altered the tenor and course of national AIDS policy. For example, the *TAC* decision not only achieved a national MTCT program in over 80 per cent of government clinics (South African Ministry of Health 2007), but laid the groundwork for a national AIDS treatment program, which was announced in 2003 (South African Department of Health 2003). By October 2006, approximately 165–175,000 people were accessing antiretrovirals through this program (International Treatment Preparedness Coalition 2006: 45). These are outstanding outcomes for enforcement of the right to health, since it secured a critical health service for poor and vulnerable people, and effectively gave a legal priority to the health needs of the poor against competing governmental priorities. Moreover the right conferred a powerful social claim on a stigmatised population that had been unfairly excluded from the benefits of public healthcare.

Nonetheless, there is an interesting distinction in the implementation of these cases. After the *Grootboom* decision, the government's formulation and implementation of housing policy was troublingly slow – a year after the decision there had been little tangible change in housing policy to cater for people in desperate and crisis situations (Pillay 2003: 12). The picture was considerably different in *TAC*, perhaps because of the power of domestic treatment advocates, who effectively used the media to highlight implementation delays, and who also instituted contempt of court proceedings against a provincial premier for not implementing the decision (Heywood 2003). Nonetheless, if political mobilisation by civil society is necessary to ensure timely implementation of Court decisions, this would suggest that judicial enforcement is quite weak, and may suggest the need to counter the indeterminacy of the reasonableness standard through mandatory orders and supervisory jurisdiction (as compared to the Constitutional Court's use in the *TAC* decision of a mandatory order without any form of overview of its implementation). The use of supervisory jurisdiction over the implementation of court orders is an option the Court left open in the *TAC* decision, which the Court may well utilise if State compliance is persistently dilatory or inadequate. In the interim, 'social' enforcement of court orders seems a feasible and effective alternative.

5.3 Positive–negative distinctions between social and civil rights

The Constitutional Court's enforcement of the right to health nonetheless sends a clear message to other legal cultures regarding the justiciability of social rights and positive duties. It illustrates the legitimacy of a judicial role in enforcing social rights, and answers pragmatic concerns about the zero-sum claims that these rights presumptively make, and about the institutional competence and democratic legitimacy of judicial review of social policy. While the Court's cautious and qualified enforcement of the State's positive duties certainly limits concerns about judicial arrogation of the executive function, it also reifies the idea of positive duties as questionably enforceable and negative duties as unquestionably so. This differential approach is evident in the Court's elaboration of alternative regimes for enforcing the negative and positive duties that each constitutional right (whether social or civil) is interpreted to entail. Thus in *Rail Commuters Action Group and others v. Transnet Ltd*[22] and *Jaftha v. Schoeman and Others; van Rooyen v. Stoltz and Others*,[23] the Court held that civil rights impose positive duties that should be assessed according to the constitutional standard of reasonableness, while viewing social rights as imposing negative duties not subject to progressive realisation, and which should instead be assessed under the Constitution's general limitations clause.[24] In this light, positive duties are seen as inherently limited and subject to progressive realisation, while negative duties are not. These aspects of the Court's jurisprudence suggest that its interpretation of the Constitution's social rights remains rooted in a sharp distinction between positive and negative duties, despite the fact that there may not be sharp distinctions between the kind of actions and resources needed to realise these duties. This distinction suggests that the Court has not fully discarded the ideological baggage associated with positive rights, and this persistent legal cultural bias may obscure the analytical work needed to effectively attend to rights violations. What is needed instead is an approach to rights and violations that focuses on what needs to be done, rather than shoehorning judicial analysis and enforcement into outdated and ultimately unhelpful categories.

6 Conclusion

The South African jurisprudence suggests that the force of the country's constitutional right to health is not just a function of its constitutional entrenchment, but of the judiciary's willingness to give it teeth. This outcome suggests that constitutional protection alone cannot guarantee the priority or strength given to particular rights, and more fundamentally, that judicial choices may be motivated by internalised ideological conceptions of the appropriate role of law and the State. This influence suggests that if the right to health is to assume judicial force, it must influence these deeper ideological conceptions of law itself, including by targeting the legal education that often continues to train judges in outmoded paradigms on social rights. In this light, social rights litigation can be viewed as providing an important but insufficient strategy for realising the right to health. The right to health will not be realised through judicial enforcement alone, and achieving its full social justice potential requires that it become internalised within individuals and societies as a basic social and political entitlement, and therefore, as a collective expectation of what should appropriately be politically prioritised and legally protected. When claims for health can combine this legal and social force, through rights discourse, advocacy, social mobilisation and litigation, the right to health may become significantly empowered as a remedial tool for global health, capable of placing reasonable limits on politics and economics in service of the health interests of the poor.

Notes

1 See for example, *Dandridge v. Williams* [1970] 397 U.S. 471; *Gosselin v. Québec (Attorney General)*, [2002] 4 S.C.R. 429; *Deshaney v. Winnbago County Dep't of Social Services* [1989] 489 U.S. 189, 194, and *Andrews v. Law Society of British Columbia* [1989] 1 S.C.R 123.
2 [1996] (4) S. Afr. L. R 744 (S. Afr. Const. Crt.), para 77 [*Ex Parte Chairperson of the Constitutional Assembly*]
3 *Ex Parte Chairperson of the Constitutional Assembly*, para 78
4 [1998] 1 S.Afr.L.R. 765 (S. Afr. Const. Ct.), para 11. [*Soobramoney*]
5 *Soobramoney*, paras. 28 and 31.
6 *Soobramoney*, para 29.
7 *Soobramoney*, paras 24–25.
8 [2000] 11 B.Const. L.R. 1169 (S. Afr. Const. Ct.). [*Grootboom*]
9 *Grootboom*, para 24.
10 *Grootboom*, paras 40–44.
11 *Grootboom*, paras 35 and 44.
12 *Grootboom*, para 44.
13 *Grootboom*, para 32, 68.
14 [2002] 5 S.Afr.L.R. 721 (S.Afr.Const.Ct). [*TAC*]
15 *TAC*, para 79.
16 *TAC*, para 96.
17 *TAC*, para 35.
18 *TAC*, para 38.
19 *TAC*, para 40.
20 [2003] Constitutional Court of South Africa, Cases CCT 12/03; CCT13/03, para 38. [*Khosa*]

21 *Khosa*, para 82.
22 [2003] Constitutional Court of South Africa, CCT 56/03. [*Rail Commuters*]
23 [2005] (2) S. Afr. L. R. 140 (Const. Crt.). [*Jaftha*]
24 *Rail Commuters*: paras 70 and 88; and *Jaftha*.

Bibliography

Abdool Karim, S. Abdool Karim, Q., Adhikari, M., Cassol, S., Chersich, M., Cooper, P., Coovadia, A., Coovadia, H., Cotton, M., Coutsoudis, A., Hide, W., Hussey, G., Maartens, G., Madhi, S., Martin, D., Pettifor, J.M., Rollins, N., Sherman, G., Thula, S., Urban, M., Velaphi, S. and Williamson, C. (2002) 'Vertical HIV Transmission in South Africa: Translating Research into Policy and Practice', *The Lancet*, 359: 992–3.

Berlin, I. (1969) *Four Essays on Liberty*. Oxford: Oxford University Press.

Bilchitz, D. (2002) 'Towards a Reasonable Approach to the Minimum Core: Laying the Foundations for Future Socio-economic Rights Jurisprudence', *South African Journal on Human Rights*, 19: 1–126.

Braveman, P. and Gruskin, S. (2003) 'Defining Equity in Health', *Journal of Epidemiology and Community Health*, 57: 254–8.

Cameron, E. (2003) 'AIDS Denial and Holocaust Denial – AIDS, Justice and the Courts in South Africa', *South African Law Journal* 120(3): 525–39.

Cohen, M. (2001) 'Mbeki Questions HIV Testing', *Associated Press*, 24 April 2001

Constitution of the Republic of South Africa Act 200 (1993), assented to 25 January 1994, date of commencement, 27 April 1994.

Cranston, M. (1973) *What are Human Rights?* London: Bodley Head.

Davis, D. (1992) 'The Case Against Inclusion of Socio-Economic Rights in a Bill of Rights Except as Directive Principles', *South African Journal on Human Rights* 8: 475–90.

Dorrington, R.E. Bourne, D., Bradshaw, D., Laubscher, R. and Timæus, I. R. (2001) *The Impact of HIV/AIDS on Adult Mortality in South Africa*, Technical Report. Burden of Disease Research Unit, Medical Research Council.

Dorrington, R.E, Bradshaw, D., Johnson, L. and Budlender, D. (2004) *The Demographic Impact of HIV/AIDS in South Africa: National Indicators for 2004*, Cape Town: Centre for Actuarial Research, South African Medical Research Council and Actuarial Society of South Africa.

Dorrington, R.E. Bradshaw, D., Johnson, L., and Budlender, D. (2006) *The Demographic Impact of HIV/AIDS in South Africa: National and Provincial Indicators for 2006*, Centre for Actuarial Research, South African Medical Research Council and Actuarial Society of South Africa.

Eide, A., Krause, C. and Rosas, A. (1995) *Economic, Social and Cultural Rights: A Textbook*. Dordrecht: Martinus Nijhoff.

Fitzpatrick, J. and Slye, R.C. (2003) 'Republic of South Africa v. Grootboom / Minister of Health v. Treatment Action Campaign', *American Journal of International Law*, 97(3): 669–80.

Forman, L. (2008a) 'Justice and Justiciability: Advancing Solidarity Through South Africans' Right to Health Jurisprudence', *Medicine and Law*, 27(3): 661–83.

Forman, L. (2008b) ' "Rights" and Wrongs: What Utility for the Right to Health in Reforming Trade Rules on Medicines?', *Health and Human Rights: An International Journal*, 10(2): 37–52.

Goodman, T. (2005) 'Is there a Right to Health?', *Journal of Medicine and Philosophy*, 30: 643–62.

Guay, L. A. Musoke, P., Fleming, T., Bagenda, D., Allen, M., Nakabiito, C., Sherman, J., Bakaki, P., Ducar, C., Deseyve, M., Emel, L., Mirochnick, M., Fowler, M.G., Mofenson, L., Miotti, P., Dransfield, K., Bray, D., Mmiro, F. and Jackson, J.B. (1999) 'Intrapartum and Neonatal Single-Dose Nevirapine Compared with Zidovudine for Prevention of Mother-to-Child Transmission of HIV-1 in Kampala, Uganda: HIVNET 012 Randomised Trial', *The Lancet*, 354: 795–802.

Harvey, M. (2000) 'How Can a Virus Cause a Syndrome? Asks Mbeki' iClinic online Aegis, see www.aegis.com/news/woza/2000/IC000906.html

Heywood, M. (2003) 'Contempt or Compliance? The TAC Case after the Constitutional Court Judgment', *ESR Review*, 4(7): 7–10.

Holmes, S. and Sunstein, C.R. (2000) *The Cost of Rights*. New York: W.H. Norton.

Human Rights Program, Harvard Law School,Harvard Law School, and the Francois-Xavier Bagnoud Center for Health and Human Rights, Harvard School of Public Health (1995) *Economic and Social Rights and the Right to Health: An Interdisciplinary Discussion Held at Harvard Law School in September, 1993*, Cambridge, MA: Human Rights Program, Harvard Law School and the Francois-Xavier Bagnoud Center for Health and Human Rights, Harvard School of Public Health.

International Treatment Preparedness Coalition (2006) *Missing the Target* #3: Stagnation in AIDS treatment Scale Up Puts Millions of Lives at Risk, 28 November 2006.

Liebenberg, S. (2002) 'South Africa's Evolving Jurisprudence on Socio-economic Rights', *Law, Democracy and Development* 6(2): 159–91.

Limburg Principles on the Implementation of the International Covenant on Economic, Social and Cultural Rights (1986) Maastricht, 2–6 June 1986.

Maastricht Guidelines (1997) Maastricht Guidelines on Violations of Economic, Social and Cultural Rights, 22–26 January 1997, reprinted in *International Commission of Jurists, Economic, Social and Cultural Rights: A Compilation of Essential Documents*, Geneva: ICJ, 1997.

Moellendorf, D. (1998) 'Reasoning about Resources: Soobramoney and the Future of Socio-Economic Rights Claims', *South African Journal on Human Rights*, 14: 327–33.

Moodley, D. (2001) 'The SAINT Trial: Nevirapine (NVP) versus Zidovudine (ZDV) + Lamivudine (3TC) in Prevention of Peripartum Transmission', International AIDS conference XIII, Durban, South Africa, 9–14 July 2000, abstract no. LbOr2.

Ngwenya, C. (2000) 'The Recognition of Access to Health Care as a Human Right in South Africa: Is it Enough?', *Health and Human Rights* 5(1): 27–44.

Nozick, R. (1974) *Anarchy, State, and Utopia*, New York: Basic Books Inc.

Pillay, K. (2002) 'Implementing Grootboom: Supervision Needed', *ESR Review*, 3(1): 1–2.

Roux, T. (2002) 'Understanding Grootboom – A Response to Cass R. Sunstein', *Forum Constitutionnel*, 12(2): 41–51.

Sen, A. (2000) *Development as Freedom*, New York: Anchor Books.

Shue, H. (1980) *Basic Rights, Subsistence, Affluence and US Foreign Policy*, Princeton, NJ: Princeton University Press.

Smith, R.D, Correa, C. and Oh, C. (2009) 'Trade, TRIPs and Pharmaceuticals', *The Lancet*, 373: 684–91.

South African Department of Health (2003) Operational Plan for Comprehensive HIV and AIDS Care, Management and Treatment for South Africa 19 November 2003, (Care Plan) online: Government of Republic of South Africa.

South African Department of Health (2008) 'National HIV and Syphilis Antenatal Sero-Prevalence Survey in South Africa 2007', see http://www.doh.gov.za/aids/index.html.

South African Ministry of Health (2007) '100% Coverage for Prevention of Mother to Child Transmission of HIV', 12 March 2007.

Steiner, H. J. and Alston, P. (eds.) (2000) *International Human Rights in Context: Law, Politics, Morals*, Oxford: Clarendon Press.

Sunstein, C.R. (2000) 'Social and Economic Rights? Lessons from South Africa', *Constitutional Forum* 4: 123–32.

The Mercury Editorial (2002) 'Government Should Provide Anti-retrovirals' (6 December 2002).

Toebes, B.C.A. (1999) *The Right to Health as a Human Right in International Law*, Antwerp: Intersentia.

United Nations (1991) *Committee on Economic, Social and Cultural Rights. General Comment 3: The Nature of States Parties' Obligations*, U.N. Doc. E/1991/23.

United Nations (2000) *Committee on Economic, Social, and Cultural Rights. General Comment No. 14: The Right to the Highest Attainable Standard of Health.* UN Doc E/C.12/2000/4 (11 August 2000).

United Nations (2008) Office of the High Commissioner for Human Rights. Ratifications and Reservations, see http://www2.ohchr.org/english/bodies/ratification/index.htm.

Waldron, J. (1993) *Liberal Rights: Collected Papers 1981–1991*, New York: Cambridge University Press.

Williamson, J. (2002) 'Did the Washington Consensus Fail?' (Speech to the Center for Strategic & International Studies, 6 November 2002) see http://www.iie.com/publications/papers/williamson1102.htm.

5 The ancillary-care responsibilities of researchers

Reasonable but not great expectations

Roger Brownsword[1]

1 Introduction

It is axiomatic that the first responsibility of researchers, whether they are working in the developed or the developing world, is to (strive to) do no harm to those who participate in their studies or trials. However, on neither side of the Atlantic is there any such settled view with regard to the responsibility of researchers to attend to the ancillary-care needs of their participants – that is, a responsibility to advise or assist participants who have medical condition *x* in circumstances where the research concerns medical condition *y*, and the research did not contribute to the presence of condition x in participants, nor did the having of condition *x* contribute to the research (Richardson and Belsky 2004; Belsky and Richardson 2004). Consider, for example, the following hypothetical posed by Leah Belsky and Henry Richardson: 'Researchers testing a new treatment for tuberculosis in a developing country discover some patients have HIV infection. Do they have a responsibility to provide antiretroviral drugs?' (Belsky and Richardson 2004: 1494)

What is the answer? Do the researchers (or their sponsors) have a duty to offer any kind of ancillary assistance to their participants? If so, is their duty simply to inform participants that they are HIV positive, or does their responsibility extend to providing (or covering the cost of) antiretroviral drugs? (Nuffield Council on Bioethics 2002, 2005).

Prompted by such questions, there are three related strands in this paper. First, in Sections 2–4, I develop the proposition that in 'a community of rights' – my idea of the benchmark setting for making moral judgments – agents would be treated as having prima facie positive obligations to one another where a four-stage test (relating to placement, capacity, reasonable imposition and fair demand) is satisfied. Second, in Sections 5 and 6, I contend that the application of this test would point to researchers having ancillary-care responsibilities to their participants. Moreover, I argue that researchers would be fixed with such responsibilities regardless of whether the trial is in a developed or a developing country. Third, in Section 7, I suggest that the courts in a community of rights might well set an example for more cautious common law courts by ruling that research participants have a reasonable expectation – whether as a matter of contract or tort law – to ancillary-care advice and assistance.

There is just one other essential introductory remark. In line with the spirit of debate in a community of rights, the emphasis of my discussion is more on the process than on a conclusive product. We are dealing with a difficult case, with many tricky spin-off issues; there are no knock-down answers; and the best that I can do is to suggest how such a matter might be addressed. It follows that, by the end of the chapter, there is still a good deal of unfinished business – but, in a community of rights, there is a sense that this is business as usual.

2 Reasonable expectations: easy cases and more difficult cases

Let us suppose that a participant in a research trial claims to have a reasonable expectation of ancillary-care advice or assistance from the research team. For ethicists and lawyers alike, this would seem to be a novel claim. In the absence of exceptional express undertaking or bespoke legal support (of the kind that simply does not currently exist), how might such a claim be made out?

In what are relatively easy cases, the claimant will appeal to some aspect of practice or protocol, proximate to the trial, which provides the basis for the expectation and characterises it as reasonable. For example, the case is easily made out if the relevant undertaking (assuring advice, assistance or treatment) has been given prior to enrolment, or if it is an explicit term of the contract to participate, or if the responsibility to offer such ancillary care is generally accepted and acted upon as a matter of common custom and practice. However, if there is no such immediate anchoring point in practice, what then? The claimant might, in good faith, have the relevant expectation, but this is little more than a *de facto* expectation. On what basis is the claimant's expectation to be presented as *reasonable*?

A more difficult case might be made out on the basis that, although there has been no direct undertaking or promise, the commitments of the researchers or the larger community imply that such ancillary-care benefit should be provided. For example, it might be argued that, in a community with a commitment to human rights, the expectation is reasonable because it teases out the implicit responsibilities of researchers in such a community. Or, it might be asserted that a rough idea of reciprocal altruism is widely recognised, so that one act of altruism deserves another: thus, where participants enter a research trial knowing that they have nothing to gain from the project itself, the researchers owe some measure of ancillary-care to participants by way of a return act of altruism.

The most difficult case is one that is wholly independent of practice (Brownsword 2003). If the claim is that an expectation is reasonable by reference to some specified standard, it is likely to elicit the sceptical response that, even if the standard indicates that there should be ancillary-care benefit, there is no reason to recognise it as binding. Hence, if it is argued that, (contrary) community practice notwithstanding, human rights set the standard, the sceptic will respond that this smacks of a fresh outbreak of nonsense on stilts.

As I have indicated already, I will assume that the benchmark for such ethically problematic cases is a community of rights. Accordingly, before we address our principal question, we need to say a little more about the nature of such a community.

3 The nature of a community of rights

Given that a community of rights is a particular kind of *moral* community, it must systematically embed a *moral* standpoint (in the formal sense); and because it is a community of *rights*, the substantive moral approach embedded is rights-led. The significance of this latter point is that, by taking a rights-led approach, such a community distinguishes itself from its two principal rivals, namely those communities in which the governing ethic is, in the one case, utility-maximising and, in the other, duty-driven (Brownsword 2008: chapter 2).

Arguably, the assumption of a community of rights is at least encouraged, if not presupposed, by our line of inquiry, for we would scarcely take seriously the possibility of ancillary-care obligations unless it was axiomatic that researchers already have extensive responsibilities to their (*rights*-holding) participants. It is also an assumption that will not be challenged by those who are of a Rawlsian or Dworkinian disposition (Rawls 1972; Dworkin 1978): taking rights seriously, or privileging the right over the good, entails the rejection of utilitarianism; and while, to this extent, Rawlsians and Dworkinians are with Kant, they prefer to lead with rights rather than (as in Kant's case) duties. It is also an assumption that is immune to challenge wherever communities have signed up to respect for human rights, because they thereby express their commitment to a rights-led ethic. Having said this, to make out a comprehensive case in favour of treating a community of rights as the benchmark setting for moral and legal judgments would necessitate a major theoretical detour that I cannot undertake in this paper (Beyleveld and Brownsword 1983, 1986; Gewirth 1978, 1996).

An important feature of my specification of a community of rights is that, while all members recognise the fundamental importance of respecting rights, they do not regard themselves as morally omniscient. Accordingly, the community of rights should be viewed as a reflective and interpretive society, not so much a finished product as an ongoing process. These various defining characteristics call for some short elaboration.

3.1 The essential characteristics of a community of rights

First, we are dealing with a *moral* community. No doubt, there could be considerable debate about the precise specification of the generic characteristics of the formally speaking 'moral', whether it is a moral standpoint or a moral community. However, I take it that a community of rights, as a moral community, must hold its commitments sincerely and in good faith; that it must treat its standards as categorically binding and universalisable; and that there must be an integrity and coherence about its commitments as a whole.

Second, as a community that is committed to the protection and promotion of individual rights, its moral approach is rights-led. In this respect, as I have just said, it distinguishes itself from both utilitarian and duty-driven instantiations of moral community. Crucially, this means that the interests of research participants will not be subordinated to the greater good; nor, on the other side, will researchers be constrained by the kind of dignitarian duty-driven concerns that have become so influential in modern bioethics (Brownsword 2006a).

Third, the fundamental baseline value of a community of rights will be to respect the conditions and the context that comprise, so to speak, the agency commons (Brownsword 2009a). We can argue about the details of this context (or commons), but it will include elements pertaining to our well-being (clean air and water, food, environmental integrity, and the like) and our freedom (security, an absence of fear and intimidation, and so on). Not to harm one another directly is fine, but the setting for flourishing agency requires more than this minimal interactive restraint. Ideal-typically, this baseline value and its guiding standards will be regarded as rationally justifiable (members viewing the guidance as a dialectically necessary entailment of agency (Gewirth 1978)). Having said this, for most practical purposes, it matters little how a community that is committed to respect for the generic rights of agents arrives at this position.

Fourth, following on from the previous point, let me repeat that I conceive of a community of rights as a society that views itself as an ongoing process rather than a finished product. By this, I mean that it is a community that constantly keeps under review the question of whether the current interpretation of its commitments is the best interpretation. There is also an awareness by members of their limited knowledge and understanding; members do not regard themselves as morally omniscient; what seems like the best interpretation today might look less convincing tomorrow.

Fifth, in a community of rights, the discourses of ethics and of regulation are regarded as both contiguous and continuous. Debates about the ethics of rights flow straight into the regulatory consciousness; and regulatory reflection on rights flows back into ethical debate. It is not enough that regulation is effective and fit for purpose; the first priority is that regulators should have the right purposes (rights-respecting purposes) and that the regulatory standards are legitimate relative to the community's rights values. In a community of rights, regulation, like ethics, is an enterprise that is dedicated to doing the right thing; and the right thing is the protection, preservation and promotion of the community's commitment to rights.

Sixth, in a community of rights, a will (or choice) theory of rights, rather than an interest theory of rights, is adopted (Hart 1973; MacCormick 1977) and, as a corollary, the paradigmatic bearer of rights is one who has the developed capacity for exercising whatever rights are held, including making choices about whether to give or to refuse consent in relation to the rights that are held.

Finally, it should be said that, even with these shared characteristics, there is considerable margin for each community of rights to express and articulate its commitments in its own way – for example, from one community to another, there might be different views about the status of non-paradigmatic rights-holders, and especially so in relation to the details of the array of recognised rights (Beyleveld and Brownsword 2006).

3.2 Questions for a community of rights

Without attempting to be exhaustive, some of the more pressing and recurring questions to be addressed, debated and (at least, provisionally) resolved within a community of rights are the following.

First, there is a large cluster of questions concerning which rights, negative and positive, are to be recognised and what the scope of those particular rights is (Brownsword 2009b). If research participants and patients have a right not to be harmed, do the former also have a right to ancillary-care advice and assistance? If so, how far does this right extend, for how long does it endure (e.g. only for the length of the trial), and so on?

Second, there are questions arising from conflicts between rights as well as from competition between rights-holders. Sometimes the conflict might be between one kind of right and another – for example, between the right to privacy and the right to freedom of expression. At other times, there might be competing rights – that is, cases where two rights-holders conflict over the same general right. If relative need is the criterion, this might facilitate an easy resolution where, say, a seriously ill person claims a right to the one available hospital bed in competition with a less ill person; but how should we decide whether the claims of needy research participants are prior to the claims of needy non-participants, or if the claims of HIV-positive agents are prior to the claims of agents with tuberculosis (TB)?

Third, because consent is an extremely important dynamic in a community of rights, the community needs to debate the terms on which a supposed 'consent' will be recognised as valid and effective. In particular, how does the community interpret the requirement that consent should reflect an unforced and informed choice, and how is consent to be signalled (will an opt-out scheme suffice, for instance), and so on (Brownsword 2004; Beyleveld and Brownsword 2007)?

Fourth, a community of rights must debate whether there are limits to the transformative effect of the reception of rights (Beyleveld and Pattinson 2002). In particular, this invites reflection on the relationship between one community of rights and another.

Finally, there is the vexed question of who has rights. Do young children, foetuses or embryos have rights? What about the mentally incompetent or the senile? And what about non-human higher animals, smart robots, and, in some future world, hybrids and chimeras of various kinds? Each community of rights must debate such matters and respond to the encompassing question (who has rights?), as well as determine an approach to those life-forms that are to be excluded.

Even though the members of a community of rights have a shared moral outlook, there is still plenty to debate. It is in this spirit that such a community would approach the question of researchers having ancillary-care obligations towards participants.

4 Positive rights and responsibilities

Two questions that present themselves to a community of rights are: (a) whether positive rights should be recognised at all within the *background* set of standards; and (b) if so, what kind of limiting principles govern the range of an agent's positive responsibilities. It is important to emphasise that we are dealing here with background rights and responsibilities, with rights and responsibilities that are imposed rather than freely assumed by promise or agreement, for I assume that it will be readily accepted in a community of rights that one agent may freely put himself under a positive obligation to another.

To deal with the first question, let us suppose that A, who is an experienced swimmer, observes B, who is a novice, getting into difficulty. Does A now have a positive responsibility for B's safety? Certainly, it would seem to be insouciant in the extreme if A were to shrug off any responsibility for B's well-being. But, would a community of rights fix A with a positive obligation as a matter of its background (imposed) moral standards?

I take it that no community of rights would reject the very idea of background positive requirements. In which case, the real question concerns the conditions that the community would set for the recognition of background positive obligations. I suggest that the conditions set would reflect the community's understanding and application of three guiding considerations. *First*, there are considerations of rational prescription. In any community that accepts the basic canons of rational prescription, an agent will only be required to assist another where 'ought implies can' is satisfied. It follows that no agent will be burdened with a positive obligation unless they are capable of rendering assistance. If we are to prescribe that A ought to assist B (by swimming over to assist B, or by throwing a line to B, or by calling a lifeguard, or whatever), then the demands that we make of A should at least be within A's capabilities. Second, there are considerations of reasonableness. How much can we reasonably demand of A? In the hypothetical, it seems that it would be little more than a minor inconvenience for A to rescue B. However, the circumstances might be very different. Is there a point beyond which it would be unreasonable to impose upon A? For example, if A would put his own life at risk by entering the waters, would we *require* such a heroic act (or would this be a case of supererogation)? Third, there are considerations of fairness. Even in a community that recognises positive rights, the default position is represented by 'can implies ought' – i.e. the default expectation is that those who are capable of helping themselves should do so. So, if the roles were reversed, we would expect B, an experienced swimmer, to rely on his own resources before seeking assistance from others.

Arguably – and I must emphasise that, given my specification of a community of rights, this is no more than arguably – by drawing on these considerations, a four-stage test along the following lines might be formulated for the recognition of particular background prima facie (and, it is important to note that these are simply prima facie) positive rights and responsibilities:

(a) Is A in a position to assist B?
(b) Does A have the capability to assist B in any material respect?
(c) Even though A is in a position to assist B and has the relevant capability, would the burden of responsibility on A be unreasonable relative to A's own essential interests?
(d) Even though A is in a position to assist B, has the relevant capability, and the imposition of responsibility on A would not be unreasonable (relative to A's essential interests), would B be taking unfair advantage of A if A were required to assist B?

Quite clearly, there is still a great deal of interpretive work to be done on these general principles, particularly in relation to the pivotal notions of 'unreasonable imposition', 'essential interests', and 'unfair advantage-taking'. Let us suppose that the community, recognising that these are slippery notions, tries to stabilise the four-stage test by focusing on the common needs of all agents, irrespective of their particular purposes, plans or projects – for example, the need of all agents for life and a level of basic physical and psychological well-being. With this focus, the community can say that A is not required to attempt to rescue B where this would jeopardise A's own life (this would be an unreasonable imposition) and, similarly, that A is not required to assist B where B is in no danger but simply wants A to teach him how to do the backstroke (this would be an unreasonable demand that amounts to another example of unfair advantage-taking).

Even with the test stabilised in this way, the community should also be mindful of a troubling pair of puzzles that threaten to undermine the practicability of any regime of positive rights. Stated shortly, one puzzle arises where A is not the only experienced swimmer on the beach. The question then is why we should single out A as the person responsible for assisting B. The converse puzzle arises where it is not just B, but B, C and D who are in difficulty, and A simply cannot assist all three. Here, the question is why we should single out, say, B as the agent to be assisted. For sure, the lesson to be taken from these puzzles is not that A is released from his positive obligation to assist (because, in the first case, others are also able to assist or because, in the second case, he cannot assist all three distressed agents). Rather, the lesson is that the community needs to articulate some principles of relative priority in relation to the bearers of positive duties (for the first kind of case) as well as those who are positive rights-holders (for the second kind of case).

In the light of these framework principles, we can turn to the question of how a community of rights might address the proposition that participants have a reasonable expectation, based on a background positive right – that researchers will attend to their ancillary-care requirements. For this purpose, we can focus on two test cases: first, the vexed question of whether the UK Biobank (see http://www.ukbiobank.ac.uk; McHale 2004) has a responsibility to provide any clinical feedback to participants; and, second, a developing country hypothetical of the kind suggested by Belsky and Richardson.

5 Test case I: the UK Biobank

The UK Biobank Ethics and Governance Framework (EGF, UK Biobank Ethics and Governance Council 2006) seeks to ensure that participants fully understand the purpose of the Biobank – crucially that it is not a healthcare programme but a research resource. At enrolment, participants are provided with some very basic data concerning their blood pressure, body mass index, estimated amount of fat, and the like (at 8, para IB3). However, the overriding message is that "UK Biobank will generally not provide health information to participants . . ." (ibid.). In the EGF, the rationale for this policy of non-disclosure is put in the following way:

> In normal healthcare settings, tests are conducted at the individual level immediately after sample collection; they search for specific conditions or outcomes; and, in the case of genetic tests, pre- and post-test counselling is provided. But, given the lack of knowledge at recruitment about the tests that might be done in this research context (and, hence, the inability to provide specific counselling beforehand), UK Biobank will not provide participants with information (genetic or otherwise) about their own individual results derived from examination of the database or samples by research undertaken after enrolment.
>
> (ibid., at 9)

So, on the side of the participants, there should be no therapeutic misconception; and, on the side of the researchers, there is an exercise of something akin to the therapeutic privilege.

Nevertheless, one can imagine an exceptional and urgent case where the research team realises that a particular participant has a serious health problem of which the participant is unaware. What then? According to Alastair Campbell (the first Chair of the Ethics and Governance Council):

> There will be a provision for communication of initial seriously abnormal findings, for example, indicators of diabetes or advanced cancer, but this will only be exceptional, and recruitment materials will not mention it, since it could give the false impression that no communication from Biobank meant a 'clean bill of health'.
>
> (Campbell 2006: 208, note 15)

This compromise (saying one thing but doing something else) might put an aggrieved participant in an interesting position. On the one hand, there would be no express undertaking on which to base a foreground claim for ancillary-care responsibilities; but, on the other hand, the Biobank seems to recognise a background positive obligation (albeit not expressly confessed in the EGF). If the participant were to press the matter, contending that the Biobank has a background responsibility to inform participants of such life-threatening conditions, how might such a claim fare relative to the four-stage test?

The first question, under the four-stage test, is whether the Biobank is in a position to assist one of its volunteer participants. Plainly, it is – indeed, in the light of the emphasis placed by the Biobank on building long-term and close relationships with its participants, it seems almost to have encouraged participants to believe that a special responsibility has been assumed. There is also a short answer to the second question. The Biobank has information that is material to the health and well-being of a participant. It has the capability to disclose that information; the question is whether it is required to do so.

The third stage is to consider whether the demand made of the Biobank is unreasonable relative to its own essential interests. Left to a subjective account of its essential interests, the Biobank (conceived as an aggregate of agents) might well argue that it is in the business of research, and that the reasonableness of any obligation to feed back clinical information should be judged relative to this fundamental mission. However, this is just the kind of special pleading that the community has neutralised by tying the notion of essential interests to those basic interests shared by all agents. No doubt, the burden of contacting and informing participants is more than trivial; but the imposition on responsible agents at the Biobank falls a long way short of being unreasonable.

Where, as we are assuming, the information relates to a serious medical condition, the essential interests of participants are implicated. Hence, at the fourth stage, the demand to be informed is entirely reasonable and there is no hint of unfair advantage-taking. Moreover, given that the Biobank participants receive no significant material or financial inducement; their participation is essentially public-spirited (much like blood donation in the UK) and immune against any accusation of free-riding or the like.[2]

Seemingly, then, the Biobank has a prima facie background obligation to feed back to participants important personal medical information where it happens to have it. This is not to suggest that the Biobank should actively seek out such information for all participants or offer treatment to them; nor does this discount the possibility that the Biobank might face competing or conflicting rights claims advanced by the potential beneficiaries of its research activities. Nevertheless, relative to the four-stage test, a participant's claimed right to be informed where the Biobank knowingly holds (and withholds) relevant medical information surely gets to first base.

6 Test case II: cross-community research

For our second test case, we will assume that researchers, who are based in a developed country, conduct their research in a developing country; and we will suppose that both countries fit the profile of a community of rights. The Nuffield Council on Bioethics reports the example of:

> a female sex worker in Benin, who was found to have pelvic inflammatory syndrome (resulting from an extra-uterine pregnancy) during a trial of a vaginal microbicide. The patient was referred to a gynaecology clinic, which asked for advance payment before performing an operation.
>
> (Nuffield Council on Bioethics 2005: para 3.26)

The sponsors had not envisaged such a situation; nevertheless, they paid the fee. But, did they have an obligation to do so? And, similarly, what would be the responsibility of the sponsors or researchers in the Belsky and Richardson hypothetical?

If our second test case arose within a developed country, using local participant agents, we would apply the four-stage test to determine the extent of the researchers' positive responsibilities. The same would be true, I suggest, if the participants were brought into the country to take part in the trial. However, our second case is rather different. The question, here, is whether the four-stage test, which is primarily designed for interactions between agents in a single community of rights, can be applied to the obligations owed by one community of rights to another, and to obligations owed by agents of one community to agents of another.

To start with, does it make sense to conceive of one community of rights having positive obligations to aid and assist another community of rights? Since the community is no more than an aggregate of the agents of that community, the question comes back: would it be coherent for an agent in one community to deny any kind of obligation to aid and assist an agent in another community (simply because the latter agent is in another community)? In principle, such a denial is incoherent: the fundamental basis of one agent having responsibilities of various kinds to another agent is not that these agents are members of the same club or community; it is simply that they are agents. Nevertheless, the fact that agents are located in different communities is far from irrelevant when it comes to assessing whether one particular agent's obligations have crystallised in relation to another agent. Quite simply, an agent in one community might not be in a position to assist an agent in another community. However, where the former agent is in a position to assist the latter, the four-stage test comes into play.

In practice, the agents of a developed community (defined as a community where the threshold generic conditions for agency are satisfied) will take collective steps to transfer resources to a developing community (defined as a community where conditions do not meet the generic threshold). Far from denying that it has positive obligations, the community's practice of offering aid for development speaks to the recognition of such obligations; and, other things being equal, a transfer at the community level results in a better chance of resources reaching those agents who are most in need of assistance. However, what if it is argued that once an agent in the developed community has made his contribution to the collective effort, it suffices to discharge his obligations? Certainly it would seem unfair, indeed disproportionate, to require one agent to contribute more than a fellow agent from the same community. Accordingly, if researchers (or their sponsors) in our second test case are to be required to contribute more than their fellow agents, there needs to be some reason for singling them out in this way.

Why should the researchers be singled out for an increased burden of responsibility? Not surprisingly, the answer is that, like the Biobank researchers, the visiting researchers step out of the background to put themselves in a position to assist their participants. It is not so much that the researchers are singled out, but that they single themselves out. Indeed, it is as though the researchers have taken up a position in the developing country, subject to the exigencies and demands of that community. However, unlike the Biobank researchers, they are not being asked simply to inform participants about their medical condition but actually to treat it (or to cover the cost of treatment). Are they required to do this?

Focusing on the Belsky and Richardson hypothetical, we can assume that we have a positive answer at the first two stages of the four-stage test – that is, we can assume that the researchers are in a position to assist, and that, based on their ability to access and supply antiretroviral drugs, they have the capacity to do so. Yet if the local healthcare system is also in a position to provide such treatment, it is unclear as to why the researchers become the principal duty-bearers. However, the point of the hypothetical is precisely that while the local healthcare system is unable to provide care, the researchers are able. The researchers, so to speak, having put themselves 'in the frame' for responsibility, find themselves in 'pole position' as the principal duty-bearers (c.f. Nuffield Council on Bioethics 2002).

Moving on to the third-stage question, if we take this approach, would it be overly demanding in relation to the researchers' essential interests? No doubt, the researchers will argue that their essential interest is in researching TB. However, this is not an essential interest in the relevant sense; it is not as though the researchers are being required to supply life-saving drugs that they need for their own health and well-being. Having said that, the researchers might well object that, if they are required to commit resources to alleviate participants' HIV infection, there will be less progress in developing more effective treatments for TB. This is a very serious point; but I suggest that in a community of rights, this would be viewed, not as a matter of unreasonable imposition, but as a potential conflict between the interests of persons with HIV and TB. This does not make the question any easier to resolve; but the interests of other rights-holders (persons with TB) should not block the argument to what is merely a prima facie responsibility.

There is also a question as to whether delivering antiretroviral drugs to the research participants but not to HIV-positive agents elsewhere in the developing community would unfairly privilege the former. Is this a serious objection? As we have said, where there are simply too many agents needing assistance, there will never be a perfect outcome and some principle of prioritisation is required – whether this is the folk-lore wisdom of 'women and children first', or a take on the classic philosophical puzzle about rescuing family members first. From the perspective of the researchers, they know that an identifiable group of their participants are HIV positive, and common sense indicates that they should proceed by acting on that information.

Nevertheless, this begs the question of why the researchers should not then go on to offer tests and assistance to other HIV-positive agents in the developing community. After all, a priority principle establishes who should be treated *first*, not who should be *treated*. Even if the HIV-positive non-participants are behind the participants in the queue for treatment, they might still be in the queue. For the researchers to deny these even more extensive obligations, they must show that it would be disproportionate to require them to treat anyone other than their participants. However, any attempt to draw a hard and fast line between participants and non-participants (other than for prioritisation) looks arbitrary.

If the claims to ancillary care can survive the first three stages of the four-stage test, can they survive the final stage? It is surely implausible to accuse the participants of taking unfair advantage of the researching agents. However, might it be argued that the claims of *non*-participants are limited? Those non-participants who are not willing to volunteer for the trial might be seen as free-riding (akin, perhaps, to agents who refuse to be vaccinated); they want the benefits without sharing the burdens. However, if we are dealing with non-participants who were willing to volunteer but who were not selected, this looks like a less fatal objection – particularly so when it was the researchers themselves who said no to these prospective participants.

Let us suppose that, researchers being persuaded by the above arguments, ancillary care is routinely made available to participants, but only exceptionally so to non-participants. In the event that researchers find themselves overwhelmed by willing participants, it might be necessary to select a small group of participants from a much larger group of willing volunteers. For those who are not selected, there is a response to the charge of free-riding: they were not trying to get something for nothing; they were willing; it was not their fault that they were not selected. However, in such circumstances, is there a new concern about the adequacy of the consent given by the participants? Does the known benefit of ancillary-care act as an incentive that distorts the free-choice element of informed consent? It would be a cruel irony if the researchers' conscientious attempt to do the right thing by their participants involved an unanticipated and wholly unintended violation of the principle that is universally accepted as fundamental to ethical research practice. This is not the place to open a discussion about the way in which incentives might invalidate free and informed consent (Nuffield Council on Bioethics 2002: 6.25–32; Brownsword 2007). Let it suffice to repeat that it surely would be perverse if the participants were not able to give valid consents because the researchers were offering ancillary care in line with their moral obligations.

7 Pleading a reasonable expectation: contract or tort?

Imagine that, in an attempt to accelerate the recognition of ancillary-care responsibilities, test-claims (asserting a contract- or tort-based reasonable expectation) are brought before the courts. In a community of rights, such claims would be arbitrated by reference to a body of legal doctrine that is integrated with the community's moral standards, these standards being reflected in the tort regime, which, in turn, provides the backdrop for contract law. However, in the common-law world, the architectural lines are not quite so clean. In this world, lawyers might well ponder whether, other things being equal, contract law or tort law would be more receptive to such a test claim.

We can deal with the law in three stages. First, I draw a thumbnail sketch of the relevant features of the common law regimes – a sketch that is more English than American in its particulars; but, no matter, since the critical question concerns the default ethic that implicitly guides the development and application of these legal regimes. Second, I consider the prospects for a tort claim brought against the Biobank (Johnston and Kaye 2004). Finally, I review the prospects for a contract claim brought against researchers (or their sponsors) who carry out their trial in a developing country – in both cases, the claimants arguing a reasonable expectation that ancillary-care advice and assistance should be, and would be, provided for the benefit of participants.

Before embarking on this part of the discussion, however, let me express a sweeping generalisation concerning the relative positions taken by English and American law: English law (whether tested in contract or tort) is probably the least likely of any common-law regime (worldwide) to support an ancillary-care test claim, from which it follows that American law is more likely than English law to support such a claim. It cannot be over-emphasised, though, that this statement should be covered with black-box health warnings. First, if we try to compare English *contract* law with American *contract* law, or English *tort* law with American *tort* law, we are liable to be misled. This is because contract and tort tend to enjoy a symbiotic relationship: if contract law is unhelpful to claimants, tort law might compensate by accepting claims that do not register in contract, and vice versa.[3] Second, even if the doctrinal particulars of one regime look more helpful to claimants than the doctrinal particulars of another regime, it does not follow that this difference will be reflected in the practical outcomes. If the doctrines of the former are applied restrictively, and the doctrines of the latter are applied liberally, the actual outcomes in the two regimes (whether in the form of judicial decisions or out-of-court settlements) might be broadly similar.[4] Third, any attempt to position American law runs into the problem of state variation. If we test the legal position in, say, California or New Jersey, we might get a very different view to that given by courts in Kansas or Alabama. Having said that, if a court in the United States, whether in California or in Alabama, stepped up to the mark to support a claim for ancillary care, past experience suggests that the English courts would take their time before following suit.

7.1 The common law regimes and their default ethic

In principle, a regime of contract or tort law might position itself by reference to a spectrum that runs from robust self-reliance and individualism at one end, to self-sacrificing altruism and reliance on others at the opposite end (Kennedy 1982; Brownsword 2006b: ch 7). If the default setting for the law is at the former end of the spectrum, the assumption is that agents both interact (tort) and transact (contract) with one another in a way that prioritises self-interest. Where the law adopts this setting, the tort regime in the background will be predicated on agents looking after their own interests; and the contract regime in the foreground will act only on very clear signals of assumption of responsibility for the welfare of others. Broadly speaking, we can say that, in their classical articulations, this is the shape of the common law regimes, with the courts exercising caution whenever they contemplate moving away from the pole of self-reliance.

In the heyday of doctrinal classicism, when interactions between agents were local and of limited variety, the tort system was not called upon to respond to road traffic accidents or claims of medical negligence; the development of mass-product markets (and product liability) and of mass tort claims had yet to happen; and, where tort did need to respond, particularly in relation to accidents at work, it did so in a distinctly claimant-unfriendly way. Famously, in modern English tort law, the decision of the majority of the Law Lords in *Donoghue v. Stevenson*[5] is seen as a major doctrinal watershed, since it established the general principle that one should take reasonable care to avoid acts or omissions that one can reasonably foresee as having an injurious effect on other agents. Nevertheless, whenever the courts sense that *Donoghue* or its progeny[6] are threatening an over-extension of liability, they default back to an ethic of self-reliance and put fresh hurdles in the way of recognising a duty of care.[7]

We find much the same story with transactions. Under the influence of nineteenth-century market-individualism, contractors are held to their bargains; coercion and fraud are regulated; but, such constraints aside, the default is one of individualism and self-reliance. Even as Lord Atkin was trumpeting the cause of consumer protection in *Donoghue*, he was advocating a thoroughly individualist regime in the leading contract cases of the period;[8] and, notwithstanding the subsequent modernisation of the common law of contract, echoes of classical individualism are still heard.[9]

Now, despite the broad formulation of the neighbour principle in *Donoghue*, the general rule in English law, just as in American law (see US Restatement 2nd Torts § 314) is that there is no tort-based liability for so-called pure omissions. Needless to say, how 'pure' the omission has to be before it falls into this category of 'no liability' is moot. At all events, in *Stovin v. Wise*,[10] Lord Hoffmann explained the policy thus:

> It is one thing for the law to say that a person who undertakes some activity shall take reasonable care not to cause damage to others. It is another thing for the law to require that a person who is doing nothing in particular shall take steps to prevent another from suffering harm . . . One can put the matter in political, moral or economic terms. In political terms it is less of an invasion of an individual's freedom for the law to require him to consider the safety of others in his actions than to impose upon him a duty to rescue or protect. A moral version of this point may be called the 'why pick on me?' argument. A duty to prevent harm to others or to render assistance to a person in danger or distress may apply to a large and indeterminate

> class of people who happen to be able to do something. Why should one be held liable rather than another? In economic terms, the efficient allocation of resources usually requires an activity should bear its own costs . . . So liability to pay compensation for loss caused by negligent conduct acts as a deterrent . . . But there is no similar justification for requiring a person who is not doing anything to spend money on behalf of someone else . . . So there must be some special reason why he should have to put his hand in his pocket.[11]

We might pause over a good deal of this, not least over the assumed sharpness of the distinction between acts (a person undertaking some activity) and omissions (a person doing nothing in particular) as well as the less than convincing moral argument; but the central point is that tort law is more comfortable with stating and enforcing background negative rights and duties than positive rights and duties. Of course, if the defendant has voluntarily assumed a positive (contractual or non-contractual) obligation, that is another matter; but, in the absence of either a special relationship (for example, between occupiers and those who are lawfully on the premises) that clearly connotes an assumption of responsibility[12] or an explicit signal that such responsibility is assumed, English tort law is not helpful to a claimant who pleads that he reasonably expected positive acts of assistance to be taken on his behalf.[13]

In the light of these remarks, we can say that, if English law were the applicable law – and, *a fortiori* perhaps, if it were US law – the prospects for a claim for ancillary-care assistance would be better today than during the classical period. Even so, we should not overstate the prospects of claimants. When it comes to pleading positive obligations, claimants whose expectations are modest[14] are less likely to be disappointed than those whose expectations are great.

7.2 Tort and the Biobank

Assuming that the relationship between the Biobank and participants is not contractual, our hypothetical claimant will plead a reasonable expectation of clinical feedback as a matter of tort law.

If English law governs the claim, it might be argued that the relationship between the Biobank and its participants is akin to that between a clinician and a patient. In clinical settings, English law is falling into line with other common-law jurisdictions by recognising that patients have a right to make informed choices about their treatment.[15] Moreover, the latest indications are that English law also accepts that the materiality of information is to be judged relative to a prudent patient standard.[16] Accordingly (assuming the analogy holds), if a prospective participant was not told that the Biobank was purely a research project, they might well claim a breach of informational responsibility. So far so good, but the test-case claim is for a failure to inform about a non-related medical condition. In clinical contexts, where a surgeon finds an unrelated medical condition while carrying out an operation, there is a requirement to report this back to the patient.[17] Again, then, it is arguable that the Biobank has a duty to report back on a serious unrelated medical condition.

Having said this, the analogy might not hold. After all, the Biobank is trying very hard to distance itself from any notion that it is a clinical facility. And, if the analogy did not hold, the Biobank would be well advised to spell out that under no circumstances will there be any clinical feedback to participants. Where the Biobank's liability hinges on a finding of explicit or implicit assumed responsibility, such steps will serve to prevent any such assumption of responsibility being made. Here, English law will hold that a participant, having been told that there will be no clinical feedback, and having enrolled on that basis, cannot then complain that (true to its word) the Biobank has not supplied clinical feedback.[18]

In contrast, the tort regime of a community of rights, by incorporating the four-stage test, might well hold that the Biobank has a background obligation to supply clinical feedback – not because the Biobank specially assumes that responsibility, but simply because it inheres in, and crystallises through, the researchers' activities. In a community of rights, participant right-holders would have the option of releasing the Biobank from its obligation; but (unlike in those regimes where no relevant background obligation is recognised) it would not be open to the Biobank to simply disclaim its responsibility.

7.3 Contract and the second test case

Let us assume that the relationship in our second test case is contractual. Participants are paid to take part in the trial. Contract law, let us suppose, is their best shot at cashing a claim for ancillary therapeutic care. And, for the sake of simplification, let us suppose that there are no jurisdictional complications.

Given the nature of the hypothetical, we must take it that the researchers give no relevant express undertaking in their contract with participants. The question, then, is whether the right kind of term can be implied. It is trite that a term may be implied only where it is compatible with the express terms; and here we are assuming that the contract is silent as to ancillary-care obligations. In such circumstances, much depends upon whether the default ethic is for self-reliance or for cooperation.

In line with its classical default ethic, English law resists the implication of a term unless it is one that clearly would be agreed by self-interested negotiators trying to maximise their short-term gains. Hence, any proposed implied term that shows as a benefit to one side and a burden to the other will be rejected unless it is a term without which the deal simply will not work. In more recent years, however, the courts have shown a greater willingness to recognise implied terms that befit a more cooperative relationship between the parties. For instance, in *Scally v. Southern Health and Social Services Board*,[19] the House of Lords held that the defendant employers had an implied obligation to look after the interests of their plaintiff doctor employees by drawing to their attention the existence of a limited opportunity to purchase 'added years' so that they would make up the full 40 years' contributions required for full entitlement under the applicable pension scheme. Judged by the orthodox standard for implied terms (i.e. a test of necessary implication),[20] the House took a bold view. However, this was thought to be no ordinary contract of employment; rather, it was one that fell within a special category where a more co-operative approach to implication of terms was appropriate. Even though *Scally* is not the only example of doctrine being manipulated to reflect what the court judges to be a reasonable expectation that one contractor will take a favourable account of the interests of the co-contractor (Burrows 1968; Collins 1992), English law has some way to go before it routinely assumes a co-operative default ethic for transactions.[21]

By contrast, in a community of rights, the default ethic for contract law would be set at a mid-point on the spectrum, with contracting agents treating their essential interests as no more and no less important than those equivalent interests of their co-contractors. The co-operative ideals that are associated with some good-faith regimes would be fundamental to contract law (Brownsword 2006a: Ch 6). In such circumstances, pleading an implied term for co-operation would be viewed as a perfectly legitimate step.

What if, though, in a community of rights, the researchers purported to limit or exclude any obligation to provide ancillary care? If such an obligation exists in the background tort regime, it would usually be open to the right-holder to waive the benefit of the right by consent.[22] In no circumstances, though, would it be open to the researchers to exclude the obligation by fiat or stipulation. If, however, the obligation does not exist in the background tort regime, the function of the contractual stipulation is not to displace a prior responsibility, but to make it clear that no such responsibility is assumed. Even in a community of rights, this would be an acceptable provision – for the researchers to fulfil their background obligations together with any expressly or implicitly assumed responsibilities is enough; supererogation is not only something that can never be required, it takes us from the realm of reasonable to that of altogether too great expectations.

8 Conclusion

In a community of rights, a claimant who pleads a reasonable expectation of ancillary care (whether in the form of informational feedback or therapeutic assistance) will have some chance of success. This is a community with a culture that is receptive to positive obligations and that will feed such obligations into its regimes of contract and tort law. What makes the claimant's expectation reasonable is not that the claimant has the expectation, but that the claim satisfies the four-stage test. Beyond the community of rights, in the common-law regimes, the expectation will be judged to be reasonable relative to current doctrine or comparable practice; and, in those regimes that default to an individualist ethic, a claimant with anything more than the most modest of expectations is likely to be disappointed.

In the larger picture, even if test-case litigation could be used to raise the question of the ancillary-care responsibilities of researchers, as well as to generate support for general obligations of this kind, national courts are not best placed to develop workable arrangements that bring together researchers from the developed world and participants from the developing world. In particular, the institutional competence of the courts is stretched where they are asked to rule on detailed questions of resource allocation and competing (rather than conflicting) rights. Faced with such tough choices, the courts can do little more than exercise a light-touch review of decisions made by others. However, once ancillary-care responsibilities are taken seriously, it should be possible for research ethics committees to translate the relevant background requirements into the foreground commitments of research protocols and, moreover, to do so in such a way that improves the prospect of the reasonable expectations of all stakeholders being satisfied (Brownsword *et al.* 2008).

Notes

1 This chapter, with some minor variation on Section III (where I now offer a more detailed sketch of the ideal–typical community of rights), was first published at (2007) *Journal of Law, Medicine and Ethics* 35: 679–91. I am grateful to the *JLME* for permission substantially to re-print this paper. Earlier versions of the paper were given at a workshop entitled 'The Ancillary-Care Obligations of Medical Researchers Working in Developing Countries', held at Georgetown University on 20–22 October, 2006, and at an ESRC-sponsored seminar on 'Theoretical Perspectives on Global Health and Human Rights' held at the University of Liverpool, on 19–20 April 2007. I am grateful to participants for their comments on the draft versions. I am also indebted to Professor Heidi Li Feldman for assistance in getting to grips with the current state of US tort law. Needless to say, the responsibility for whatever errors and omissions remain was always mine and it continues to remain mine alone.

2 Within a community of rights, it is arguable that agents have a positive obligation to one another to participate in projects such as the Biobank; but, for present purposes, we need not pursue that idea. Compare Pattinson (2006: 345–347); Brownsword (2009b).

3 See Lord Goff in *White v Jones* [1995] 2 AC 207, 262–4; Markesinis (1987).

4 "The Common Core of European Private Law Project", initiated at the University of Trento in 1993, adopts a comparative approach that focuses on results rather than doctrinal details. See e.g. Zimmermann and Whittaker 2000; Brownsword 2001.

5 [1932] AC 562.

6 Notably, *Anns v. Merton London Borough Council* [1978] AC 728.

7 Most importantly, perhaps, the courts have limited *Donoghue* by declaring that the overriding question is whether it would be "fair, just and reasonable" to recognise a duty in the particular circumstances. Thus, in *Caparo Industries plc v. Dickman* [1990] 2 AC 605, at 617–18, Lord Bridge said that, in addition to the elements of 'foreseeability of damage' and a relationship of "proximity" or "neighbourhood", it is essential "that the situation should be one in which the court considers it fair, just and reasonable that the law should impose a duty of a given scope upon one party for the benefit of the other" (emphasis added).

8 See e.g. *Bell v. Lever Bros Ltd* [1932] AC 161 (where Lord Atkin took an uncompromising line on non-disclosure); and *Arcos Ltd v. EA Ronaasen and Son* [1933] AC 470 (where Lord Atkin was party to the unanimous House of Lords' view that sellers who failed to deliver goods corresponding precisely to the contractual description had no cause for complaint if buyers then rejected the goods purely for their own economic advantage).

9 See e.g. *Walford v. Miles* [1992] 2 AC 128, at 138, where Lord Ackner declared that a doctrinal recognition of a duty to negotiate in good faith would be "inherently repugnant to the adversarial position of the parties."

10 [1996] 1 AC 923.
11 At 943–944.
12 But even then, compare *Smith and Others v. Littlewoods Organisation Ltd* [1987] AC 241, where the defendant occupiers of an empty cinema were held not liable when a fire that was started by trespassing children at the cinema spread to the claimants' adjacent premises. According to Lord Griffiths, at 251, foreseeability does not suffice, and the best that can be done is "to leave it to the good sense of the judges to apply realistic standards in conformity with generally accepted patterns of behaviour to determine whether in the particular circumstances of a given case there has been a breach of duty sounding in negligence."
13 Compare Beldam LJ in *Barrett v. Ministry of Defence* [1995] 3 All ER 87, at 95:

> The characteristic which distinguishes those [special] relationships is reliance expressed or implied in the relationship which the party to whom the duty is owed is entitled to place on the other party to make provision for his safety. I can see no reason why it should not be fair, just and reasonable for the law to leave a responsible adult to assume responsibility for his own actions in consuming alcoholic drink . . . To dilute self-responsibility and to blame one adult for another's lack of self-control is neither just nor reasonable and in the development of the law of negligence an increment too far.

14 For example, suppose that, during a trial, researchers came to realise that their study was creating an unreasonable risk of physical harm to participants. Then, researchers surely would be found to have positive responsibilities (in law) to take reasonable steps to alleviate that risk. Compare US Restatement 2nd Torts § 321 and *McNeilab, Inc. v. North River Ins. Co.* 645 F. Supp. 525, 551.
15 See *Canterbury v. Spence* 464 F 2d 772 (DC Cir. 1972); *Reibl v. Hughes* (1980) 114 DLR (3d) 1; and *Rogers v. Whitaker* (1992) 67 ALJR 47.
16 See especially *Pearce v. United Bristol Healthcare NHS Trust* [1999] PIQR 53 and *Chester v. Afshar* [2004] 4 All ER 587.
17 Compare *Marshall v. Curry* [1933] 3 DLR 260 and *Murray v. McMurchy* [1949] 2 DLR 442 (BCSC).
18 We might recall Lord Reid's enumeration of the options open to one who is asked for advice (viz., decline, accept without responsibility, accept with responsibility), in *Hedley Byrne and Co. Ltd. v. Heller and Partners Ltd.* [1964] AC 465, at 486.
19 [1992] 1 AC 294. Although c.f. *Reid v. Rush and Tompkins Group plc* [1989] 3 All ER 228 and, more recently, *Crossley v. Faithful & Gould Holdings Ltd* [2004] EWCA Civ 293.
20 See *Liverpool City Council v. Irwin* [1977] AC 239.
21 Compare *Baird Textile Holdings Ltd v. Marks and Spencer plc* [2001] EWCA Civ 274, [2002] 1 All ER (Comm) 737.
22 I am avoiding presenting this question in the more usual terms of mandatory or optional, or default rules, because I think that these terms are apt to mislead where, as in the text, the setting is that of a community of rights.

Bibliography

Belsky, L. and Richardson, H.S. (2004) 'Medical Researchers' Ancillary Clinical Care Responsibilities,' *British Medical Journal* 328: 1494–1496.

Beyleveld, D. and Brownsword, R. (1983) 'Law as a Moral Judgment vs Law as the Rules of the Powerful' *American Journal of Jurisprudence*, 28: 79–117.

—— (1986) *Law as a Moral Judgment*, London: Sweet and Maxwell.

—— (2006) 'Principle, Proceduralism and Precaution in a Community of Rights', *Ratio Juris* 19: 141–68.

—— (2007) *Consent in the Law*, Oxford: Hart.

Beyleveld, D. and Pattinson, S. (2002) 'Horizontal Applicability and Direct Effect,' *Law Quarterly Review* 118: 623–46.

Brownsword, R. (2001) 'Individualism, Co-operativism and an Ethic for European Contract Law,' *Modern Law Review* 64: 628–42.

—— (2003) 'After Investors: Interpretation, Expectation and the Implicit Dimension of the "New Contextualism"', in Campbell, D. Collins, H. and Wightman, J. (eds.) *The Implicit Dimension of Contract*, Oxford: Hart, 103–41.

—— (2004) 'The Cult of Consent: Fixation and Fallacy', *King's College Law Journal* 15: 223–51.

—— (2006a) 'Cloning, Zoning and the Harm Principle', in McLean, S. A. M (ed.), *First Do No Harm*, Aldershot: Ashgate, 527–42.

—— (2006b) *Contract Law: Themes for the Twenty-First Century* 2nd ed Oxford: Oxford University Press.

—— (2007) 'Informed Consent: To Whom it May Concern,' *Jahrbuch für Recht und Ethik* 15: 267–89.

—— (2008) *Rights, Regulation, and the Technological Revolution*, Oxford: Oxford University Press.

—— (2009a) *Regulatory Cosmopolitanism: Clubs, Commons, and Questions of Coherence*, TILT Working Papers, University of Tilburg.

—— (2009b) 'Rights, Responsibility and Stewardship: Beyond Consent', in Widdows, H. and Mullen, C. (eds.), *The Governance of Genetic Information: Who Decides?* Cambridge: Cambridge University Press, 99–125.

Brownsword, R., Cermak, A., Chaisson, R., Clayman, M.D., Corr, P. B., DeCharney, S., Grady, C., Higgs, E. S., Kumar, N. K., Loe, R., Merritt, M., Molyneux, M., Petros, B., Richardson, H. S., and Sugarman, J. (2008) 'The Ancillary Care Obligations of Medical Researchers Working in Developing Countries', *PLOS Medicine* 5(5): e90.

Burrows, J. F. '(1968) 'Contractual Co-operation and the Implied Term', *Modern Law Review* 31: 390–407.

Campbell, A. V. (2006) 'The Ethical Challenges of Biobanks: Safeguarding Altruism and Trust', in McLean, S. A. M. (ed.), *First Do No Harm*, Aldershot: Ashgate, 203–214.

Collins, H. (1992) 'Implied Duty to Give Information During Performance of Contracts', *Modern Law Review* 55: 556–62.

Dworkin, R. (1978) *Taking Rights Seriously*, London: Duckworth.

Gewirth, A. (1978) *Reason and Morality*, Chicago: Chicago University Press.

—— (1996) *Community of Rights*, Chicago: Chicago University Press.

Hart, H. L. A. (1973) 'Bentham on Legal Rights', in Simpson, A. W. B. (ed.), *Oxford Essays in Jurisprudence (Second Series)*, Oxford: Clarendon Press, 171.

Johnston, C. and Kaye, J. (2004) 'Does the UK Biobank have a Legal Obligation to Feedback Individual Findings to Participants?', *Medical Law Review* 12: 239–67.

Kennedy, D. (1982) 'Distributive and Paternalist Motives in Contract and Tort Law, with Special Reference to Compulsory Terms and Unequal Bargaining Power', *Maryland Law Review* 41: 563–658.

MacCormick, D. N. (1977) 'Rights in Legislation', in Hacker, P.M.S. and Raz, J. (eds.), *Law, Morality, and Society*, Oxford: Clarendon Press, 189.

Markesinis, B. S. (1987) 'An Expanding Tort Law – The Price of a Rigid Contract Law' *Law Quarterly Review* 103: 354–97.

McHale, J. V. (2004) 'Regulating Genetic Databases: Some Legal and Ethical Issues', *Medical Law Review* 12: 70–96.

Nuffield Council on Bioethics, (2002) *The Ethics of Research Related to Healthcare in Developing Countries*, London: Nuffield.

—— (2005) *The Ethics of Research Related to Healthcare in Developing Countries: A Follow-Up Discussion*, London: Nuffield.

Pattinson, S. D. (2006) *Medical Law and Ethics*, London: Sweet and Maxwell.

Rawls, J. (1972) *A Theory of Justice*, London: Oxford University Press.

Richardson, H. S. and Belsky, L. (2004) 'The Ancillary-Care Responsibilities of Medical Researchers: An Ethical Framework for Thinking about the Clinical Care that Researchers Owe Their Subjects', *Hastings Center Report* 34: 25–33.

UK Biobank Ethics and Governance Council (2006) UK Biobank Ethics and Governance Framework (version 2.0, July 2006), see http://www.ukbiobank.ac.uk/docs/EGF_Version2_July%202006.pdf

Zimmermann, R., and Whittaker, S. (eds.) (2000) *Good Faith in European Contract Law*, Cambridge: Cambridge University Press.

6 Human rights and health sector corruption

Brigit Toebes[1]

> Money that should be spent on alleviating poverty and illness ends up instead in private pockets. In this way, corruption literally violates human rights, as people are denied the care that their governments are obliged to provide.
>
> (Robinson 2006)

1 Introduction

Corruption is not a new phenomenon – it has affected societies and social relations since ancient civilisations (Carr 2006: 5). One of the branches where corruption is endemic is the health sector. An elucidating report by Transparency International (2006), which in itself builds upon a wide amount of existing research, makes it clear that the health sector is extremely vulnerable when it comes to corruption.[2] This is the case in rich as well as poor nations.[3] In some countries, the health sector is considered to be the most corrupt sector of all (Savedoff and Hussman 2006: 5).[4]

Although a systematic investigation has yet to be made, empirical research indicates that acts of corruption can adversely affect the provision of publicly provided services, including healthcare services (Gupta *et al.* 2000). As such, health sector corruption deprives people of access to healthcare and leads to poor health outcomes. To single out one negative effect, corruption has been negatively associated with child health. Gupta *et al.* demonstrate that a high level of corruption has adverse consequences for a country's child and infant mortality rates, and its percentage of low-birth-weight babies in total births. Child mortality rates in countries with high levels of corruption are about one-third higher than in countries with low levels of corruption, and infant mortality rates are five times as high (Gupta *et al.* 2000: 7–26). As such, corruption potentially violates the right to health and other related human rights.

The problems of health sector corruption are not necessarily well-known in the field. While medical and public health literature lack references to health sector corruption, healthcare professionals themselves may not perceive corruption as a systemic problem. As such, there is a disconnection between the above-mentioned findings on health sector corruption research and the perceptions of the health sector itself.[5] A similar disconnection exists between corruption and human rights law. While it is obvious that acts of corruption can lead to human rights violations, human rights specialists are only just starting to explore the link (e.g. ICHRP 2009).

This chapter assesses how health sector corruption impacts upon human rights and how the human rights framework can be used as a tool to address corruption in this area. This analysis fits into the current literature on the relation between health systems and human rights. Increasingly, human rights scholars and activists are exploring the links between human rights and the organisation of the health sector (Hunt and Backman n.d.) Based on existing research, this chapter will first discuss the character of corruption, and of health sector corruption more specifically. Subsequently, a connection will be made between the existing findings on health sector corruption and the human rights framework. Particular attention will in this respect be paid to the framework of the right to health, as laid out in particular by the United Nations Committee on Economic, Social and Cultural Rights (CESCR) General Comment 14 on the Right to Health. On the basis of these findings (national and international), State obligations in relation to corruption in the health sector are identified. Such obligations are also identified for non-State actors, including private hospitals, insurance companies, commercial suppliers of medical healthcare goods and services, healthcare consumers and health workers. Finally, the question is addressed of when and to what extent an act of corruption can amount to a human rights violation. Having made the connection between corruption and human rights, the conclusions contain some suggestions as to how human rights principles and norms can be used as tools to combat corruption.

2 Corruption: the international framework

2.1 Definition of corruption

Before we can embark upon an analysis of health sector corruption, we need to identify the international framework of corruption more generally. This chapter will use Transparency International's definition of corruption: 'the misuse of entrusted power for private gain'.[6] It is submitted that this definition provides a clear basis for establishing a link between corruption and human rights. On the basis of human rights, governments and other actors have to respect the powers bestowed upon them. For example, human rights may imply a governmental responsibility for providing a certain public service, such as legal assistance, schooling, healthcare services and water services. An act of corruption, or 'the abuse of entrusted power for private gain', disrespects this responsibility and may as such lead to a violation of human rights. Another important feature of the definition is that it not only focuses on 'public power', but rather on 'entrusted power' more generally. As such, it leaves room for addressing non-State actors, which is of essential importance when it comes to health sector corruption.[7] This is also important in light of the fact that the health sector is increasingly privatised (see Section 5.3 under 'privatisation').

Yet with this clear definition at hand it will not always be easy to define whether a certain act actually constitutes an act of corruption. As Savedoff observes, the definition of what constitutes 'corruption' may vary from the one society to the other (Savedoff 2007). While in some countries a certain act, e.g. informal payments to doctors, may clearly constitute an act of corruption, in others it may be considered an essential part of the country's culture and society.[8] In this connection, it has been suggested that corruption may effectively reduce bureaucracy and speed the implementation of administrative practices conforming to the economic forces of the market (IDEA n.d.) As such, some have argued that corruption may actually benefit the economies of developing countries, and that it is a Western notion in the way it is currently defined (Savedoff 2007: 2). A parallel can be drawn here with the discussion as to whether human rights are universal notions or rather subject to cultural relativism (Baehr 1999, Howard 1997). The present chapter takes a two-pronged approach to this discussion. On the one hand, it identifies a broad set of human rights obligations of various actors in the health sector in relation to corruption (Section 5.5). On the other hand, however, it only identifies the most serious acts of corruption as human rights violations (see Section 5.6).

2.2 *Treaty law on corruption*

International economic institutions like the World Bank and the IMF have made tackling corruption into a focal point of their policies.[9] In addition, a number of international treaties address the issue of corruption.[10] Most importantly, in 2003 the General Assembly adopted the United Nations Convention against Corruption, which entered into force in 2005 and has now been ratified by more than 100 Member States (UN 2003). The Convention does not contain a general definition of corruption.[11] It first enumerates a number of preventative measures that Member States are required to take in order to prevent corruption from occurring (UN 2003: Chapter II). Subsequently, in its chapter entitled 'Criminalisation and Law Enforcement' it identifies and defines five acts of corruption as criminal acts:

(a) the bribery of national and foreign public officials and bribery in the private sector (the promise, solicitation or acceptance of an undue advantage);[12]
(b) embezzlement, misappropriation or other diversion of property by a public official (of any property or any other things of value entrusted to the public official by virtue of his or her position);
(c) trading in influence (the promise, solicitation or acceptance of an undue advantage with a view to obtaining an undue advantage from the public official);
(d) abuse of functions (the performance or failure to perform an act, in the discharge of his or her functions, with the purpose of obtaining an undue advantage); and
(e) illicit enrichment (a significant increase in the assets of a public official that he or she cannot reasonably explain in relation to his or her lawful income)

(UN 2003: Chapter III)

Without discussing the scope and effects of this treaty elaborately, it is observed that, contrary to the Council of Europe framework, which also embraces a civil law convention (Council of Europe 1999b), this convention only defines criminal acts. Sandgren criticises the emphasis on criminal law when it comes to combating corruption (Sandgren 2005:726). But, as Carr observes, the UN convention is quite comprehensive in the sense that it requires States Parties to put in place, maintain and coordinate anti-corruption policies (Carr 2006: 40). Yet there may be a certain tension between the penal tools provided for by this Convention that seek to punish wrong-doing and the more policy-oriented measures aimed at addressing the ill-effects of corruption. Furthermore, the UN Convention is directed primarily at Member States, not at non-State actors. When it comes to health sector corruption, it is of crucial importance to address non-State actors, including hospitals, insurance companies and commercial suppliers of medical healthcare goods and services (see Section 5.5). Nonetheless the Convention involves society as a whole and the private sector more particularly by urging Member States to prevent corruption involving the private sector, to promote the active participation of private actors in the fight against corruption and to raise public awareness of the matter (UN 2003: Arts 12, 13, 'Participation of society'). As such, Member States have so-called 'obligations to protect' individuals against the corrupt acts of third parties, including healthcare providers of goods and services (see Section 5.3).

It goes beyond the scope of this chapter to elaborately discuss the UN anti-corruption treaty and others like it. Yet these instruments can be important tools in addressing health sector corruption. They can also help to further identify the link between health sector corruption and human rights. We will use the above-mentioned identification of corrupt acts in discussing State obligations as regards health sector corruption (see the obligations to 'respect' in Section 5.3).

3 The characteristics of health sector corruption

Transparency International identifies three main characteristics of the health sector that make it so vulnerable to corruption (Transparency International 2006: xvii). It refers first to the imbalance of information that prevails in the health system. While healthcare providers possess more information on health, drugs and illness than their patients, suppliers of medical and healthcare goods and services know more about their products than the public officials entrusted with spending decisions. Second, it refers to the uncertainty in 'health markets' as a factor for health sector corruption. As the report explains, the uncertainty inherent in selecting, monitoring, measuring and delivering healthcare services makes it difficult to detect and assign responsibility for abuses (Transparency International 2006: 5). Third, the complexity of health systems is a factor that exacerbates health sector corruption. The report refers in particular to the large number of parties involved, which makes it more difficult to generate and analyse information in a transparent manner (Transparency International 2006: xvii).

As mentioned, the complexity of the health sector is partly due to the large number of actors involved in the health sector and the complexity of their multiple forms of interaction. According to Savedoff and Hussmann, all abuses involve transactions between two or more actors (Savedoff and Hussmann 2006: 5). In the anti-corruption literature, a distinction is generally made between five main categories of actors:

(a) regulators (health ministries, parliaments, supervisory commissions, accrediting and licensing bodies);
(b) payers (social security organisations, public and private insurers, financial intermediaries, public and private donors);
(c) providers (hospitals, doctors and medical associations, pharmacists);
(d) consumers (patients, patient support groups, disease-related advocacy groups);
(e) suppliers (commercial suppliers of medical and healthcare goods and services, including pharmaceutical companies and biotechnology companies, as well as producers of medical equipment and medical device companies)

(Savedoff and Hussmann 2006: 8–10)[13]

Based on discussions with health sector professionals, this author would also include:

(f) researchers and educators (groups and organisations that address medical and healthcare research, including medical schools and their parent universities, medical journals, medical education companies).[14]

4 Health sector corruption and human rights

At the core of our analysis lies the international human 'right to health'. The term 'right to health' is shorthand for the 'right to the highest attainable standard of health' as provided in Article 12 of the UN International Covenant on Economic, Social and Cultural Rights (ICESCR). As pointed out by the former Special Rapporteur on the Right to Health, the right to health is a firmly established feature of binding international law (UN 2004: para 15). In addition to Article 12 ICESCR, the right to health is recognised by provisions in a number of other international human rights instruments, including Article 25 of the Universal Declaration on Human Rights (UDHR); Article 5(e) of the International Convention of All Forms of Racial Discrimination (CERD); Articles 11.1 and 12 of the Convention on the Elimination of All forms of Discrimination Against Women (CEDAW) and Article 24 of the Convention on the Rights of the child (CRC). At the regional level we come across the right to health in Article 11 of the (revised) European Social Charter (ESC), in Article 16 of the African Charter of Human and Peoples' Rights and in Article 10 of the Additional Protocol to the American Convention on Human Rights in the Area of Economic, Social and Cultural Rights. Furthermore, over 100 national constitutional provisions include a right to health (UN 2004: para 15). Finally, an increasing amount of case law on the right to health generated by national and international judicial bodies points to the increasing enforceability or 'justiciability' of the right to health (UN 2004: para 16).

An elaborate explanation of the right to health is provided by UN General Comment 14 on the right to health, which is an explanatory document on Article 12 ICESCR adopted by the Committee on Economic, Social and Cultural Rights (CESCR), the treaty-monitoring body to the ICESCR (CESCR 2000). Although strictly speaking not legally binding, this document is the most authoritative document on the right to health. Therefore, this chapter closely follows the approach taken in the General Comment. The General Comment does not address the issue of corruption explicitly, but it does provide a suitable framework for addressing this issue in relation to the health sector.

As the General Comment explains, the right to health is closely related to, and dependent upon, the realisation of other human rights (CESCR 2000: para 3). With respect to corruption in the health sector, the following other human rights are of particular importance: the right to life, the principle of non-discrimination, freedom of expression and the right to information, the right to political participation and the right to a remedy.[15] While the right to health lies at the core of our analysis on corruption in the health sector, the other rights support and reinforce this right. For example, serious acts of corruption in the health sector can lead to infringements of people's health (right to health), but can also result in a person's death (right to life). Furthermore, freedom of expression and the right to information overlap with the right to health in the sense that they embrace the notion of expressing and accessing health-related information that is of crucial importance when it comes to combating health sector corruption. For example, on some occasions the corrupt act leads to an attempt to cover up this act, and as such to a violation of freedom of expression and the right to information (see Section 5.1 under access to information). Furthermore, the right to health includes a prohibition of discrimination in access to health services and as such is connected to the principle of non-discrimination. This is important, because corruption may directly and indirectly affect vulnerable groups, as will be pointed out below in Section 5.2. The right to (political) participation reinforces the right to health in the sense that it gives people the right to have a say in important decisions regarding the (organisation of the) health sector (see section 5.1). And finally, in relation to the right to a remedy, the right to health reflects the notion that individuals whose health has been adversely affected by a health practitioner or other actor in the health sector should have adequate means of redress.

While this chapter primarily uses the framework of the right to health to analyse health sector corruption, it is recognised that the corrupt acts that are identified may equally lead to violations of the rights identified above. Given the lack of enforceability of economic, social and cultural rights (Toebes 1999: c. IV; Coomans 2006), claims based on rights to life and a fair trial and freedom of expression may on some occasions be more successful than claims based on a right to health.

The right to health should also be read in conjunction with Article 2 (1) ICESCR, a general Article in the Covenant that underlines States Parties' obligation to take 'steps' in relation to the substantive rights in the Covenant. Such steps need to be taken to 'the maximum of a State's available resources (. . .)'. Implicit in this obligation is the duty to use available resources effectively and in a transparent manner, i.e. without corruption. Article 2(1) also stresses the need to adopt legislative measures to realise the substantive rights in the Covenant. As such, if we agree that corruption potentially violates human rights, it can be argued that States parties have an obligation to adopt anti-corruption legislation to ensure that the rights in the Covenant are realised in a transparent and efficient manner.

As mentioned above, the right to health is an inclusive right which not only extends to timely and appropriate healthcare services, but also to the underlying determinants of health, such as access to safe, potable water and adequate sanitation, healthy occupational and environmental conditions, and access to health-related education and information. This implies that when we analyse corruption in relation to a right to health, it is not only the healthcare sector that should, in principle, be under scrutiny, but also e.g. water provision and the occupational and environmental health sectors. A discussion of the underlying conditions inherent in the right to health would be beyond the scope of this chapter. However, it can be argued that the framework developed here can equally be applied, for example, to corruption in the provision of water services (Transparency International 2008).

5 Applying the human rights framework

5.1 The 'AAAQ'

The General Comment on the Right to Health identifies a set of principles that apply at all levels of the health sector and that are also important in relation to the problem of corruption: availability, accessibility, acceptability and quality of health facilities (the so-called 'AAAQ' (CESCR 2000: para 12)). One finds similar principles in the UN General Comments on the substantive rights in the ICESCR, as well as in a national health law context.[16] In addition, (political) participation[17] and accountability are important for addressing health sector corruption. Although not elaborately discussed in the General Comment (CESCR 2000: paras 11 and 59–62), they are increasingly referred to in the health and human rights literature as important principles underlying the right to health (Potts n.d.)

As pointed out by the former Special Rapporteur on the Right to Health, Paul Hunt, while this framework is especially relevant to policy analysis, the identification of obligations further on in this chapter (obligations to 'respect, protect and fulfil') is more suited to legal analysis (UN 2004: para 39). In a policy context it does not make a great deal of difference whether a particular obligation requires negative (obligation to respect) or positive State behaviour (obligations to protect and fulfil). This distinction is of much greater relevance in legal analysis, since 'negative' State obligations may be more easily enforceable before a court of law than the more 'programmatic' or 'positive' State obligations (Toebes 1999: 239).

5.1.1 Availability

Availability requires that health facilities, goods and services, as well as programmes, have to be available in sufficient quantity. Corruption may affect the availability of health goods and services. Money that is used to bribe regulators, healthcare providers (of goods as well as services) could have been spent on health facilities directly. Therefore, States need to ensure that the availability of health goods and facilities is not negatively affected by acts of corruption in the health sector.

5.1.2 Accessibility

Accessibility requires that health facilities, goods and services are accessible to all persons without discrimination. Accessibility has four overlapping dimensions:

Non-discrimination requires that health facilities, goods and services are within safe physical reach of all sections of society, especially vulnerable or marginalised groups (see below in Section 5.2). First of all, health sector corruption can generally mean that fewer dues are paid into the system, thereby reducing public expenditure on health (FIDH 2005: 24). Research points out that in countries where corruption is endemic, the poorer sections of the population and those who live in rural areas suffer longer waiting periods at public health clinics and are also more frequently denied vaccines than are rich and urban sections of the population (Azfar and Gurgur 2006: 38). Health sector corruption can also lead to discrimination more directly when healthcare providers and professionals treat patients differently according to their income and their contacts with the medical profession (FIDH 2005: 24). Altogether, therefore, States need to ensure that individual patients or certain sections of the population are not disadvantaged by acts of corruption in the health sector.

Physical access implies that health facilities, goods and services are within safe physical reach of all sections of the population, especially vulnerable or marginalised groups, such as ethnic minorities and indigenous populations. Health sector corruption may lead to choices that are less favourable to the community, e.g. hospitals may be built in remote or wealthy areas of a city rather than in the vicinity of the communities that need them most. Therefore, States need to ensure that decisions to build health centres and hospitals are not negatively affected by health sector corruption.

Economic access (affordability) implies that health facilities, goods and services must be affordable to all, whether publicly or privately provided. Corruption can affect the affordability of health services in many ways. At a macro-economic level, health services may become more expensive if the health sector is affected by corruption. Public officials can demand fees for drugs that have been provided free of charge by pharmaceutical companies or donor organisations. At the level of healthcare provision doctors can make healthcare services more expensive by demanding informal payments ('under-the-table payments'). They may also refuse to attend patients who do not have insurance. Altogether, States need to ensure that the affordability of healthcare services is not negatively affected by health sector corruption.

Access to information requires that patients and the public as a whole have the right to seek, receive and impart information and ideas. At the level of the system as a whole, corruption will lead to skewed information about health needs and use of facilities going to planners, leading to misallocation of resources. The level of healthcare provision is vulnerable to corruption because it is characterised by the above-mentioned 'asymmetric information': for example, healthcare providers are better informed than their patients on issues like diagnosis and treatment (Savedoff and Hussmann 2006: 4–5).

When seeking health services, patients should be in a position to make informed choices and select appropriate providers at appropriate prices and standards of quality (U4 2006: 13). Patients should be informed of their rights, of the services available, and of prices and conditions of access (U4 2006: 13). They should also be informed about the health services that they are entitled to free of charge and about the eligibility criteria for certain medical programmes. Also, patients have to be informed about the toxicity or adverse effects of drugs.[18] In turn, doctors need to have accurate, complete and unbiased information about the harms of specific tests and treatments, in order to make the best medical decisions for their patients.[19] Whistle-blowers in the health sector should be in a position to report to the competent authorities any facts that constitute health sector corruption (UN 2003: art 33). Altogether, States need to ensure that health information is available at all levels of the health sector, and that the provision of such information is not negatively affected by health sector corruption.

5.1.3 *Acceptability*

Health facilities must be respectful of medical ethics, and they must be culturally appropriate. Among other things, health facilities must be designed to respect confidentiality and improve the health status of those concerned. Due to the above-mentioned 'imbalance of information', the health professional's position is more powerful than that of the patient. For example, under pressure from a pharmaceutical company, a health professional may be tempted to prescribe drugs to a patient that are not in his or her best interests. States should put in place guarantees that ensure that health professionals do not abuse their position of power, and thereby disrespect the 'acceptability' of the health service for the patient.

5.1.4 *Quality*

Health facilities must be scientifically and medically appropriate, and of good quality. Corruption can affect the quality of medicines, for example, when regulators are bribed to carry out less than rigorous checks, or when hospital administrators purchase cheaper, less effective drugs and embezzle the proceeds.

States should ensure that the quality of health services is guaranteed at all levels of the health sector and that the quality of health services is not negatively affected by health service corruption.

Participation[20]

The public must have a say in important decisions concerning the health sector, for example, the decision to privatise or decentralise (parts of) the health sector. States should ensure political participation in decision-making on the organisation of the health sector. Political participation is not only realised through a democratic system of elections, but also by providing for public enquiries regarding planned health sector reform (see also Potts n.d.).

When it comes to the health budget, it has been pointed out that the public and/or civil society can be actively included in all stages of the budget cycle for the health sector. Public budget hearings can be held at the local level to involve citizens in the way public services are delivered (U4 2006:23).

Accountability

Potts explains the concept of 'accountability' as a broad process, which requires governments to show, explain and justify how they have discharged their obligations regarding the right to health. According to Potts, an effective accountability process comprises the following essential elements: monitoring, accountability mechanisms, remedies, and participation (Potts n.d.: 13–17 and Vian 2008). Monitoring is aimed at providing governments with the information that they need to create transparent health policies, as well as providing rights-holders with essential health-related information (Potts n.d.: 13–17). 'Accountability mechanisms' can be judicial or quasi-judicial (for example, a health ombudsman or other independent complaint mechanism), as well as administrative, political or social in character (Potts n.d.: 17–27). States should establish supervisory bodies which monitor the actions and decisions of actors in the health sector, be they public or private actors, ranging from hospitals to health equipment providers, and impose sanctions upon them where necessary.

Providing remedies implies that States provide for a mechanism of redress when people have been affected by health sector corruption.[21] A problem that arises in the context of corruption is that on many occasions the victim of the corrupt act has participated in the act: the individual who 'had' to pay the bribe participated in the wrongdoing. In such situations it seems more effective to search for other accountability mechanisms.

5.2 Identification of vulnerable groups

Pursuant to its Arts 2.2, 3 and 12, the ICESCR prohibits any discrimination in access to health services on the grounds of race, colour, sex, language, religion, political or other opinion, national or social origin, property, birth, physical or mental disability, health status (including HIV/AIDS), sexual orientation and civil, political, social or other status. The General Comment on the Right to Health points out that inappropriate health resource allocation can lead to discrimination that may not be overt (CESCR 2000: para 18). As health sector corruption may enhance inappropriate health resource allocation, it can lead to discrimination indirectly. But health sector corruption can also lead to discrimination directly, for example when so-called 'informal payments' are unaffordable to certain sections of the population.

The following are examples of population groups that are particularly vulnerable when it comes to health sector corruption:

Poor people are the most susceptible when officials hoard drugs or waste resources on the wrong kind of medicines (Cohen 2006: 84). They may also be refused medical services based on their inability to afford the bill afterwards. And, as mentioned above, they also have the most difficulty affording the informal payments that are often required to receive the medical care they need.

Persons with chronic diseases and disabled persons. Given their condition, persons with chronic diseases and disabled persons often require more health services than others – and for an indefinite period. This makes them particularly vulnerable to being excluded from health insurance, for example.

HIV-positive persons and persons with AIDS are likely to suffer due to health sector corruption because they are highly dependent on the availability and affordability of anti-retroviral drugs (ARVs). It is reported that, particularly in low-income countries, a lot of corruption surrounds the procurement and distribution of ARVs. Money available for ARVs is embezzled during all stages of the procurement and distribution chain, by government officials, doctors and others involved in this process (Tayler and Dickinson 2006: 104). It is reported that where ARVs are provided free of charge, requests for 'top-up payments' are nevertheless common, as is trade in ARVs derived from patients or leaked out of the health system. There is also an extensive market in fake ARVs (Tayler and Dickinson 2006: 105–106).

People living in remote areas. Building a health centre in a remote area may put a strain on the healthcare budget where it would be more lucrative to build health centres and hospitals in central areas. As such, persons living in remote areas are vulnerable to health sector corruption when the commercial aspects of a planning decision are taken into account rather than the general geographic accessibility of healthcare services.

Women. Given their specific health needs in relation to their sexual and reproductive function, women often require more healthcare services than men. As such, they can be affected disproportionately by the effects of health sector corruption, for example when they do not have the money to afford informal payments exacted for assistance at the birth.

Other factors need to be taken into account as well, for example the fact that women often face a disproportionate burden caring for sick family members, which reduces their participation in the paid labour force (UN 2004: para 57 (a)). As such, they may lack the means to afford healthcare services, in particular when informal payments are required.

The General Comment on the Right to Health stresses the need to develop and implement a comprehensive national strategy for promoting women's health, including a policy to provide high-quality, affordable healthcare, of which sexual and reproductive services also form a part (CESCR 2000: para 21). Such strategies should not be affected by acts of corruption in the health sector.

Another issue that should be mentioned is that women constitute a large proportion of healthcare personnel. As such, they can also be affected disproportionately when health sector corruption negatively affects the timely payment of proper wages.

5.3 State obligations

On the basis of this framework, a set of legal obligations can be identified that are incumbent upon States and possibly upon other actors in the health sector. As it is States that ratify human rights treaties, and not other actors in the health sector, States and their governments bear the primary responsibility for realising these obligations towards individuals.

In this regard, the General Comment distinguishes between so-called State obligations to 'respect', to 'protect' and to 'fulfil' the right to health. The obligation to respect the right to health is a negative obligation to refrain from interfering directly or indirectly with the enjoyment of the right to health. The obligation to protect requires States to take legislative and other measures that prevent third parties, including private insurers, private healthcare providers, and suppliers from interfering with the guarantees under the right to health. Finally, the obligation to fulfil requires States to adopt appropriate legislative, administrative, budgetary, judicial, promotional and other measures towards the full realisation of the right to health (CESCR 2000: paras 34–37).

As to the definitions of 'State' and 'government', it is observed that both terms are used interchangeably and in a broad fashion, covering both law- and policy-making sections, as well as those government institutions responsible for the implementation of policies. These concepts also include governmental bodies at all levels, from national, to regional and local (Potts n.d. 38). Furthermore, in section 3 a distinction was made between regulators, payers, providers and consumers. It should be noted that a State or Government can be a regulator and a payer, as well as a provider (i.e. when health services are publicly provided).

5.3.1 State obligations to respect

In relation to corruption, the obligation to respect implies that government regulators and public payers, providers and suppliers are to refrain from corrupt acts that lead to a denial of health services. To draw again on the acts of corruption identified in the UN Convention Against Corruption (see Section 2.2), government authorities and their public officials should, among other things, refrain from:

(a) the bribery of national and foreign public officials in relation to the health sector; bribery of regulators to approve drugs or devices; and bribery in the public and private health sector;
(b) embezzlement, misappropriation or other diversion of funds from the health budget by a public official [for example the illegal diversion or sale of medicines from public clinics to private practice by doctors and health officers or diverting drugs that were destined for their country back into the international drug market (Bale 2006: 92)];
(c) trading in influence in the health sector (for example, if the public official receives an undue advantage from a health insurance company in exchange for certain privileges, such as permission to own part of the insurance market);
(d) abuse of functions in relation to the health sector [for example, colluding with organisations that fake or sell counterfeit drugs (Akunyili 2006: 87)].
(e) illicit enrichment from the health budget (for example stealing money from the health budget).

5.3.2 State obligations to protect

In relation to the right to health, the 'obligation to protect' implies a State obligation to adopt legislation and to establish the necessary regulatory mechanisms to monitor the (partly) independent health sector. This obligation is closely related to the principle of 'accountability' discussed above (see Section 5 under 'accountability'). The obligation to protect is a key obligation when it comes to the prevention and detection of health sector corruption. Corruption can be found at all levels of the health sector, and the State has an obligation to prevent and address corruption at each of these levels.

Three general State obligations can be identified when it comes to supervising the health sector in order to prevent and to combat corrupt acts. It is submitted that States are under a duty to:

(a) regulate: the adoption of legislation to ensure that the actors in the health sector, whether public or private in character, refrain from health sector corruption;
(b) monitor: the adoption of monitoring mechanisms aimed at supervising or regulating the behaviour of the actors in the health sector in such a way that health sector corruption may be detected;
(c) provide redress: the creation of possibilities to complain about failure or malpractice by the actors in the health sector.

(Toebes 2008: 451)

In relation to the obligation to protect, we need to identify the actors that are to be supervised by the State as part of its obligation to protect (Savedoff 2007: 3). As mentioned above, a distinction is generally drawn between government regulators, payers, providers, consumers and suppliers (see Section 3).

Government regulators. We can first identify state, regional and local governments and government regulators (health ministries, parliaments and specialised commissions). Although strictly speaking part of the State itself, it is submitted that that same State is also required to adopt legislation and to take other measures to ensure that its own officials refrain from health sector corruption.[22] It can do so by, for example, disseminating performance data on state and local governments, by providing information about the financial resources over which (local) governments have direct control, and by submitting (local) governments to closer supervision (Human Rights Watch 2007: 5).

Payers. As mentioned, with 'payers' reference is generally made to social security organisations and public and private health insurers. Health insurance organisations are important 'payers' in the health sector. Governments are required to take measures to ensure that public and private health insurers refrain from acts of corruption. More specifically, they are required, as mentioned above, to regulate, to monitor and to provide redress.

As noted, adverse selection practices by (private) health insurers may lead to an uninsured population disproportionately made up of those most in need of care (CGD 2006: 4). Government intervention is required to ensure that health insurers do not differentiate between customers on the basis of health status, age, financial capability or other factors related to the insured (Toebes 2006: 114–19, 2008: 449).

Providers. Governments are under an obligation to regulate healthcare providers, including hospitals, physicians and other health workers, as well as commercial suppliers of medical and healthcare goods and services. As Savedoff explains, since healthcare providers have such a strong influence over medical decisions, they have ample opportunity to engage in abuse (Savedoff 2007: 4). This section focuses on hospitals and the medical profession.

It has been pointed out that the hospital sector is quite vulnerable to corruption, in both developing and developed countries alike (Vian 2006: 49). Corruption in hospitals may vary from corruption in procurement to embezzlement and theft by medical personnel, and corruption in payment systems (Vian 2006: 50). Eventually corruption in the hospital's administration can leave patients with expired medicines or without any medicines, which affects their enjoyment of the right to health.[23]

States are under an obligation to adopt transparency and accountability measures to hold hospitals accountable administratively. States can adopt legislation to achieve this aim, but they can also set up (citizen) health boards, procurement, pharmacy and therapeutic committees to enhance transparency within hospitals. For example, research has demonstrated that centralising hospital procurement is one way to reduce opportunities for corruption (Vian 2006: 52). Health Ministries may also decide to publish open waiting lists to curb the trend of patients paying bribes to reduce time spent on waiting lists (Vian 2006: 55).

Furthermore, the question arises of how governments can regulate the medical profession when it comes to corruption in their practices. States could take measures in order to reduce informal payments (fees, gifts and bribes) to the medical profession (Allin *et al.* 2006: 67). This can be achieved by creating awareness among health system workers of their duty towards patients and by informing health system users of their rights (Transparency International 2006: 75). In addition, the State may try to reduce informal payments by tackling the shortages in the health sector, developing more appropriate and affordable benefits packages, formalising informal payments as co-payments, shifting to private healthcare or social insurance models, and by creating information and monitoring systems with penalties for infringement (Allin *et al.* 2006: 69). In connection with this, States should consider prohibiting preferential treatment to well-connected individuals (CGD 2006: 20). Furthermore, States could take measures to prevent absenteeism among health personnel (CGD 2006: 16–20), create accountability for medical personnel and ensure proper wages so that health professionals are less inclined to take on second jobs. States could take measures to prohibit practices of selling public positions and requiring bribes for promotion (CGD 2006: 19–20). Finally, Governments may prevent payments by pharmaceutical, biotechnology, medical device and other companies to physicians to support marketing of their products. Physicians may be paid to give talks, to 'consult', and to serve on advisory boards[24] and they may receive gifts 'in kind' from pharmaceutical companies, such as. holidays or trips to conferences.

Consumers or patients. Patients may try to get free or subsidised care by under-reporting their personal income or they may misrepresent their enrolment in an insurance plan by using other people's insurance cards. Patients may also bribe a doctor to obtain benefits for non-health issue (e.g. to obtain a disability benefit or to avoid military service), or they may pay bribes to get privileged access to public care (Savedoff and Hussmann 2006: 4, 10). Governments should take measures to prevent patients and healthcare consumers more generally from taking such acts.

Suppliers. States are under a general obligation to ensure that healthcare supply systems are institutionally sound and transparent and that there are appropriate mechanisms to reduce the likelihood of corruption (Cohen 2006: 77). They should take measures to prevent the production and sale of adulterated drugs.[25] When it comes to the supply of drugs, they should ensure that the manipulation of information on drug trials is prohibited and sanctioned. They could adopt legislative and other measures to reduce the likelihood of corruption in the drug selection process, for example by establishing drug selection committees that are composed of impartial persons with the appropriate technical skills, and who make use of the WHO criteria for selection (Cohen 2006: 81). They should address inappropriate marketing practices by some pharmaceutical companies and avoid inappropriate prescribing by physicians (Cohen 2006: 83). Furthermore, they could see to it that drugs are allocated, transported and stored appropriately, and they could try to prevent the distribution of counterfeit drugs, including drugs that have been relabelled and unregistered drugs (Akunyili 2006: 97). Finally, they could try to ensure that pharmacies, hospitals and healthcare providers are reimbursed for drugs in an appropriate and transparent way (Cohen 2006: 84). Similarly, States are under an obligation to regulate the behaviour of suppliers of medical equipment. They should hold them accountable when they commit acts that can be classified as health sector corruption. Finally, as mentioned above, States can take measures to prevent payments by pharmaceutical and other companies to physicians to support marketing of their products.

Researchers and educators are additional important actors in the health sector. Among other things, governments are to ensure that clinical research is carried out independently, i.e. that researchers are not influenced by manufacturers who have an interest in bringing the tested drug onto the market. Once the stage of publishing the research results is reached, researchers should be obliged to adopt a similarly independent approach. As far as this author is aware, few guidelines call for clinical researchers to be totally independent from the companies that make the products or services that are the subjects of their research.[26]

5.3.3 State obligations to fulfil

On the basis of the obligation to fulfil, States are under a general obligation to devote a sufficient percentage of their budget to health services. As mentioned above, this should be done to the 'maximum of their available resources'. It should be noted that States do not always meet this requirement. It is reported that while most rich countries spend at least five per cent of GDP on health, many developing countries spend less then half this amount (U4 2006: 3).

With regard to corruption more specifically, States should formulate, implement and periodically review a coherent national policy to minimise the risk of corruption throughout the entire health system. While it is recognised that the resources available for preventing corruption may not be as plentiful in low-income countries as in high-income countries (Vian 2006: 57), States should adopt such policies 'to the maximum of their available resources' (Article 2(1) ICESCR). In countries where health sector corruption is endemic, national health policies and health financing strategies should include a policy to reduce the wasting of resources due to corruption (U4 2006: 5). This policy should be coherently and consistently applied across all levels of the health sector.

As to the (financial) organisation of the health sector, the General Comment on the Right to Health points out that human rights law is neutral on the way in which States organise their healthcare systems (CESCR 2000: para 12). For example, the right to health may be satisfied through whatever mix of public and private sector services is appropriate in the national context. Yet States should take into account that certain choices may imply a higher risk of health sector corruption, and should build in mechanisms to prevent this. As pointed out by the former Special Rapporteur on the Right to Health, Paul Hunt, international human rights law requires that a chosen rule or policy delivers positive right to health outcomes, also for the disadvantaged (UN 2004: para 12). In this regard, three trends are important when it comes to health sector corruption:

Health funding mechanisms. When it comes to health funding mechanisms, a distinction can be made between 'integrated systems', which finance the supply of services directly, and 'payer/provider systems', where the payer and the provider are separate entities (Savedoff and Hussmann 2006: 11; Savedoff 2007: 8).

It has been pointed out that a system of directly financing the supply of health services will be more vulnerable to corruption in procurement and abuses that undermine the quality of services. Common forms of corruption are theft, illegally charging patients and diverting them to private practices, and absenteeism (Transparency International 2006: 11). The second system, which is common in high- and middle-income countries with social insurance systems, relies on billing and health insurance. Due to the fact that under this model public financing is separated from provision, these systems are generally more vulnerable to the diversion of funds. The most common forms of abuse are excessive or low-quality medical treatment, and fraud in billing government or insurance agencies (Transparency International 2006: 11–13). States should take into account such vulnerabilities when they take steps to reorganise their health funding mechanisms.

Decentralisation. There has been a widespread devolution of authority to local governments.[27] As local governments attain more power over healthcare provision, it is important to ensure that local health authorities are not corrupt. As such, the decentralisation of healthcare services should always include a strategy to prevent corruption at the local government level (Human Rights Watch 2007: 40–64).

Privatisation. Under human rights law, States are free to privatise their health systems. However, they must ensure that healthcare privatisation does not lead to more corruption. The privatisation of public services implies a move away from direct government control. States should therefore establish the necessary mechanisms for monitoring the private healthcare sector (Toebes: 2006: 118–119).

Furthermore, health sector corruption has been linked to the lack of a clear-cut separation between public and private practice. Patients may find themselves paying for a service twice – first in the public hospital, and then in the private clinic where the same doctor is employed (FIDH 2005: 24). States are to create mechanisms to prevent such practices.

Payment of health professionals. Where earnings are low, health professionals may take on second jobs and be more tempted to demand contributions from patients (CGD 2006: 36). States should ensure access to decent wages to the 'maximum of their available resources', as stipulated under Article 2(1) ICESCR.

Second, research demonstrates that physicians whose earnings are based on salary rather than fee-for-service, bonus or capitation tend to be less productive and show lower levels of care (CGD 2006: 36). On the other hand, fee-for-service payments may lead to excess utilisation, and even to useless and harmful therapies.[28] Therefore, States should be aware of the risks when deciding in favour of either a salary-based or a fee-for-service system.

5.4 International obligations

On the basis of, *inter alia*, Article 2(1) ICESCR, States are obliged to provide 'international cooperation and assistance' in order to realise the rights provided for in the ICESCR, including the right to health. As pointed out by the General Comment on the Right to Health, developed States have a duty to assist developing nations, in particular when it comes to realising minimum essential levels of health facilities, goods and services (CESCR 2000: 39; Sepúlveda 2003: 370–5). It is arguable that while providing such aid, developed States are under an obligation to ensure that this process is not affected by corruption. Here it should be taken into account that States often donate vast funds to developing countries, often through donor organisations. Large amounts of such funds do not reach their goal, but instead disappear into the pockets of public officials and health workers in poor nations (Kasper 2006; Tayler and Dickinsen 2006: 107 and 109–11).[29] It is also important for States to consider their (indirect) role in the growing number of public–private partnerships ('Global PPP' (Widdus 2003)). States may try to exert pressure to ensure that these partnerships are not dominated by the commercial interests of private companies (see also Richter 2003). In sum, we can identify the following international State obligations to respect, protect and fulfil:

- International State obligations to respect: refrain from health sector corruption in the provision of health services to developing nations.
- International State obligations to protect: ensure that healthcare providers and providers of healthcare goods and services refrain from health sector corruption;[30] and ensure that receiving States, including their central and local governments, utilise and distribute the assistance received in a transparent and fair manner. (Sepúlveda 2003: 376–7)
- International State obligation to fulfil: assist developing nations to realise minimum levels of health facilities in a transparent manner.

5.5 Obligations of non-State actors

The primary focus of this chapter is on the position of States in relation to health sector corruption. However, health sector corruption cannot be combated by solely focusing on the responsibilities of governments. It is of crucial importance to also address the other actors in the health sector. In fact it is increasingly argued that other actors besides States have obligations under human rights law (e.g. Jägers 2000). Several legal bases for this assumption can be found in international (human rights) law.[31] For example, the preamble to the Universal Declaration of Human Rights recognises the human rights responsibilities of 'all organs of society' (UDHR 1948: preamble). As demonstrated below, we can in fact identify obligations to respect, protect and fulfil in relation to all these actors. While it is important to identify these obligations, recognition of the human rights obligations of other actors besides States should never undermine the primary responsibility of States under international law.

It would be impossible to give an exhaustive overview of the human rights responsibilities of all the actors in the health sector. This section gives a non-exhaustive overview of the human rights obligations of health insurers (as one of the payers), hospitals and the medical profession (as important providers), and pharmaceutical companies (as powerful suppliers).

5.5.1 Health insurers

If we assume that both public and private health insurers bear a certain responsibility under the right to health, we can identify the following obligations: *Respect*: Health insurers should refrain from:

- embezzlement, theft and illicit enrichment from the health insurance budget;
- displaying bias in favour of certain procedures, medical professionals or products due to conflicts of interest;[32]
- refusing patients on the basis of their health status, age or other factors, and as such employing adverse selection practices that may lead to an uninsured population made up of those most in need of care (CGD 2006: 4);
- refusing patients on the basis of their financial capability, though this will depend on the structure of the particular healthcare system.[33]

Protect: Health insurers should adopt internal regulations and other measures to:

- provide for explicit protection of whistle-blowers;
- ensure due process if the health insurer has an internal disciplinary process;
- prohibit and prevent the illegal billing of healthcare providers and customers;
- prevent the overproduction of care by physicians (CGD 2006: 4);
- prevent the over-consumption of medical services by customers.

Fulfil: Health insurers are to adopt an anti-corruption strategy that addresses corruption in all departments and that includes the measures mentioned above.

5.5.2 Hospitals

Assuming that hospitals bear a certain responsibility under the right to health, we can identify the following obligations of hospital authorities (Transparency International 2006: 50).

Respect: Hospital authorities should refrain from, among other things:

- embezzlement, theft and illicit enrichment from the hospital budget;[34]
- overpayment for goods and services;
- illegally billing insurance companies, governments or patients for uncovered services;
- performing unnecessary medical interventions in order to maximise fee revenue;[35]

- selling public positions and requiring bribes for promotion;
- encouraging physicians and employees to obtain payments or outside income from pharmaceutical companies and other outside organisations or individuals with vested interests;
- displaying bias in favour of particular procedures, devices or drugs.[36]

Protect: Hospital authorities are to adopt internal regulations and take other measures to:

- protect the position of whistle-blowers;
- prohibit and prevent the diversion of budgets or user-fee revenue for personal advantage, stealing medicines or medical supplies or equipment;
- prohibit and prevent the acceptance of informal payments by their health personnel;
- prohibit and prevent preferential treatment to well-connected individuals;
- prohibit and prevent the use of hospital equipment for private business;
- prevent and prohibit physicians from improperly referring public hospital patients to their private practice;
- prohibit and prevent absenteeism of medical personnel while being paid.

Fulfil: Hospital authorities are to adopt an anti-corruption strategy that addresses corruption in all departments and that includes the measures mentioned above. It should be noted that approaches to prevention and control should not only require monitoring and control systems for detection and punishment, but may also require reforms to payment systems and reforms to strengthen professionalism (Vian 2006: 54). The creation of individual contracts with personnel and increased pay scales while sanctioning poor performance may also prevent corruption among hospital personnel (Vian 2006: 55).

Furthermore, part of the strategy can be the adoption of an administrative system of procurement and inventory control (Vian 2006: 52). Such a system may provide for review committees to certify the need for new drugs or equipment, competitive bidding and other best-practice procurement procedures and inventory systems to safeguard supplies (Vian 2006: 59). It may also include the formalisation of user fees and the promotion of professionalism among staff (Vian 2006: 55).

5.5.3 The medical profession

Whether the medical profession has direct responsibility under international human rights law will depend on whether doctors are employed by a national health system or whether they work in a private setting. It can be argued that doctors who work in a national health system are directly part of the State, and as such bear direct responsibility under human rights law. But even if the medical profession does not bear direct legal obligations under human rights law, it can be argued that it has a moral responsibility to comply with human rights.

In the first place, the profession's own professional codes commit it to abstain from unethical and unprofessional behaviour ('obligation to respect'). Existing codes of conduct in fact display a commitment to transparency and combating health sector corruption. For example, the new Physician Charter on Medical Professionalism, which was adopted in 2001 by three professional organisations covering the US and Europe, contains many implicit references to the prevention of corruption.[37]

Furthermore, given the key position that the medical profession occupies in the health sector, its members are often the first to detect human rights violations and can therefore play an important role in detecting and preventing such violations ('obligation to protect'). Finally, also on the basis of its professional codes, the medical profession has committed itself to providing good quality health services ('obligation to fulfil'). In relation to corruption, the medical profession can be said to have the following obligations:

Respect:

- to avoid conflicts of interests with their patients, for example where a doctor is given an incentive by the manufacturer to prescribe a particular drug, even though it is not in the best interests of his or her patient;
- to refuse informal payments (Allin *et al.* 2006: 63);
- to remain independent from all outside organisations and individuals with vested economic or political interests in their clinical and educational activities (Williams 2006: 95);
- to avoid bias in favour of particular procedures, devices or drugs;
- to refrain from an overproduction of care when third parties cover costs (CGD 2006: 4).

Protect:

- to offer protection to whistle-blowers
- to protect patients from unethical behaviour by other healthcare providers or the pharmaceutical industry.

Fulfil:

- to provide good quality healthcare services and to provide independent advice; the medical profession as a whole could consider the adoption of strategies and codes to prevent corruption among its members.

5.5.4 *Pharmaceutical companies*

Pharmaceuticals are essential to health systems, and they play an important role in enhancing the quality of life for many patients (Cohen 2006: 77). As such, the pharmaceutical industry plays an important role in realising people's right to health. An important initiative concerns the Human Rights Guidelines for Pharmaceutical Companies in Relation to Access to Medicines (Right to Health Unit of the Essex University Human Rights Centre n.d.) With regard to corruption, the pharmaceutical industry (both as a whole and as individual companies) have the following human rights obligations:

Respect: Pharmaceutical companies should refrain from:

- embezzlement, theft and illicit enrichment from their budgets;
- manipulating or suppressing research results;[38]
- influencing healthcare providers to provide certain drugs;
- excessively promoting drugs;
- deceptive or stealth marketing;[39]
- paying physicians, academics, and other health professionals as consultants or speakers to further their marketing objectives;
- stealth advocacy;[40]
- exerting pressure on the drug selection process to have their drugs selected.

Protect: Pharmaceutical companies should take measures to:

- offer protection to whistle-blowers;
- address counterfeiting (Right to Health Unit of the Essex University Human Rights Centre n.d.: para 44).

Fulfil: Pharmaceutical companies should adopt internal regulations and other measures to (Right to Health Unit of the Essex University Human Rights Centre n.d.: paras 7–11, 43):

- provide for adequate registration procedures which regulate the labelling, marketing, usage, warning and prescription requirements for a drug (Cohen 2006: 80; WHO 1988);
- ensure that drugs are allocated, transported and stored appropriately;
- adopt, implement and enforce their own codes of conduct that detail best practice in the pharmaceutical industry (Cohen 2006: 83; Bale 2006:, 93).

5.6 Human rights violations in relation to health sector corruption

On the basis of the above-defined obligations resulting from the right to health in relation to corruption, it is possible to identify potential violations in relation to such obligations. As observed by Sepúlveda, the definition of violations does not stand alone, but is rather meant to complement the definition of obligations (Sepúlveda 2006: 22). Its purpose is to make our analysis more concrete and tangible. First, we need to identify what constitutes a 'violation' of the obligations that were identified above.[41] For this, we can go back to the 'Maastricht Guidelines on Violations of Economic, Social and Cultural Rights', which were issued by a group of experts in 1997 (Maastricht Guidelines 1997). The guidelines formulate a violation of economic, social and cultural rights as follows:

> A violation of economic social and cultural rights occurs when a State pursues, by action or omission, a policy or practice which deliberately contravenes or ignores obligations of the Covenant, or fails to achieve the required standard of conduct or result . . .[42]
>
> (Maastricht Guidelines 1997: para 11)

This definition focuses on violations of States. As it is States who are the primary responsible actors under international human rights law, we may indeed first want to address States, after which we can gradually identify other responsible actors in the health sector. Furthermore, although it is up to courts and other (quasi-) judicial bodies to assess whether a human rights violation is at stake, we may want to focus on violations that reach a certain degree of severity. By focusing on the most severe violations first, we can create clarity over how corruption impacts upon human rights, after which we can gradually move on to less severe violations, e.g. the acceptance of informal payments by physicians. Two suggestions are made as to how we can identify the most serious violations.

First, the above definition makes a distinction between violations through acts of commission and through omission (Maastricht Guidelines 1997: paras 14–15). A parallel can be drawn here with violations of the obligation to respect (violations through acts of commission) and violations of the obligations to protect and to fulfil (violations through an act of omission). Arguably a failure to realise an obligation to 'respect' is more easily identifiable as a human rights violation than a failure to realise an obligation to protect and to fulfil. For example, while stealing from the health budget by a government official (an action) can be identified as a straightforward human rights violation, a failure by the government to protect individuals from being refused by health insurance companies is more difficult to identify as a (governmental) human rights violation. In this connection, when positive obligations to 'protect' and to 'fulfil' are at stake, we may want to focus on corrupt acts that occur in a structural fashion rather than on one-off incidents. As such, as is discussed below, States and other actors can be held to violate the right to health where they structurally disrespect the obligations to protect and fulfil that right.

In a similar vein, we may want to identify how the act impacts upon human rights. The International Council of Human Rights Policy distinguishes between acts that violate human rights directly and corrupt acts that have an indirect bearing upon human rights (International Council on Human Rights Policy 2008: paras 43–44). For example, when an individual needs to bribe a doctor in order to obtain medical treatment, that act of corruption directly infringes upon the right to health. On the other hand, situations can occur where corruption constitutes an essential factor contributing to a chain of events that eventually lead to a violation of a right (indirect violations (International Council on Human Rights Policy 2008: paras 43–44)). For example, where public officials allow the illegal importation of toxic waste from other countries in return for a bribe, and the waste is placed in a residential area, the corrupt act of bribery may lead indirectly to a violation of the right to health. Third, the report of the Council identifies 'remote violations', where corruption is one factor among others (International Council on Human Rights Policy 2008: para 48). Corrupt acts that have a direct bearing upon human rights will be easier to identify as human rights violations. Therefore, in the analysis below, the emphasis lies on acts that violate the rights directly.

In the following subsections, we detail specific primary human rights violations in relation to health sector corruption.

5.6.1 *States*

Violations of the 'obligation to respect': States may violate the obligation to respect the right to health if they or one of their agents:

- misappropriate funds that have been allocated to the health sector;
- accept bribes in exchange for, for example, a construction permit for a health facility;
- embezzle or steal money from the health budget;
- trade in influence in the health sector;
- abuse their function in relation to the health sector;
- collude with an organisation that fakes drugs or sells counterfeit drugs;
- divert drugs that are destined for their country back into the international drug market.

Violations of the 'obligation to protect': States may violate the obligation to protect the right to health if they or their agents structurally fail to adopt legislation and other measures to:

- protect individuals from health sector corruption;
- regulate and monitor the actors in the health sector;
- provide redress for victims of health sector corruption.

Violations of the 'obligation to fulfil': States may violate the obligation to fulfil the right to health if they structurally fail to adopt a national strategy that tackles corruption throughout their entire health system.

5.6.2 *Other actors*

The following are examples of violations to respect, protect and to fulfil by other actors in the health sector.

Violations of the 'obligation to respect': Actors in the health sector may violate the obligation to respect the right to health if they structurally:

- accept informal payments;
- select patients on the basis of their health status, age or financial capability;
- over-produce care when third parties cover the costs;
- let themselves be influenced heavily by the pharmaceutical industry or,

as a pharmaceutical company or producer of medical equipment, influence healthcare providers to have their drugs or medical equipment selected.

Violations of the 'obligation to protect': Healthcare providers and other actors in the health sector may violate the obligation to protect the right to health if they structurally fail to adopt regulations and to take other measures to offer protection against:

- illegal billing;
- the over-consumption of medical services;
- over-production of care by physicians when third parties cover the costs;
- considerable over-payment for goods and services;
- a wide practice of unnecessary medical interventions in order to maximise fee revenue;
- selling public positions and requiring bribes for promotion;
- the diversion of budgets or user-fee revenue for personal advantage, or theft of medicines or medical supplies or equipment;
- the structural acceptance of informal payments by their health personnel;
- structural preferential treatment to well-connected individuals;
- consistent use of hospital equipment for private business;
- physicians consistently improperly referring public hospital patients to their private practice;
- structural absenteeism of medical personnel while being paid.

Violations of the 'obligation to fulfil': Healthcare providers and other actors in the health sector may violate the obligation to fulfil the right to health if they structurally fail to adopt an anti-corruption strategy that addresses corruption across all departments of their hospital, health centre, pharmaceutical company or other health-related institution.

6 Conclusions: human rights as a tool to combat health sector corruption

This chapter, and previous research, have demonstrated that corruption is a serious issue in the health sector that can adversely affect the availability, accessibility, acceptability and quality of health services. As such, this chapter has made it clear that corruption seriously impacts upon the right to health and a number of other relevant human rights. It has been pointed out that when tackling health sector corruption, it is important to address both public and private behaviour. A set of State obligations and potential obligations of other actors have subsequently been identified in relation to preventing and addressing health sector corruption. On the basis of this set of obligations, a set of potential human rights violations in relation to corruption have been identified.

By establishing how corruption impacts upon human rights, we may firstly assist States and other actors in the health sector in protecting individuals from health sector corruption. We may also empower those who have legitimate claims in relation to health sector corruption. By way of concluding remarks, we will identify how we can employ human rights law as a tool to combat corruption.

When it comes to governments, this chapter has made it clear that States have an ongoing obligation to monitor and to address existing health sector corruption. Furthermore, States are to assess new laws and policies in light of their vulnerability to corruption. Increasingly, States are recommended to undertake 'human rights impact assessments' in order to identify the possible human rights consequences of, for example, health sector decentralisation, healthcare commercialisation bills and planned policies (see *inter alia* Gostin and Mann 1994, Hunt and McNaughton 2006). As part of such a 'human rights impact assessment' States are able to review whether the introduction of health sector reforms will increase health sector corruption. For example, they can assess whether the transfer of responsibilities to local health boards will lead to more corruption which in turn may affect the 'affordability' of healthcare services.[13]

In addition, governments have human rights responsibilities outside their national borders, for example if they act as donors. In this position they must ensure that their policies are transparent and accountable, and that they have the necessary institutional capacities to prevent any misappropriation of funds or corruption.[11]

Other actors in the health sector may similarly apply human rights in their regulation policies. For example, health sector suppliers and payers can implement a human rights approach in their existing codes of conduct. Health workers could embed an anti-corruption strategy in their existing professional codes or could adopt a new code that focuses on corruption as a violation of the right to health.

UN bodies may integrate a human rights approach in their existing anti-corruption strategies. As suggested by Savedoff, they can develop aggregate health sector indicators of corruption (e.g. absenteeism, share of people paying bribes) and they can collect and publish data (Savedoff 2006: 12). When it comes to health sector corruption, they could apply the 'AAAQ' (page 108) and define obligations to 'respect, protect and fulfil' the right to health in relation to corruption and with regard to the various actors in the health sector. The CESCR could adopt a General Comment that addresses the issue of corruption in relation to economic, social and cultural rights.

Although (international) donor organisations may not have direct responsibilities under international human rights law they have an important role to play in minimising corruption. On many occasions donor organisations provide for vast funds to recipient countries. Donor organisations should be open and explicit about what they are giving and to whom (Tayler and Dickinson 2006: 111). They can publish information about the dates and amounts of their disbursements. They can involve parties from government, civil society, the private sector, the UN and patient organisations in monitoring the submission of proposals and the use of funds (Kasper 2006: 108–109). They should ensure that aid is used in line with good procurement guidelines. They can also try to enhance responsible behaviour within pharmaceutical companies (Tayler and Dickinson 2006: 111).

Civil society groups can try to address the link between health sector corruption and human rights in their campaigns and other actions, and they can use human rights as a framework for relaying their message. Individual victims of health sector corruption or interest groups could try to bring claims before national and international courts and quasi-judicial bodies.

Notes

1 The author wishes to thank Roy Poses (Clinical Associate Professor – Brown University School of Medicine (US)), who is quoted at several points in the text. The author also wishes to thank Dr. William D. Savedoff (Social Insight (US)), and the editors of this publication for their valuable comments and insights. This chapter is based on the author's preliminary research paper written for research project carried out by the International Council on Human Rights Policy (ICHRP) on the more general relationship between corruption and human rights (for the preliminary research paper see Toebes (2007). See also more generally: International Council on Human Rights Policy (2008). All mistakes are the responsibility of this author.

2 Transparency International is the global civil society organisation leading the fight against corruption, see http://www.transparency.org. Main source consulted: Transparency International (2006). See also U4 (2008) – U4 is operated by the Chr. Michelsen Institute in association with Transparency International – and the World Bank (n.d). For a recent study see Vian (2008).

3 Kaufmann (2004) asserts that available data indicate that corruption more generally poses a challenge not only to poor but also to rich nations. For an example in the Western world see Weber (2005).

4 For a specific example on Serbia see FIDH (2005): in a survey carried out by a Serbian NGO ('Lingva') 28.1 per cent of persons questioned considered health as the most corrupt area.

5 As indicated by Roy Poses, see note 1.

6 Transparency International (n.d).

7 Contrary to the definition by P. Bardhan: 'the abuse of public office for personal gain', which less clearly embraces the role of private behaviour. See Bardhan (1997); also Savedoff (2007: 2), and Kaufmann and Vicente (2005).

8 For example, informal payments constitute 84 per cent of total health expenditure in Azerbaijan. See for example Allin, Davaki and Mossialos (2006: 64).

9 See for example the World Bank (n.d.)

10 See the Inter-American Convention Against Corruption (1996); the OECD Convention on Combating Bribery of Foreign Public Officials (1997); the Council of Europe Criminal Law Convention on Corruption (and Additional Protocol) (1999) and the Civil Law Convention on Corruption (1999); the Convention drawn up on the basis of Article K.3 (2) (c) of the Treaty on European Union, on the fight against corruption involving officials of the European Union Communities or officials of Member States of the European Union (1999); the Southern African Development Protocol Against Corruption 2001; the African Union Convention on Preventing and Combating Corruption (2002) and the UN Convention on Corruption (2003) that is discussed below. For an overview see Carr (2006: 11).

11 For example, the Council of Europe Conventions contain a description of corruption in Article 2. See Council of Europe (1999a, 1999b).

12 Articles 15, 16 and 21. A distinction is generally made between active bribery (offering a bribe) and passive bribery (passive bribery). If the undue advantage is given in the

context of international business the act is called trans-national bribery, while bribery solely involving the private sector is addressed as bribery in the private sector. See International Council on Human Rights Policy (2008: para 22).

13 For an overview of how these actors interact see Savedoff 2007: 3.

14 As suggested by Roy Poses, see note 1.

15 Right to life: *inter alia*, article 6 of the International Covenant on Civil and Political Rights (ICCPR), Article 2 European Convention for the Protection of Human Rights and Fundamental Freedoms (ECHR); principle of non-discrimination: *inter alia*, common Article 2 of the ICCPR and the International Covenant on Economic, Social and Cultural Rights (ICESCR), freedom of expression and the right to information: *inter alia*, Articles 19 ICCPR and 10 ECHR; the right to (political) participation: *inter alia*, Article 25 ICCPR, the right to a remedy: *inter alia*, Articles 2(3) ICCPR and 13 ECHR.

16 See in particular the UN General Comments on the rights to water, education, food and housing, CESCR (1997–2002). For an example of the use of these principles in a national context, see Toebes (2006).

17 See Arts 25 ICCPR, 23(2) American Convention on Human Rights, and 13(1) African Convention on Human and People's Rights.

18 Examples include suppression of information about suicide as a side effect of anti-depressants in children, particularly the drug Seroxat used in the UK, and heart attacks as a side effect of rofecoxib (Vioxx), which is marketed widely in the US as a reliever of mild to moderate pain. See the *Guardian* (2002) and *Washington Post* (2005).

19 As suggested by Roy Poses, see note 1.

20 See Articles 25 ICCPR, 23(2) American Convention on Human Rights, and 13(1) African Convention on Human and People's Rights. For a more elaborate analysis see Potts (n.d.).

21 The right to a remedy is *inter alia* set forth in Arts 2(3) ICCPR and 13 ECHR. See also Section 4. Potts mentions the following forms of remedies: restitution, compensation, rehabilitation, and satisfaction, and guarantees of non-repetition. See Potts (n.d. 28–9).

22 As part of its 'obligation to protect' under General Comment 14, see CESCR 2000: para 33.

23 A hospital pharmacy in Egypt had 46 different kinds of medicines that had expired since 2003 and 2005, and which were still being given to the patients. See FDHRD (2006).

24 As suggested by Roy Poses, see note 1.

25 As in the case of the Chinese manufactured adulterated drug heparin sold in the US. See for example *New York Times* (2008).

26 As suggested by Roy Poses, see note 1. More generally see also the WHO Guidelines for Good Clinical Practice 1995 and World Medical Assembly 1964, although these documents do not refer explicitly to the influence exerted by drug manufacturers.

27 For an example concerning the Italian health care system, see Mesters (2008: 494).

28 As suggested by Roy Poses, see note 1. See also Savedoff (2007:4).

29 For an example on Kenya see Kipkoech Tanui and Nixon Ng'ang'a (2006: 112–15).

30 For an example on how the UK seeks to supervise the pharmaceutical industry see Department for International Development (DFID) 2005.

31 In this regard, reference is often made to the body of International Humanitarian Law and to the Genocide Convention, which both contain references to the human rights responsibilities of non-State actors.

32 As suggested by Roy Poses, see note 1.

33 This may depend on the character of the health insurance system and it may vary from public to private health insurer. Public health insurers may be more easily obliged not to refuse patients on the basis of their financial capabilities. In countries where there are no affordable alternatives under the public health insurance system it may be more urgent for private health insurance companies to accept patients irrespective of their financial capabilities.

34 For concrete examples about hospital thefts in Egypt see FDHRD (2006: 5–6).
35 In a survey carried out by the American College of Physician Executives, 59 per cent of physician executives consulted indicated that they were very concerned about physicians potentially refusing to attend patients who do not have insurance. See Weber (2005: 8).
36 Last two points: as suggested by Roy Poses, see note 1.
37 Examples are the 'Principle of social justice', the 'Commitment to honesty with patients', the 'Commitment to maintaining appropriate relations with patients', the 'Commitment to a just distribution of finite resources', and the 'Commitment to scientific knowledge'. See ABIM Foundation, ACP Foundation and the European Federation of Internal Medicine (EFIM) n.d.
38 As suggested by Poses, see note 1.
39 As suggested by Poses, see note 1.
40 As suggested by Poses, see note 1.
41 For a step by step approach see International Council on Human Rights Policy (2008: para 48).
42 This paragraph also indicates that an act of discrimination constitutes a violation.
43 For an analysis in relation to health sector privatisation see Toebes (2006, 2008).
44 For an example see the German Federal Ministry for Economic Cooperation and Development (2006).

Bibliography

ABIM Foundation (American Board of Internal Medicine), ACP Foundation (American College of Physicians), and the European Federation of Internal Medicine (EFIM) (n.d.), *Medical Professionalism in the New Millennium: A Physician Charter.* See http://www.abimfoundation.org/professionalism/charter.shtm

Akunyili, D. (2006) 'The fight against counterfeit drugs in Nigeria', in Transparency International, *Global Corruption Report 2006, Special Focus – Corruption and Health*, London: Pluto Press: 96–100.

Allin, S., Konstantina, D. and Mossialos, E. (2006) 'Paying for "free" health care: the conundrum of informal payments in post-communist Europe' in Transparency International, *Global Corruption Report 2006, Special Focus – Corruption and Health*, London: Pluto Press: 63–70.

American Medical Association (2001) *Principles of Medical Ethics of the American Medical Association.* = http://www.ama-assn.org/ama/pub/physician-resources/medical-ethics/code-medical-ethics/principles-medical-ethics.shtml

AU (2002) *African Union Convention on Preventing and Combating Corruption.*

Azfar, O. and Tugrul G. (2006) 'Local-level corruption hits health service delivery in the Philippines', in Transparency International, *Global Corruption Report 2006, Special Focus – Corruption and Health*, London: Pluto Press: 37–39.

Baehr, P. R. (1999), *Human Rights – Universality in Practice*, London: Macmillan Press.

Bale, H. (2006), 'Promoting trust and transparency in pharmaceutical companies: an industry perspective', in Transparency International, *Global Corruption Report 2006, Special Focus – Corruption and Health*, London: Pluto Press: 91–3.

Bardhan, P. (1997) 'Corruption and development: a review of issues', *Journal of Economic Literature* 25: 1320–46

Carr, I. (2006) 'The United Nations Convention on Corruption: Making a Real Difference to the Quality of Life of Millions?', *Manchester Journal of International Economic Law* 3(3): 3–44.

CESCR (2000) *Committee on Economic, Social and Cultural Rights, The right to the highest attainable standard of health, UN General Comment No. 14 (2000)*, UN Doc. E/C12/200/4, 11 August.

CESCR (1997–2002) *Committee on Economic, Social and Cultural Rights, General Comments on the Rights to Water, Education, Food, and Housing (General Comments 15, 13, 12 and 4 respectively)*. See http://www2.ohchr.org/english/bodies/cescr/comments.htm.

CGD (Center for Global development, Maureen Lewis) (2006), *Governance and Corruption in Public Health Care Systems, Working Paper no. 87*, January 2006. See http://www.cgdev.org/content/publications/detail/5967

Cohen, J. C. (2006) 'Pharmaceuticals and corruption: a risk assessment', in Transparency International, *Global Corruption Report 2006, Special Focus – Corruption and Health*, London: Pluto Press: 77–85.

Coomans, F. (Ed.) (2006) *Justiciability of Economic, Social and Cultural Rights*, Antwerp and Oxford: Intersentia.

Council of Europe (1999a) *Criminal Law Convention on Corruption (and Additional Protocol)*.

—— (1999b) *Civil Law Convention on Corruption*.

DFID (Department for International Development) (2005), *Increasing people's access to essential medicines in developing countries: a framework for good practice in the pharmaceutical industry, A UK Government policy paper*, March 2005. See http://www.dfid.gov.uk

EU (1999) Convention drawn up on the basis of Article K.3 (2) (c) of the Treaty on European Union, on the fight against corruption involving officials of the European Union Communities or officials of Member States of the European Union (1999).

FDHRD (Forum for Development and Human Rights Dialogue) (2006) *'Right to Health' Wasted rights and absent care – An overview on corruption and negligence in the Health Sector in Egypt, April 2006* (ed. by Said Abdel Hafez Darwish). See http://www.moltaka.org/en/issues/06/0403.htm (accessed April 2009).

FIDH (International Federation for Human Rights) (2005), *Serbia: Discrimination and Corruption, the Flaws in the Health Care System*, April 2005, No. 416/2.

German Federal Ministry for Economic Cooperation and Development (2006), *Preventing corruption – promoting transparency: What is German development policy doing?*. See http://www.bmz.de/en/service/infothek/buerger/FlyerKorruption.pdf (accessed June 2009).

Gostin, L. and J. Mann (1994) 'Towards the development of human rights impact assessments for the formulation and evaluation of public health policies', *Health and Human Rights* 1(1): 59–80.

Guardian, The (2002) 'Glaxo "played down Seroxat side-effects" ', *Guardian*, 12 October. http://www.guardian.co.uk/society/2002/oct/12/mentalhealth.research

Gupta, S., Davoodi, H. and Tiongson, E. (2000) 'Corruption and the provision of health care and education services', IMF Working Paper, WP/00/116, June 2000.= http://www.imf.org/external/pubs/ft/wp/2000/wp00116.pdf

Howard, R. E. (1997) 'Human rights and the culture of wars', 8 *International Journal* 94–112.

Human Rights Watch (2007) *Chop Fine, The Human Rights Impact of Local Government Corruption and Mismanagement in Rivers State, Nigeria*, January 2007, 19(2(A)).

Hunt, P. and Backman, G. (n.d.) *Health Systems and the Right to the Highest Attainable Standard of Health*, University of Essex Human Rights Centre = http://www2.essex.ac.uk/human_rights_centre

Hunt, P. and McNaughton, G. (2006) *Impact Assessments, Poverty and Human Rights, a Case Study Using the Right to the Highest Attainable Standard of Health, Submitted to UNESCO*, 31 May 2006. See http://www2.essex.ac.uk/human_rights_centre

IDEA (International Debate Association) (n.d.), see http://www.idebate.org/debatabase/topic_details.php?topicID=507

International Council on Human Rights Policy (2008) *Corruption and Human Rights Conceptual Paper, Draft Report*, April 2008, see. http://www.ichrp.org/en/projects/131

International Council on Human Rights Policy (2009) *Corruption and Human Rights: Making the Connection*, Geneva: International Council on Human Rights Policy.

Jägers, N. (2000) *Corporate Responsibility for Human Rights Violations*, Antwerp and Oxford: Intersentia/Hart.

Kasper, Toby (2006) 'Accountability in a time of crisis: corruption and the Global Fund', in Transparency International, *Global Corruption Report 2006, Special Focus – Corruption and Health*, London: Pluto Press: 108–9.

Kaufmann, D. (2004) 'Corruption, governance and security: challenges for the rich countries and the world', World Bank Institute. See http://papers.ssrn.com/sol3/papers.cfm?abstract_id=605801

Kaufmann, D. and Vicente, P. C. (2005) *Corruption, Governance and Security: Challenges for the Rich Countries and the World*, see www.worldbank.org/wbi/governance

Maastricht Guidelines (1997), *Maastricht Guidelines on Violations of Economic, Social and Cultural Rights*, Maastricht, January 22–26, 1997. See http://www1.umn.edu/humanrts/instree/Maastrichtguidelines_.html

Mesters, B. (2008) 'Don Corleone in de zorg' [Don Corleone in medical care], *Medisch Contact* 21 March 2008, 63(12): 492–496.

New York Times (2008) 'The Frightening Heparin Case', 28 April. See http://www.nytimes.com/2008/04/28/opinion/28mon2.html

OAS (1996) *Inter-American Convention Against Corruption.*

OECD (1997) *Convention on Combating Bribery of Foreign Public Officials.*

Potts, H. (n.d.) *Participation and the Right to the Highest Attainable Standard of Health, and Accountability and the Right to the Highest Attainable Standard of Health*, University of Essex, Human Rights Centre. See http://www2.essex.ac.uk/human_rights_centre/rth/docs

Richter, J. (2003) '*"We the Peoples" or "We the Corporations": Critical Reflections on UN–Business "Partnerships"*', International Baby Food Action Network and Geneva Infant Feeding Association, Geneva.

Right to Health Unit of the Essex University Human Rights Centre (n.d.), *Human Rights Guidelines for Pharmaceutical Companies.* See http://www2.essex.ac.uk/human_rights_centre/rth/projects.shtm

Robinson, Mary (2006) 'Foreword', in Transparency International, *Global Corruption Report 2006, Special Focus – Corruption and Health*, London: Pluto Press: xiv–xv.

SA (2001) Southern African Development Protocol Against Corruption.

Sandgren, C. (2005) 'Combating corruption: the misunderstood role of law', *International Lawyer* 39(3): 717–31.

Savedoff, William D. and Karen Hussmann (2006) 'Why are health systems so prone to corruption?', in Transparency International, *Global Corruption Report 2006, Special Focus – Corruption and Health*, London: Pluto Press: 4–13.

—— (2007) *Transparency and Corruption in the Health Sector: A Conceptual Framework and Ideas for Action in Latin American and the Caribbean, Health Technical Note 03/2007* Inter-American Development Bank, Washington, D.C. See http://www.iadb.org/sds/doc/CorruptionHealthFrameworkSavedoff.pdf

Sepúlveda, Magdalena (2003) *The Nature of the Obligations under the International Covenant on Economic, Social and Cultural Rights*, Antwerp, and Groningen/Oxford: Intersentia/Hart.

Tanui, K. and Ng'ang'a, N. (2006) 'Corruption in Kenya's National AIDS Control Council', in Transparency International, *Global Corruption Report 2006, Special Focus – Corruption and Health*, London: Pluto Press: 112–15.

Tayler, L. and Dickinson, C. (2006), 'The link between corruption and human rights', in Transparency International, *Global Corruption Report 2006, Special Focus – Corruption and Health*, London: Pluto Press: 104–111.

Toebes, B. C. A. (1999) *The Right to Health as a Human Right in International Law*, Antwerp, and Groningen/Oxford: Intersentia/Hart.

—— (2006) 'The right to health and the privatisation of national health systems: a case study of the Netherlands', *Health and Human Rights* 9(1): 114–27.

—— (2007), preliminary research paper entitled 'Human rights and health sector corruption', written for a larger project on human rights and health sector corruption of the International Council on Human Rights Policy, = http://www.ichrp.org/files/papers/122/131_-_Brigit_Toebes_-_2007.pdf#search='toebes

—— (2008) 'Taking a human rights approach to health care commercialisation', in Cholewka P. A. and Motlagh M. M. (eds.) *Health Capital and Sustainable Socioeconomic Development* London, Taylor and Francis 442–54.

Transparency International (2006) *Global Corruption Report 2006, Special Focus – Corruption and Health*, London: Pluto Press.

—— (2008) *Global Corruption Report 2008, Corruption in the Water Sector*. See http://www.transparency.org/publications/gcr

—— (n.d.), *Frequently asked questions about corruption*. See http://www.transparency.org/news_room/faq/corruption_faq

UDHR (1948) *Universal Declaration of Human Rights, art. 7*, G.A. Res. 217A(III), U.N. GAOR, 3d Sess., at 71, U.N. Doc. A/810.

U4 (2006) *Corruption in the Health Sector*. See http://www.u4.no/document/u4-issue/u4_issue1_2006_health.pdf

UN (2003) United Nations Convention against Corruption.

UN (2004) *Report of the Special Rapporteur on the Right to the Highest Attainable Standard of Health, Paul Hunt, Mission to the World Trade Organisation*, UN Doc. E/CN.4/2004/49/Add.1,1 March 2004.

Vian, T. (2006) 'Corruption in hospital administration', in Transparency International, *Global Corruption Report 2006, Special Focus – Corruption and Health*, London: Pluto Press, pp. 49–53

—— (2008), 'Review of corruption in the health sector: theory, methods and interventions, *Health Policy and Planning* 23(2): 83–94

Washington Post (2005) 'Merck found liable in Vioxx case', 20 August.

Weber, D. O. (2005), 'Unethical business practices in U.S. health care alarm physician leaders', *Physician Executive*, March–April 2005. See http://www.medical newstoday.com/articles/20968.php

WHO (1988) *Criteria for Medicinal Drug Promotion*. See http://apps.who.int/medicinedocs/en/d/Jwhozip08e/1.html#Jwhozip08e.1

—— (1995) *WHO Guidelines for Good Clinical Practice (GCP) for Trials on Pharmaceutical Products, WHO Technical Report Series, No. 850 1995, Annex 3*. See http://homepage.vghtpe.gov.tw/~mre/goodexp/Fercap-Survey/WHO-GCP–1995.pdf

Widdus, R. (2003) 'Public–private partnerships for health require thoughtful evaluation', *Bulletin of the World Health Organisation* 81(4): 235.

Williams, J. (2006) 'Fighting corruption: the role of the medical profession', in Transparency

International, *Global Corruption Report 2006, Special Focus – Corruption and Health*, London: Pluto Press: 94–6.

World Bank (n.d.) 'Governance & anti-corruption', webpage. See http://web.worldbank.org/WBSITE/EXTERNAL/WBI/WBIPROGRAMS/PSGLP/0,,menuPK:461646~pagePK:64156143~piPK:64154155~theSitePK:461606,00.html

World Medical Assembly (1964) *Declaration of Helsinki. Ethical Principles for Medical Research Involving Human Subjects*. See http://www.wma.net/e/policy/b3.htm

7 The child's right to health and the courts

Aoife Nolan

1 Introduction

The child's right to health has started to come into its own. In addition to being set out in a wide range of international and regional human rights instruments, the right is included in a growing number of national constitutions. This has resulted in it being the subject of ever-greater levels of judicial and quasi-judicial attention. However, the extent of the protection afforded to the child's right to health by such bodies has by no means been uniform. While some judicial and quasi-judicial bodies have not hesitated to address children's right to health and construe it in such a way as to impose extensive obligations on the state, others have been far more reticent. This raises the question of how the approaches of such bodies have differed – and why.

This chapter considers the way in which the child's right to health has been interpreted and applied by a wide range of domestic courts and international judicial and quasi-judicial decision-making bodies.[1] In doing so, the chapter identifies the role that has been, and may be, played by the courts in fleshing out the substantive content of the child's right to health.[2] In particular, the author focuses on the courts' role in delineating the state's duty to fulfil the right to health of children. That is, the duty of the state to adopt appropriate legislative, administrative, budgetary, judicial, promotional and other measures towards the full realisation of that right.[3] The adjudication of this state obligation arguably poses the greatest challenge to judicial and quasi-judicial decision-making bodies, requiring as it does the evaluation of whether the state has taken adequate positive steps (and, frequently, has allocated sufficient resources) to facilitate the child's right to health. Indeed, regardless of the frequently exaggerated and inaccurate claims about the alleged institutional incapacity of courts to deal with the positive obligations imposed by economic and social rights,[4] concerns about the judicial review of state 'inaction'[5] and resource allocation have been central to objections to the legal legitimacy of economic and social rights adjudication, including that involving the right to health (see e.g. Hogan 2001: 189). It is thus fitting that this chapter should focus on if, and how, courts have risen to the challenge of the obligation to fulfil.

The substantive aspects of the right to health may be broken down into two main elements: the right to healthcare or health services (which is generally understood as the provision of preventative, curative and rehabilitative medical services) and the right to the underlying preconditions for health, including access to safe and potable water, adequate supplies of safe food, access to health-related education and information (Heyns 2000).[6] In this chapter, the main focus will be on the child's right to healthcare or health services, although the underlying preconditions will be dealt with where relevant.

Rather than simply focusing on how the courts have construed the obligations imposed by the child's right to health, the author will also seek to identify trends in the approaches adopted towards the child's right to health by such bodies. What perceptions of children as rights-holders and members of democratic society underpin such approaches? How do the courts advance particular conceptions of children and their rights through their decision-making? A key element of analysing the courts' role in relation to the child's right to health is a consideration of how that right has been enshrined in the different instruments, which the courts then interpret and apply. This is necessary due to the implications that the particular formulation of a rights provision may have for the court's treatment of such. Furthermore, the way in which the child's right to health is enshrined is frequently reflective of legal or societal perceptions of children and their rights, which may be confirmed or rejected by the court.

Before beginning my analysis, I note that international, regional and domestic law deal extensively with the health rights of particular groups of children[7] – most notably those of children living with disabilities[8] or working children.[9] This chapter, however, will concentrate on the right to health of the 'child' generally, focusing only on the health rights of particular groups of children (for instance, children in state custody) where these arise in cases under discussion in the framework of the general right to health of children. Similarly, this chapter will deal exclusively with the state's obligation to give effect to the child's right to health, and will not consider the horizontal application of that right to parents, carers or other non-state actors.[10] Finally, the author will not deal with court decisions concerning the overriding of a child's refusal of necessary treatment[11] or cases in which a child seeks medical treatment in the face of parental opposition.[12] While such decisions undoubtedly have clear implications for multiple aspects of the child's right to health, including the state's obligation to ensure that children have opportunities to participate in decisions affecting their health,[13] space constraints render an adequate discussion of them beyond the scope of this chapter.

Section 2 of this chapter centres on children as bearers of the right to health, highlighting the implications that the perceived characteristics of childhood and the position of children in society have had, and may have in future, on the courts' construal of that right. Section 3 is a brief analysis of the child's right to health under international law. In Section 4, the author addresses the very different ways in which the child's right to health has been enshrined in national constitutions. Section 5 discusses whether the accepted heightened vulnerability of children with regard to their right to health has resulted in their being accorded priority *vis-à-vis* other groups when it comes to the courts' delineation and enforcement of that right. Before moving on to consider the direct treatment of the child's right to health by courts, Section 6 analyses courts' approaches to the state's duty to fulfil the child's right to health. Section 7 draws together the key questions addressed in the chapter, and presents conclusions on the role of the courts in enforcing the child's right to health.

2 Children and the right to health

Before discussing the courts' approach to the child's right to health, it is necessary to consider the child as a right-to-health-bearer in the broader context. Much has been written with regard to whether children are or should be right-holders, and the basis upon which such rights should be granted. The author's aim is not to reopen that debate.[11] Rather, this chapter proceeds on the understanding that children have been accorded legal rights to health under international, regional and domestic law, on the basis of their status as human persons who are children, and that these rights require implementation by the state.

The position of children in relation to the right to health differs from that of many other groups of right-holders in several ways. The most obvious of these is the fact that children are frequently more vulnerable to violations of their rights, and are less able to protect themselves – or capable of taking advantage of protections that are available – than are members of other groups. Because of their nature and condition, children have a reduced capacity to meet their health needs by either obtaining or creating sustenance from the resources of their environment (Wringe 1981: 135–6). Furthermore, they are less likely to have the skills necessary to gain a stake in the health-related resources, and other resources of the community, by negotiating special rights for themselves (i.e. rights that arise from transactions or relationships (Ibid)). In addition, children are often affected in a different way from adults by violations of their right to health (Office of the High Commissioner of Human Rights 2001). The physical and psychological effects that children suffer as a result of violations of their right to health will generally be greater than those experienced by adults due to their lower level of physical and mental development.[15] This is true both in relation to (a) the immediate impact that violations of the right to health may have on a child's physical and psychological state, and (b) the long-term detrimental effects on the child's development and future capacity for autonomy resulting from such a violation.

The idea that children are in a particular position with regard to the right to health as a result of the biological and socially constructed characteristics of childhood has frequently informed, and been reflected in, the way that the child's right to health has been enshrined in domestic constitutions and international human rights instruments. Perceptions of children and childhood have also often implicitly and/or explicitly influenced how courts have interpreted and applied such provisions. For instance, in its *Advisory Opinion on the Juridical Condition of the Child*,[16] the Inter-American Court of Human Rights stated that 'education and care for the health of children require various measures of protection and are the key pillars to ensure enjoyment of a decent life by the children, *who in view of their immaturity and vulnerability often lack adequate means to effectively defend their rights'* [emphasis added].[17] This statement clearly reflects a perception of children as vulnerable, largely passive, beings who require positive intervention on their behalf to ensure the realisation of their rights. However, the Court had previously commented in its Advisory Opinion that

> [The best-interests principle] is based on the very dignity of the human being, *on the characteristics of children themselves, and on the need to foster their development, making full use of their potential*, as well as on the nature and scope of the Convention on the Rights of the Child.[18]

Here, the Court specifically justified the paternalistic best-interests principle in terms of, amongst other things, the need to develop the child's potential – that is, to maximise the child's future capacity for autonomy.

The exclusion of children from the democratic decision-making processes that determine budgetary allocations and policies also considerably weakens their ability to ensure that their right to health is enforced. If political organs cannot be held to account by children, they are likely to be less attentive to their rights and interests than they would be in relation to those of other, enfranchised vulnerable groups (for instance, the elderly). Awareness of the position of children 'outside democracy' has encouraged the courts to play an active role in asserting the child's right to health in some cases. In one Colombian case involving the child's right to health, the Constitutional Court stated that, in a rights-based social state, the political community owes preferential treatment to those who find themselves in circumstances of clear weakness and who are impeded from participating, under equal conditions, in the adoption of public policies that are applicable to them.[19] The Court held that the reason that justifies giving precedence to the application of the 'democratic principle' (which provides that the elected political organs are those responsible for tax policies and budgets) at the time of assigning positive rights is 'irrelevant in the case of the fundamental rights of minors'.[20] According to the Court, the democratic principle cannot oppose the claim to essential demands of a group of the population that is unable to participate in public debate and that, as a result, does not have its own voice in the adoption of political decisions that affect it.

It is also worth noting the strong linkage between non-discrimination and the child's right to health. Like all economic and social rights, violations of the child's right to health are often the result of deeply-rooted systemic inequality.[21] Those children who are most likely to suffer violations of their right to health are frequently also victims of discrimination – whether on the grounds (or a combination of grounds) of disability, socio-economic status, race, ethnicity, nationality, or other status. Furthermore, children whose right to health has been violated may become victims of discrimination on that ground also (for instance, as a result of stigmatic attitudes about persons living with mental illness or HIV/AIDS).[22] The issue of non-discrimination has been a particular feature in right to health cases that centre on the unequal availability of certain treatments within a particular country (see, for example, Ely Yamin 2003: 349). This is largely due to the linkage between the access to such treatment and the resources that are available to an individual or her family. It is notable that both the Committee on Economic, Social and Cultural Rights (CESCR) and the Committee on the Rights of the Child (ComRC) have emphasised that the state is under an immediate obligation to ensure that the child's right to health is exercised without discrimination of any kind.[23]

At this stage, it is important to establish why the child's right to health is useful in responding to the specific position and right-to-health-related needs of children that are outlined above. First, the child's right to health serves as a springboard for children (and others) to hold government to account, whether at the domestic or the international level. Claims based on that right serve to challenge – and offer litigants the opportunity to recalibrate – the power relationship between children and right-to-health duty-bearers. In addition, where children are recognised as rights-bearers, they are promoted from merely being the object of the rights and duties of others, and are afforded the respect and dignity associated with the status of 'right-holder' (Freeman 1992). Furthermore, recognition and enforcement of the child's right to health by bodies such as those under consideration is a key avenue by which children's health-related issues may be put on the agenda of otherwise indifferent and unresponsive law- and policy-makers. Finally, while it has frequently been argued that the existence of economic and social rights-related legislative entitlements renders express economic and social rights protections unnecessary, it is important to note that such non-rights-based entitlements are often narrowly phrased and do not afford full coverage to all aspects of economic and social rights. In contrast, the protection afforded by the child's right to health is comprehensive and wide-ranging.

Having looked at the position of the child in relation to enjoyment of the right to health and the importance of that right, it seems appropriate to turn to consider how that right has been set out and interpreted at the international level. This will provide the necessary backdrop to an analysis of how the national and regional guarantees have been dealt with by judicial and quasi-judicial bodies.

3 The child's right to health under international law – a brief discussion

The most celebrated and authoritative statement of the right to health under international human rights law is Article 12 of the International Covenant on Economic, Social and Cultural Rights (ICESCR). The steps that States must take so as to give effect to that right include those necessary for the reduction of the stillbirth rate and of infant mortality, and for the healthy development of the child.[24] These child-specific duties are addressed in greater detail by the Committee in General Comment quote 14 on the Right to the Highest Attainable Standard of Health.[25]

The right to health in all its forms, including the child's right to health, must contain the interrelated and essential elements of availability, accessibility, acceptability and quality.[26] Like all rights, the child's right to the highest attainable standard of health imposes three levels of duty on the state – the obligations to respect, protect and fulfil.[27] The obligation to respect requires States to refrain from interfering with the enjoyment of socio-economic and cultural rights.[28] The obligation to protect requires States to take measures that prevent third parties from interfering with the enjoyment of such rights. The obligation to fulfil involves States taking steps to facilitate individuals and communities in enjoying the right, and, when an individual or group is unable to realise the right themselves, to provide that specific right.[29] The first two obligations are immediate in nature. The duty to fulfil the right to the highest attainable standard of physical and mental health also includes duties of an immediate nature. For instance, the immediately realisable 'minimum core' obligations imposed by the right. However, the primary duty imposed by Article 12 ICESCR is one of *progressive* realisation, limited by the state's maximum available resources.[30] There is also a corresponding prohibition on retrogressive measures in all but very limited circumstances.

It is in the context of the Convention on the Rights of the Child (CRC), however, that the substantive content of the right to health of the child has been considered most fully. Like Art 12 ICESCR, Art 24 is essentially concerned with the right to health as a right to health-related goods and services – i.e. as a 'medicalised' conception of health. This is in strong contrast to, for example the 'social medicine' focus of the World Health Organization (WHO) Constitution (Meier and Fox 2008: 260). Numerous aspects of the right to health are dealt with in the CRC, both implicitly in the obligation imposed on states parties by Art 6 to ensure, to the maximum extent possible, the survival and development of the child, and expressly in provisions such as Art 24.[31] My analysis here will focus primarily on Art 24, however. The importance of the child's right to health in the overall schema of children's rights is indicated by the fact that it has been the subject of two General Comments of the Committee on the Rights of the Child (ComRC 2003a, 2003b).[32] It has also been dealt with extensively in three other non-health-specific General Comments.[33]

Art 24 has been described as 'the most elaborate and specific provision on the right to health' (Doek 2001: 162). It establishes that States Parties recognise the right of the child to the enjoyment of the highest attainable standard of health and to facilities for the treatment of illness and rehabilitation of health. States Parties are obliged to strive to ensure that no child is deprived of his or her right of access to healthcare services. The obligation to ensure full implementation of this right includes taking measures to reduce infant and child mortality; to ensure the provision of the necessary medical assistance and healthcare to all children, with emphasis on the development of primary healthcare; to combat disease and malnutrition, including within the framework of primary healthcare;[34] to ensure appropriate pre-natal and post-natal healthcare to mothers; and to develop preventive healthcare, guidance for parents and family planning education and services. Art 24(3) imposes a duty on States Parties to 'take all effective and appropriate measures with a view to abolishing traditional practices prejudicial to the health of children'. Art 24 emphasises the role of international cooperation in relation to the child's right to health, enjoining States Parties to promote and encourage such cooperation with a view to progressively realising the right. Although aspects of the child's right to health are also dealt with in a range of other CRC provisions, my analysis here will focus primarily on Art 24.

Art 4 of the CRC states that, with regard to the economic, social and cultural rights contained in the instrument, States Parties shall undertake such measures 'to the maximum extent of their available resources' and, where needed, within the framework of international co-operation. This is reflected in the language used in the provisions themselves. In addition, Art 24 explicitly refers to the obligations of states 'to pursue full implementation' of this right. In General Comment No. 5 on General Measures of Implementation for the Convention on the Rights of the Child, the Committee on the Rights of the Child states that '[t]he second sentence of Article 4 reflects a realistic acceptance that lack of resources – financial and other resources – may hamper the full implementation of economic, social and cultural rights in some States', and that this introduces the concept of the 'progressive implementation' of such rights (ComRC 2003c: para 8).[35]

The Committee has also made it clear that the obligation on states to implement protection 'to the maximum extent of their available resources' requires states to demonstrate that they have done so and, where necessary, have sought international cooperation.[36] Whatever their economic circumstances, states are required to take all possible measures towards the realisation of the rights of the child, with particular regard to the most disadvantaged groups.[37] The Committee has highlighted the similarity of its approach to the Interpretation of Art 4 CRC to that of the CESCR in relation to the issue of maximum available resources under ICESCR.

The Committee on the Rights of the Child has strongly emphasised the linkage between the right to survival and development set out in Art 6 of the CRC and the economic and social rights set out in that instrument.[38] The close linkage between Arts 6 and 24 is demonstrated in the Committee's General guidelines for the Form and Content of Periodic Reports.[39] In the section of the guidelines on 'basic health and welfare', the Committee asks states to provide relevant information in respect of both Arts 6 and 24 (ComRC 2005a: para 31).

Like all rights set out in the CRC, the child's right to health must be interpreted in the light of the general principles of the Convention: the duty of non-discrimination (Art 2), the best interests of the child [Art 3(1)], the child's right to life, survival and development (Art 6) and the child's right to express her/his views freely in all matters affecting her/him (Art 12). The Committee has incorporated these principles into its interpretation of Art 24 and the other health-related provisions of the CRC. For instance, the Committee has emphasised that all decision-making concerning a child's health and actions undertaken in relation to health services must take account of the best-interests principle.[40]

The key focus of this chapter is the role played by domestic courts and other judicial and quasi-judicial decision-making bodies in relation to the interpretation and application of the child's right to health. Clearly, the role played by such bodies is contingent on their ability to address and take account of the child's right to health in their decision-making – whether in the framework of abstract judicial review or in adjudication based on concrete situations. It is regrettable that the Committee does not, as yet, have an associated complaints mechanism, which would enable rights victims to bring complaints before that body. In addition, the relatively recent adoption of the Optional Protocol to the ICESCR means that the CESCR has not yet had an opportunity to hear any complaints brought under that Protocol. This has limited those Committees' ability to flesh out the child's right to health in the context of the real-life experiences of children. It has not, however, prevented them from highlighting the need for the provision of domestic legal remedies for violations of the rights set out in the instruments they monitor. For instance, in its General Comment No. 5, the Committee on the Rights of the Child states that economic, social and cultural rights, as well as civil and political rights, must be regarded as justiciable.[41] In addition, the CESCR has stated that courts should take account of Covenant rights where this is necessary to ensure that the State's conduct is consistent with its Covenant obligations: '[n]eglect by the courts of this responsibility is incompatible with the principle of the rule of law, which must always be taken to include respect for international human rights obligations'.[42] Crucially, for the purposes of this chapter, when a court is faced with a choice between an interpretation of domestic law that would place the State in breach of the Covenant and one that would enable the State to comply with the Covenant, international law requires the choice of the latter.[43]

4 The child's right to health under national constitutions

In addition to being set out in the international and regional human-rights instruments set out above, the child's right to health has been included in a large number of national constitutions. This is consistent with the significant evidence of a growing tendency towards the express delineation of children's rights in constitutions (for more, see Tobin 2005), including the right to health. This is undoubtedly attributable to the influence of the CRC and the growing awareness of children's rights at the domestic level that has followed that instrument's entry into force. In addition, there is a growing tendency towards the constitutionalisation (and judicial recognition and enforcement) of jusiticiable economic and social rights at both the national and international levels. A survey of 86 national constitutions reveals that 18 explicitly enshrine the child's right to health or healthcare services or aspects thereof.[44] In some, the child's right to health is located under the umbrella of the general right to health provision.[45] In others, it forms part of the children's rights guarantee. In a number of constitutions, it is arguably covered in both.[46] While some provisions outlining the child's right to health are judicially enforceable, others are not, due to, for example, being included in the constitution as a directive principle of social policy.[47] Where the child's right to health is included as a justiciable provision in the constitutional framework, there is far greater scope for judicial protection of that right. However, even where such a right is not justiciable, it still establishes a policy imperative for the legislative and administrative action and exhibits a national commitment to the right to health (Kinney 2004: 301).

Some constitutions explicitly refer to the 'right' of the child to healthcare, while others adopt the approach of delineating the state's duties in such a way as to make it clear that they correspond to a right inhering to the child.[48] A number of constitutional provisions are phrased in terms of a prohibition on interference with the enjoyment of the right to health. For instance, Art 48 of the 1993 Cambodian constitution directs the state to 'protect children from acts that are injurious to their . . . health, and welfare'.[49] Another constitutional provision that is similar in approach, but which reflects a particular concern with how interference with the child's right to health might arise, is Art 34(3) of the Ugandan Constitution (1995): 'No child shall be deprived by any person of medical treatment . . . by reason of religious or other beliefs'. Both of these provisions are primarily concerned with the obligations of the state to respect and protect children's rights. Other constitutions, however, clearly envisage the state moving beyond a preventive or protective role to take steps towards the full realisation of the child's right to health. An example of such an approach was Art 49 of the 1998 Ecuadorian Constitution, which stated, amongst other things, that the state will 'ensure and guarantee' the child's right to comprehensive health – language that suggests strongly that the state must move beyond merely preventing interference with the enjoyment of that right.[50]

A large number of the constitutions surveyed contain provisions that refer or relate to the child's right to special measures of protection or assistance or the child's right to development (whether physical, mental, cultural, spiritual or other), which could be interpreted to encompass some elements of the right to health. In fact, a number of 'protection/development' provisions explicitly require the state to take measures related to the child's right to health.[51] The argument that the child's right to health should be afforded protection by such 'general protection' provisions is particularly strong where the right to health of 'everyone' is enshrined elsewhere in the constitution.[52] For instance, Art 37 of the Constitution of Suriname (1987) provides that '[y]oung people shall enjoy special protection for the enjoyment of economic, social and cultural rights among which are: a. Access to education, culture and work; b. Vocational schooling; c. Physical training, sports and recreation', while the right to health of 'everyone' is set out in the preceding Art 36. It would seem surprising if one were able to argue successfully that the right to health was not included in the 'economic, social and cultural' rights referred to in Art 37.[53] A significant number of other constitutions include an obligation on the state to protect minors from hazardous working conditions.[54] It is notable, however, that many 'special protection' constitutional provisions are premised on the notion of children as passive objects in need of special protection rather than as active subjects of rights (Tobin 2005: 105–110).

There are a couple of additional points to be made regarding how constitutions afford protection to children's rights, which reflect particular attitudes towards children and their rights. First, child-rights-related issues, including the right to health, are often dealt with in the context of constitutional provisions focusing on the rights of a number of vulnerable groups such as older persons.[55] Similarly, the linkage that is frequently made between childhood and maternity, or children and mothers, in constitutional provisions is also evident in the context of the right to health.[56]

Inevitably, constitutional articles on the child's right to health vary in terms of prescriptiveness and detail. Having stated in Art 44 that the right to health is a basic right of children, Art 50 of the Colombian Constitution (which forms part of a series of detailed provisions related to the right to health) provides that:

> any child under a year old who may not be covered by any type of protection or social security will be entitled to receive free care in all health institutions that receive state subsidies.

In contrast, Art 22(2) of the Nepalese Final Interim Constitution (2007) consists simply of the broad statement that 'every child shall have the right to . . . basic health', with no additional information on how that right is to be realised. Art 16(2) of that instrument adds little information, merely stating that 'every citizen shall have the right to get basic health service free of cost from the State as provided for in the law'.

The right to health of the child has also been recognised indirectly within domestic constitutional frameworks that do not deal explicitly with the right to health and/or children's rights by means of explicit constitutional recognition that particular international human rights treaties ratified by the relevant state form part of and/or take precedence over domestic law.[57] One recent example is Art 22 of the Republic of Kosovo constitution (2008), which provides that the CRC is directly applicable in Kosovo and, in the case of conflict, has priority over provisions of laws and other acts of public institutions. Under a number of Latin American regimes, instruments enshrining the child's right to health are accorded constitutional priority and the rights enshrined therein form part of the constitutional rights framework (frequently referred to as 'hierarchy' (Courtis 2008a: 165)).[58] This domestic reliance upon international standards that form part of the constitutional hierarchy has been a particular feature of the Argentine and Colombian cases on the child's right to health, which we will consider in more detail below. A slightly different approach is evidenced in Section 18 of the Timor-Leste Constitution (2002), which provides that 'children shall enjoy all rights that are universally recognised, as well as all those that are enshrined in international conventions commonly ratified or approved by the State'.[59] One such convention is the CRC.

This section has discussed the different ways in which the child's right to health has been enshrined both at the international and the domestic levels, as well as the perceptions of children that underpin those protections. My analysis will now turn to how such standards have been applied by the courts.

5 The child's right to health: imposing an additional claim to protection and creating priority?

We have already spoken of the child's particular vulnerability *vis-à-vis* other right-holders when it comes to violations of their right to health and, indeed, of any of their rights. This vulnerability or particular disadvantage of children in relation to the right to health has been reflected in the way that the child's right to health has been enshrined in some domestic and international instruments. The best-known example is Section 28(1)(c) of the South African Constitution. While the right of 'everyone' to have access to healthcare set out in Section 27(1) is expressly qualified by available resources and a duty of progressive (rather than immediate) realisation, the right of children to basic healthcare services is not.[60] This latter right prima facie imposes a direct and immediate obligation upon the State to meet the economic and social rights needs of those groups, although, as we will see in section 6, this is not how the court has treated Section 28(1)(c) in practice. In contrast, Art 49 of the Colombian Constitution, which deals with the right to health, is generally considered progressive in nature, except when there is a nexus with a 'fundamental right' – i.e. a civil and political right (Sepúlveda 2008: 147). However, according to the Colombian Constitutional Court, 'the right to health held by children, as opposed to that of other people . . . was established in the constitution as fundamental'.[61] The child's right to health thus imposes a more stringent obligation on the state than the health rights of others do.[62]

An awareness of the particular situation of children with regard to the right to health is also demonstrated in the decision-making of regional human rights bodies. The European Committee of Social Rights' decision in *International Federation of Human Rights Leagues (FIDH) v. France*[63] centred on Arts 13 and 17 of the Revised Social Charter. Art 13 guarantees access to social and medical assistance and care to those without adequate resources. Art 17, which provides for the right of children and young persons to social, legal and economic protection, requires the State to take measures to ensure that children have the care and the assistance they need, including medical care and assistance.[64] Here, FIDH claimed that France had violated Art 13 by ending the exemption of illegal immigrants with very low incomes from charges for medical and hospital treatment. FIDH also submitted that a 2002 Legislative Reform restricting access to medical services for children of illegal immigrants violated Art 17. Such children had to wait three months to qualify for medical assistance, and were only accorded assistance in 'situations that involve an immediate threat to life'.

The Committee found no violation of Art 13, however, since illegal immigrants could access some forms of medical assistance after three months of residence, while all foreign nationals could at any time obtain treatment for 'emergencies and life-threatening conditions'. This finding was reached despite evidence of significant problems with the implementation of the legislation. The Committee found a violation of Art 17, however, even though children had similar access to healthcare as adults. In doing so, the Committee referred to the various provisions under the Revised Social Charter that guarantee the child's right to protection in different contexts. The Committee emphasised that Art 17 was inspired by the CRC, and that it protects in a general manner the right of children and young persons to care and assistance, and highlighted that the French legal framework did not ensure such care and assistance.[65] In doing so, the Committee recognised the additional claim to protection that children have on the basis of their status as children.

There is thus evidence from international and domestic experiences that both the drafters of human rights instruments/constitutions and courts will be prepared to impose stricter obligations on states in relation to the child's right to health than they will in relation to the health rights of others. In addition, there have been a number of instances of constitutions and courts holding that the child's right to health must take priority over those of others. Art 44 of the Colombian Constitution explicitly states that 'the rights of children have priority over the rights of others',[66] while the Argentine Supreme Court has stated – in a child right-to-health case – that where the best interest of the child is at stake, 'this interest shall be protected beyond other considerations by all branches of government'.[67] In Brazil, both national superior courts have made clear the absolute priority enjoyed by children and adolescents in terms of the exercise of the right to health, with the Superior Court of Justice stating in one case that:

> The constitutional right to the absolute priority of children and adolescents in the exercise of the right to health is established by constitutional norm. . . . To submit a child or adolescent in a waiting list in order to attend others is the same as to legalise the most violent aggression of the principle of equality, essential in a democratic society provided by the Constitution, putting also into risk the clause in defence of human dignity.[68]

In contrast, where constitutions or instruments do not explicitly include a provision on the child's right to health, but strongly entrench the rights of parents or the family, there is a risk that the child's right to health will be subordinated to the rights of others. This has been the case in Ireland, where the Constitution provides very limited protection to children's rights but contains strident statements in relation to 'parental' and 'family' rights and duties.[69] This contrasts sharply with the approach of the CRC. Admittedly, that instrument regards the family 'as the fundamental group of society and the natural environment for the growth and well-being of . . . children',[70] recognises the 'rights and duties' of the 'parents, legal guardians, or other individuals legally responsible for' the child,[71] and acknowledges 'the primary responsibility' of parents and legal guardians 'for the upbringing and development of the child'.[72] However, unlike the Irish Constitution, it sets out a wide range of rights for children, and makes it clear that the best interests of the child are to be accorded priority (if not absolute priority) in all actions concerning them.[73]

6 The interpretation of the duty to fulfil the child's right to health by courts

In this section, I will focus on a number of the ways in which courts have interpreted and applied the duty to fulfil the child's right to health. As stated above, the duty to fulfil the right to health includes the state's duty to 'progressively realise' the right, in particular by devoting 'maximum available resources' to the fulfilment of the child's right to health.[74] It also encompasses a number of immediate obligations. The question arises as to how courts rise to the challenge of enforcing both the progressive and immediate obligations positive obligations imposed by the right to health.

In addressing this question, I will discuss how courts from three different jurisdictions – Argentina, Colombia and South Africa – have grappled with these issues. I will begin by looking at the state's duty to progressively realise the child's right to health to the maximum extent of its available resources. I will then turn to the immediate obligations imposed by the child's right to health, which give rise to a directly enforceable claim against the state.

6.1 Judicial enforcement of the duty of progressive realisation – a tale of two jurisdictions

The most celebrated judicial decision on the duty to progressively realise the child's right to health is that of the South African Constitutional Court in the case of *Minister of Health v. Treatment Action Campaign (No. 2)*.[75] In its constitutional claim, the Treatment Action Campaign (TAC) argued that the state's continued failure and refusal to make Nevirapine (NVP) generally available in the public sector in accordance with the decision of the relevant health professional as to the best interests of his or her patient, as well as its continued failure and refusal to plan and implement a nation-wide comprehensive programme to prevent mother-to-child transmission (MTCT) of HIV was unconstitutional. It was unconstitutional because, amongst other things: (a) it violated the constitutional right of women and their babies to have access to healthcare services, including reproductive healthcare under Section 27; (b) it constituted a failure to take reasonable measures to achieve progressive realisation of the right of access to healthcare services, including reproductive healthcare set out in Section 27(2);[76] and (c) it was in breach of the right of the babies' concerned to basic healthcare services under Section 28.

The Constitutional Court's judgment primarily focused on whether the state had taken reasonable measures in terms of Section 27(2). Quoting the dicta in the earlier case of *Grootboom* – that a programme that excludes a significant segment of society cannot be said to be reasonable[77] – the Court pointed out that, to the extent that Government limited the supply of NVP to its research sites, it was the poor outside the catchment areas of these sites who could not afford to pay for services that would suffer.[78] The Court held that the Government's policy constituted a breach of the state's obligation under Section 27(2) read with Section 27(1), in so far as it confined the use of NVP to the pilot sites, and excluded those who could reasonably have been included (i.e. those outside the catchment sites who could not afford to pay for services (van Wyk 2003: 404)).[79] Declaring that Section 27 of the Constitution required the Government to devise and implement, within its available resources, a comprehensive and coordinated programme to realise progressively the rights of pregnant women and their newborn children to have access to health services, the Court made a number of far-reaching orders directed at ensuring the State took the steps necessary to progressively realise the child's right to health. The *TAC* decision is thus a notable example of a domestic tribunal employing its own constitutional test in adjudicating whether the state had taken adequate steps to progressively realise the child's right to health.

Another example of a domestic court dealing with the progressive realisation of the child's right to health is the Argentinean case of *Campodónico de Beviacqua, Ana Carina c. Ministerio de Salud y Banco de Drogas Neoplácias.*[80] This decision centred on the right to health of a child who had been born with a serious disability in his marrow, which reduced his immunological defences. The medicine necessary for the child's treatment was initially provided by the State. Later, however, the child's mother was informed that state delivery would be interrupted, with the State claiming that it had only ever provided the medicine on 'humanitarian' grounds (rather than on the basis of a legal duty). The mother of the child brought an *amparo* action,[81] seeking to prevent the interruption of delivery on the basis that such State action would deprive her child of his rights to life and health guaranteed by the national constitution and under international human rights treaties.[82] This action was based on a threatened violation by the State of its duty to respect (that is, not to interfere with) the child's enjoyment of his right to health. However, the Argentine Supreme Court's judgment focused extensively on the obligation of the State to take steps to fulfil the child's right to health by provision of treatment.

The Supreme Court found in favour of the complainant, upholding the judgment of a lower court prohibiting the interruption of the delivery of the necessary medicine. Having strongly emphasised the link between the right to life and the right to health (going so far as to state that the right to health was 'within' the right to life), the Supreme Court referred to previous judgments in which it had highlighted the urgent obligation of the public authorities to guarantee the right to health through the taking of positive actions – without prejudice to the obligations of other bodies.[83]

The Court relied heavily on provisions of the international treaties that form part of the Argentine constitutional hierarchy, particularly the ICESCR and the CRC.[84] According to Art 75(22) of the Argentinian Constitution, these treaties 'have constitutional hierarchy . . . and are to be understood as complementing the rights and guarantees recognised [in the Constitution]'. The Court emphasised that the measures that must be adopted in order to guarantee the right to health, include the development of a plan to reduce child mortality, to guarantee the healthy development of children, and to provide them with assistance and medical services in case of illness.[85] The Court referred to the obligation of states parties under Art 2(1) ICESCR to progressively achieve the full realisation of the rights set out in the Covenant to the maximum of their available resources, as well as stating that the government was obliged to 'immediately' take appropriate measures, in conformity with its constitution and law,[86] to ensure that the competent authorities of the federal State comply with the provisions of that Treaty.[87] The Court highlighted that the CRC includes the obligation of the state to encourage and guarantee the effective access of children with physical and mental disabilities to health services and rehabilitation.[88] It also obliges the state to ensure that such children are not deprived of those services, and to achieve full realisation of the right to benefit from social security, for which account must be taken of national legislation, resources and the situation of each child and the persons responsible for his maintenance.[89]

Both the *TAC* case and the *Beviacqua* case are excellent examples of the courts outlining what steps must be taken to progressively realise the child's right to health. In addition, *Beviacqua* makes it clear that the child may have a directly enforceable immediate claim against the state for violations of its right to health. The Argentinean Supreme Court was thus prepared to give effect to both the immediate and progressive obligations imposed by the child's right to health. As Section 6.2 demonstrates, such an approach has not been uniformly adopted by other courts.

6.2 Children's immediately enforceable claims – judicial rejection vs. judicial recognition

Commentators differ strongly on whether economic and social rights-holders should be provided with immediately enforceable individual claims against the state. This has been a particular issue in the context of the provision of essential healthcare services for children. On the one hand, it is arguable that the provision of such a direct entitlement ensures that economic and social rights are substantive (in terms of providing a specific economic and social rights-related good or service to children) and not merely procedural in nature. If a child is not entitled to directly claim health goods and services, then her right to health arguably runs the risk of being essentially meaningless (or valueless) to her, due to its lack of concrete content and its inability to result in the actual satisfaction of the child's material need.[90] On the other hand, it might be argued that direct entitlement risks a flood of litigation, resulting in those children that do not sue being disadvantaged as a result of the State having to put a disproportionate amount of its resources towards meeting claims.[91] Below, I will focus on the approach of two courts that have both been active in enforcing the child's right to health, but which have adopted very different approaches to the question of whether or not the child's right to health gives rise to an immediate entitlement against the State.

The South African Constitutional Court's response to the question of whether the right to health furnishes children with an immediately enforceable claim against the state has been an emphatic 'no'. The child rights provision of the South African Constitution, Section 28(1)(c), has received much attention (see, for example, Friedman and Pantazis 2006: 47-6–47-14). Section 28(1)(c) provides that every child has the right to basic nutrition, shelter, basic healthcare services and social services. The lack of qualification in terms of any reference to 'progressive realisation' or 'maximum available resources' in Section 28(1)(c) (in contrast to other economic and social rights guarantees under the Constitution) meant that many commentators initially concluded that the rights in that provision imposed an immediate obligation on the State to fulfil them, thereby providing children with a direct immediate entitlement against the state (see, for example De Vos (1997: 87–8) and Viljoen (2002: 203–4)).

This is not, however, the interpretation that has been adopted by the South African Constitutional Court. In *Grootboom* (which focused on the right child's to shelter and the right of 'everyone' to have access to adequate housing under Sections 28(1)(c) and 26, respectively) the Court held, amongst other things, that Section 28(1)(c) does not create any primary State obligation to provide shelter on demand to parents and their children if the children are being cared for by their parents or families. According to the Court, it follows from Section 28(1)(b) (which enshrines the right of the child to family care or parental care, or to appropriate alternative care if the child is removed from the family environment) that the Constitution considers that a child has the right to parental or family care in the first place. The child has the right to appropriate alternative care only where the former is lacking.

Following an outcry from children's rights activists post-*Grootboom*, the Constitutional Court used its judgment in the *TAC* case to clarify [or, arguably, correct (Budlender 2002)] its stance on Section 28(1)(c). The *TAC* case concerned children born in public institutions to mothers who 'were for the most part indigent and unable to gain access to private medical treatment which is beyond their means. They and their children are in the main dependent upon the State to make healthcare services available to them'.[92] The Court emphasised that the Constitutional Court in *Grootboom* had made it clear that its construal of Section 28(1)(c) did not mean that the State incurs *no* obligation in relation to children who are being cared for by their parents or families. However, the Court adhered to its reasoning in *Grootboom* and did not conclude that the children had a direct individual entitlement to healthcare services in circumstances where their parents could not afford those services (Liebenberg 2004: 4–5). Instead the Court relied on the right of children to basic healthcare services in Section 28 to support its finding that the Government's policy was 'unreasonable' in terms of Section 27 because the policy excluded and harmed a particularly vulnerable group (Ibid).

In the same case, the Court rejected the argument of Amici (the Institute for Democracy in South Africa and the Community Law Centre) that the individual constitutional rights created by Sections 27(1)(a) and 28(1)(c), and enforceable against the state under Section 7(2), include a right of access to a minimum core of healthcare services comprising the minimum necessary for dignified human existence. The Court referred to *Grootboom* in which it treated the notion of a minimum core as possibly being relevant to reasonableness under Section 26(2), but not as a self-standing right conferred on everyone under Section 26(1). In the Court's view in *TAC*, it would be impossible to give everyone access even to a 'core' service immediately – all that is possible, and that can be expected of the state, is that it acts reasonably to provide access to the socio-economic rights identified in Sections 26 and 27 on a progressive basis.[93] The Constitutional Court emphasised the limited institutional capacity of the courts to make the factual and political enquiries necessary in order to determine what a minimum core standard should be, to decide how public revenues should be spent[94] and to adjudicate upon issues where court orders could have multiple social and economic consequences for the community.[95]

The *TAC* decision is an example of a court displaying reluctance to require the State to do more than to achieve the progressive realisation of the child's right to health within that State's maximum resources. Indeed, in doing so, the Court arguably ignored the text and purpose underlying the particular constitutional provision setting out the child's right to health at issue in the case. Despite this, the judgment of the Court in *TAC* did lead to a significant rise in the level of access to health services for pregnant women living with HIV/AIDS and their newborn infants due to the increase in facilities (see, for example, Shung-King *et al.* 2004: 145).[96]

The approach of the South African Court contrasts with that of the Colombian Constitutional Court, which has held that the child's constitutional right to health imposes a directly enforceable immediate obligation on the state. The most significant decision of the court on this issue is that of *SU-225/98*.[97] This was an action brought by the parents of 418 children living in a severely disadvantaged area of Bogotá against the national and district health authorities. The parents claimed that their children were in a high-risk situation due to the particular living conditions experienced by residents of the area, and that they were unable to meet the cost of the vaccines. The parents alleged that by failing to provide their children with a vaccine to prevent meningitis free of charge, the defendants had violated the children's constitutional rights to life (Art 11), health (Arts 44 and 49) and social security (Art 48).

In *SU-225/98*, the court made it clear that the rights in Art 44 (including the right to health) have an essential content of immediate application that limits the discretion of the political organs and that rely on a reinforced judicial mechanism for their protection (the *tutela* action). This is consistent with previous jurisprudence of the court on the constitutional doctrine of the 'minimo vital' (minimum conditions for a dignified life), in which the court has indicated that the flagrant violation of a human right that compromises the very existence of a person in a radical way obliges the judge to mobilise the positive action of the state.

The court concluded, however, that *only* the essential content of the right can be directly applied by the judge, while it is the legislature which must define the full scope of the right. The court found that the deficient cover of the vaccination service constituted a flagrant violation of the right child's right to health because it exposed them to the risk of contracting a lethal illness and dire consequences. Crucially, it also held that the State's abstention from acting in this case violated the constitutional mandate to eradicate marginalisation and discrimination. It thus emphasised the relationship between the enjoyment of health services and equality. The court confirmed the order of a lower court requiring the relevant state entities to establish a free infant vaccination programme for the poor.

The Colombian court has gone on to find that the right to health of the child is subject to immediate application (in the sense of giving rise to immediate obligations) in cases involving the right to treatment of children with disabilities[98] and the right of children to treatment overseas when the necessary treatment is unavailable in Colombia.[99]

7 Conclusions

Having considered a range of different case-law from international, regional and domestic courts and judicial and quasi-judicial bodies, it is possible to draw some conclusions about the factors that affect the ability of courts to play an extensive role in fleshing out the substantive content of the right to health.

The first key factor relates to the existence of a justiciable right-to-health provision within the legal framework that the judicial or quasi-judicial body is responsible for enforcing. Thus, for example, the European Court of Human Rights, whose key instrument does not contain a provision providing for an explicit right to health, has played an extremely limited role in fleshing out the right to health – of children or otherwise.[100] In contrast, the jurisprudence of the Inter-American court is a very positive example of the way in which the child's right to health has been afforded protection indirectly via the judicial application of other, civil and political, rights.[101] In doing so, however, the Court has explicitly cited ESR-related concerns and legal standards where interpreting civil and political rights. Unsurprisingly, courts at the national level have played the strongest role where they are empowered to apply and enforce justiciable constitutional provisions expressly setting out the child's right to health. This is due to the fact that where such rights and duties are set out in the constitution, debate moves fairly rapidly beyond the issue of whether it is legitimate for the courts to apply and enforce the child's right to health (in terms of the separation of powers and the 'counter-majoritarian' objection) to the question of defining the specific content of the duties imposed on the state by such a right.[102] This is demonstrated by the approaches adopted by courts in countries such as South Africa, Colombia, Brazil and Argentina, where the child's right to health is clearly established as a justiciable right in the constitutional framework. In those jurisdictions where the existence of such a constitutional rights is undisputed, judicial analysis centres on how – rather than if – such a right should be enforced. That is not to suggest that courts completely disregard issues of the separation of powers or the question of counter-majoritarianism where they are dealing with constitutional provisions specifically outlining the child's right to health. For instance, in the *TAC* case, the Constitutional Court explicitly addressed and refuted state lawyers' claims that courts cannot make orders that have the effect of requiring the executive to pursue a particular policy.[103] Indeed, courts cannot afford to do so if their decisions are to be authoritative and they are to maintain their institutional legitimacy in the eyes of society and the other branches of government (or, in the case of international bodies, in the eyes of States Parties and the international community). However, the existence of explicit constitutional provisions on the child's right to health shifts the debate from 'does/should such a constitutional right exist?' to 'what is the precise scope of that right and of the duties it imposes?'.

The role played by international law is also extremely important in terms of determining how, and to what extent, judicial and quasi-judicial decision-making bodies interpret and apply the child's right to health. Where international law standards on the child's right to health form part of the constitutional framework of a particular country (for example, Colombia and Argentina) or can be referred to directly by regional decision-making bodies in their consideration of the child's right to health (for instance, the Inter-American Court of Human Rights),[104] this will generally lead to the courts affording more expansive protection to that right. That said, reference to international law standards by domestic courts does not mean that courts will inevitably follow those standards in their interpretation of domestic standards.[105]

The role played by a particular decision-making body also depends on the institutional capacity of that body. The most detailed justiciable provision on the child's right to health under regional human rights law is set out in Art 14 of the African Charter on the Rights and Welfare of the Child. This article provides that every child 'shall have the right to enjoy the best attainable state of physical, mental and spiritual health' and outlines in detail the steps that states parties must undertake in order to ensure full implementation of this right. The provision potentially provides the African Committee on the Rights and Welfare of the Child (the body responsible for monitoring the implementation of the Children's Charter) and the African Court of Human and Peoples' Rights (which has competence to interpret and apply the Children's Charter)[106] with an excellent opportunity to flesh out the child's right to health in the context of specific fact situations. However, despite its establishment nine years ago, the African Committee has yet to make any decisions on any individual complaints involving the right to health. As a result, it is unclear whether, for example, the obligations set out in Art 14 are immediate in nature or whether, instead, that provision is only concerned with the progressive realisation of the child's right to health. In *Purohit and Moore v. The Gambia*,[107] a case involving the right to health of mental health patients in state health facilities, the African Commission on Human and Peoples' Rights considered the obligation imposed on States by Art 16 (the right to enjoy the best attainable state of physical and mental health) of the African Charter on Human and Peoples' Rights. Textually, Art 16 is unqualified by any reference to 'progressive realisation' or 'maximum available resources'. However, the Commission read into Art 16 the obligation on States Parties, 'to take concrete and targeted steps, while taking full advantage of their available resources, to ensure that the right to health is fully realised in all its aspects without discrimination of any kind'. In doing so, the Committee made it clear that Art 16 primarily imposes a duty of progressive, rather than immediate, realisation. It remains to be seen whether the African Committee on the Rights and Welfare of the Child or the African Court will adopt a similar approach in relation to Art 14 of the Children's Charter.

It is clear from the experiences outlined in this article that the courts have an important role to play in the delineation and application of the child's right to health. However, it is important to note that the cases highlighted above – and the author herself – do not suggest that the application of the right to health by judicial or quasi-judicial bodies can provide a panacea to all right to health violations suffered by children. Such violations are frequently linked to multifaceted and deeply entrenched social determinants and issues such as poverty and systemic societal inequality. Remedying such problems – and the rights violations caused by them – will require action from a wide range of governmental and (ever more frequently) non-state actors such as inter-governmental organisations and international financial institutions. Leaving aside both the generally reactive role of the bodies under consideration here as well as the issues that may arise as a result of the lack of binding force in some of those bodies' decisions, there are undoubtedly other actors that are institutionally better equipped and located to give effect to the child's right to health. This does not mean, however, that the courts cannot make a significant contribution to the enforcement of the child's right to health. This author agrees with Forman's statement (made in relation to the South African right-to-health jurisprudence) that courts can 'play an important role in enabling discrete instances of access to healthcare services, and in remedying gross policy defects that may have very broad impacts on health and healthcare access' (Forman 2005: 721).

In conclusion, it is important to note a future development that will have a considerable impact on the interpretation and application of the child's right to health at the international law level. On 10 December 2008, the General Assembly adopted the Optional Protocol to the International Covenant on Economic, Social and Cultural Rights. This Optional Protocol will enable individual communications to be brought before the CESCR for violations of the child's right to health. This is very likely to result in a more detailed understanding of the child's right to health under Art 12(1), and the jurisprudence of the ComESCR will almost certainly influence the approach of regional and domestic courts in the context of economic and social rights. Similarly, the growing momentum around the establishment of a complaints mechanism to the ComRC bodes well for the evolution of more developed international jurisprudence on the child's right to health.[108] It is thus clear that the discussion about the child's right to health and the courts is only really beginning.

Notes

1 Due to space constraints, the chapter will not address the efficacy of such bodies' adjudication of the child's right to health in terms of the concrete impact that such activity has on either the actual enjoyment of that right by the individual child claimants or by children more generally. There is only currently limited (and case-specific) empirical evidence available on the impact of litigation and adjudication on the realisation of the child's right to health. For a useful example of an attempt to measure how many (and which) people benefit from economic and social rights

litigation and adjudication, including right to health litigation, at the domestic level in various jurisdictions, see Brinks and Gauri (2008: 324–42).

2 Admittedly, the statements and findings of quasi-judicial bodies such as UN-treaty monitoring bodies and some regional human rights monitoring bodies (for instance, the European Committee of Social Rights and the African Commission on Human and People's Rights) do not have the binding legal force of the decisions of domestic and other regional and international judicial bodies. It is, however, crucial to take the decisions of such bodies into account. This is due to the important role played by them in terms of both defining the child's right to health and in outlining how that right should be given effect to. For the sake of fluency, all of these bodies will be referred to as 'courts' throughout this piece.

3 CESCR (2000 para 33). See section 3 below for a discussion of the duty to 'fulfil'.

4 For a discussion, and refutation, of claims about the alleged institutional shortcomings of courts in dealing with socio-economic rights, see Nolan *et al.* (2007: Section 2.3).

5 For an excellent critique of the philosophical underpinnings of objections to courts reviewing 'state inaction', including those related to conceptions of a 'neutral' liberal state and the overriding value accorded to individual autonomy, see Sunstein (1993) and Bandes (1990).

6 These are set out in the CESCR (2000 at para 3). The underlying preconditions for children's health have been fleshed out by the Committee on the Rights of the Child, which has identified various factors that are essential for the health of children, including younger children. Among these are access to clean drinking water, adequate sanitation, appropriate immunisation, good nutrition and medical services, and a stress-free environment (ComRC 2005b, para 27(a)).

7 In addition to being accorded the right to the highest attainable standard of physical and mental health under the ICESCR, specific groups of children are entitled to the health rights set out in particular instruments such as the Convention on the Elimination of All Forms of Discrimination Against Women (girl children), the Convention on the Rights of Persons with Disabilities (children with disabilities) and the International Convention on the Protection of the Rights of All Migrant Workers and Members of Their Families (the children of migrant workers).

8 See e.g. Art 23(2) of the Convention on the Rights of the Child, under which disabled children are entitled to special care; Art 13 of the African Charter on the Rights and Welfare of the Child.

9 See e.g. Art 32 Convention on the Rights of the Child, Arts 7(1) and 2 of the European Social Charter, Art 15(1) of the European Social Charter; and Art 7(f) of the San Salvador Protocol.

10 See e.g. Art 18 Convention on the Rights of the Child, which recognises that parents or legal guardians have primary responsibility for the upbringing and development of the child.

11 See e.g. *Royal Alexandra Hospital for Children v. Joseph and Ors* [2005] NSWSC 422 (New South Wales Supreme Court decision ordering that a child over the age of 16 with leukaemia should be provided with a blood transfusion in the face of objections from both the child and his parents).

12 See e.g. *Gillick v. West Norfolk and Wisbech Area Health Authority* [1985] 3 All ER 402 (UK House of Lords decision holding that a doctor can lawfully prescribe contraception for a girl under 16 years of age, without the consent of her parents if and when the child achieves a sufficient understanding and intelligence to enable her to understand fully what is proposed).

13 ComRC (2003b, para 35(b)). For a useful discussion of child participation in the healthcare setting in a UK context, see Franklin and Sloper (2006: 11–30). Other chapters in the same volume focus on child participation with regard to a range of different health-related decision-making situations.

14 For two celebrated contrasting views on whether children should be accorded rights, see Purdy (1994) and McGillivray (1994).

15 I am aware that there are groups of adults within society that are at least as vulnerable as children (due to disability, pregnancy, age, or disadvantages/disabilities such as being illiterate in a developed country, etc.). However, I wish to compare the relative situations of an adult of reasonable good health and education by the standards of her society with that of an average child in the same society. The focus on the situation of adults without particular vulnerabilities is consistent with my focus on the right to health of the 'child' generally, rather than the health rights of particular groups of children.

16 Advisory Opinion OC-17/2002 *on the Juridical Condition and Human Rights of the Child*, 28 August 2002.

17 ibid. at para 86.

18 ibid. at para 56. [emphasis added and footnotes omitted]

19 SU-225/98.

20 ibid.

21 See, e.g. *Minister of Health v. Treatment Action Campaign (No.2)* 2002 (5) SA 721 (CC) [*Treatment Action Campaign*], in which only those HIV-infected mothers in a few designated pilot sites could receive antiretroviral treatment to prevent mother-to-child transmission of the HIV/AIDS virus, while mothers in other public hospitals could not. Women using public hospitals were likely to be members of groups previously discriminated against under the apartheid regime, and were disadvantaged by the persistent inequalities (racial/gender) in South African society.

22 The Committee on the Rights of the Child has highlighted the interrelationship between discrimination and violations of the right to health: 'discrimination is responsible for heightening the vulnerability of children to HIV and AIDS, as well as seriously impacting the lives of children who are affected by HIV/AIDS, or are themselves HIV infected. Girls and boys of parents living with HIV/AIDS are often victims of stigma and discrimination as they too are often assumed to be infected' (ComRC 2003a: para 95).

23 See CESCR (2000: para 30).

24 Article 12(1)(a).

25 See CESCR (2000: paras 14, 23 and 24).

26 ibid. para 12.

27 For a discussion of the evolution of the tripartite typology of human rights obligations, originating with the work of Henry Shue and culminating in the adoption of the 'respect, protect, fulfil' framework by the UN Committee on Economic, Social and Cultural Rights, see Nolan (2009).

28 Maastricht Guidelines (1997: para 6).

29 Paraphrased from CESCR (1999: para 47).

30 See discussion below in Section 4.

31 Aspects of the child's right to health are also dealt with in a range of other provisions of the Convention on the Rights of the Child. See e.g. Arts 3(3), 17, 23, 25, 28 and 32(1).

32 ComRC (2003b: Introduction).

33 See ComRC (2005b, 2006: paras 51–62, 2009: paras 49–55).

34 Such steps include dealing with the underlying conditions for proper healthcare such as the application of readily available technology, the provision of adequate nutritious foods and clean drinking water and taking into consideration the dangers and risks of environmental pollution. States are also obliged to ensure access to education and support in the use of basic knowledge on child health and nutrition, the advantages of breastfeeding, hygiene and environmental sanitation and the prevention of accidents. (Arts 24(2)(c) and (e))

35 The Committee on Economic, Social and Cultural Rights has noted that the phrase

'to the maximum of its available resources' was intended by the drafters of the ICESCR to refer to 'both the resources existing within a State and those available from the international community through international cooperation and assistance'. See CESCR (1991, para 13).

36 CRC (2003c: para 7).
37 ibid. at para 8.
38 See, e.g., CRC (2005b: para 10).
39 CRC (2005a).
40 CRC (2005b : para 13(b)).
41 CRC (2003c: para 6).
42 CESCR (1998: para 14).
43 ibid. at para 15.
44 See e.g. Panama (1972, amended in 2004) (Section 28(1)); Ecuador (2008) (Article 45); Colombia (1991) (Article 44 and Article 50); Brazil (1988) (Art 227(1)); Honduras (1982) Article 123).
45 See, e.g., Art 27 Constitution of Lesotho (1993).
46 See e.g. Art 64 (the right to health) and Art 69 (children's rights), Constitution of Portugal (1976).
47 See e.g. Art 39(f) of the Indian Constitution (1949).
48 See e.g. Art 199 of the 1967 Bolivian Constitution, which provides that 'the state is to protect the physical, mental and moral health of the child and to defend the rights of the child to a home and education'.
49 See also Art 42 of the Constitution of the Congo (2006).
50 The 1998 Constitution was recently replaced with a new Constitution that includes an extensive section on children's rights (Section 5).
51 See e.g. Art 50 of the Moldovan Constitution (1994).
52 See e.g. the Constitution of Slovenia, Arts 51 and 56(1); the Constitution of Romania (1991 as amended in 2003), Arts 34 and 49(1).
53 See also Arts 31 and 47 of the Angolan Constitution (1992). The 1992 Constitution was replaced with a new Constitution in January 2010.
54 See e.g. Art 15(2) and (3) of the Namibian Constitution (1990); and Art 54(3) of the Albanian Constitution (1998);
55 See e.g. Art 51 of the Guatemalan Constitution (1985).
56 See e.g. Art 44 of the Cuban Constitution (1976 as amended in 1992); Art 8(15) of the Constitution of the Dominican Republic (as enacted in 2002 – similar provisions are found in the 1994 enactment); and Art 54(2) of the Afghanistan Constitution (2004).
57 See e.g. Section 75(22) of the Argentine Constitution (1994).
58 For a discussion of the different ways in which international human rights instruments may form part of the constitutional frameworks of (Latin American) civil law jurisdictions, see García Méndez (2007: 118–119).
59 For a similar approach, see Article 119 of the Constitution of Honduras (1982) and Article 71 of the Nicaraguan Constitution (1987 with 1995 reforms).
60 Section 28(1)(c).
61 T-200/93. See also T-402/92.
62 See also, the Colombian Court's decision in T-760/2008, in which the Court ordered the legislatively established contributory and subsidised benefits regimes to be unified. According to the Court, this was to be carried out in the first case for children and youth. With regard to adults, it was to be done progressively taking into account sustainable funding.
63 Complaint No. 14/2003, 3 November 2004.
64 Complaint No. 14/2003, para 36.
65 Author's note: Art 13 is more restrictive in its wording.
66 See also Art 60 of the Constitution of Bolivia (2009).

67 *Campodónico de Beviacqua, Ana Carina v. Ministerio de Salud y Banco de Drogas Neoplácias*, C. 823. XXXV, 24 Oct. 2008, para 21.
68 Superior Court of Justice, Resp. 577836 cited in Piovesan (2008: 187).
69 See e.g. *North Western Health Board v. W. (H.)* [2001] IESC 70.
70 See Preamble, Convention on the Rights of the Child.
71 Art 3(2) Convention on the Rights of the Child. See also Article 5 CRC.
72 Art 18(1) Convention on the Rights of the Child.
73 Art 3(1) Convention on the Rights of the Child.
74 According to General Comment 14, 'the obligation to fulfil requires States to adopt appropriate legislative, administrative, budgetary, judicial, promotional and other measures towards the full realisation of the right to health' (CESCR 2000: para 33).
75 2002 (5) SA 721 (CC).
76 Section 27(2) requires the state to 'take reasonable legislative and other measures, within its available resources, to achieve the progressive realisation of' the right to have access to healthcare services.
77 *Grootboom v Oostenberg Municipality and Ors* 2000 (3) BCLR 277 (C) at para 43.
78 2002 (5) SA 721 (CC) at para 70.
79 See para 80 of the Treatment Action Campaign judgment for a summary of the court's findings on reasonableness.
80 C. 823. XXXV, 24 Oct. 2000.
81 According to Courtis, '[t]he *amparo* is a traditional constitutional injunction granting the plaintiff injunctive relief when a constitutional right is threatened. While the "classical amparo" limited *locus standi* to an individual grievance, the inclusion of a "collective amparo" enlarged *locus standi*, allowing a member of the aggrieved class, NGOs and the ombudsman to bring cases before courts when massive infringement of constitutional rights occurred' (Courtis 2008a: 165, footnote 8).
82 Art 42 of the Argentinean Constitution discusses the right to protection of health in the context of Art 42, which sets out the rights of consumers. However, the establishment of a constitutional right to health resulted from the judicial recognition of the constitutional priority accorded to international instruments setting out that right.
85 *Campodónico de Beviacqua, Ana Carina c. Ministerio de Salud y Banco de Drogas Neoplácias*, paras 16, 19 and 20.
86 See *Campodónico de Beviacqua, Ana Carina c. Ministerio de Salud y Banco de Drogas Neoplácias*, paras 17–18.
87 *Campodónico de Beviacqua, Ana Carina c. Ministerio de Salud y Banco de Drogas Neoplácias*, para 18.
88 *Campodónico de Beviacqua, Ana Carina c. Ministerio de Salud y Banco de Drogas Neoplácias*, para 19.
89 *Campodónico de Beviacqua, Ana Carina c. Ministerio de Salud y Banco de Drogas Neoplácias*, para 20.
90 *Campodónico de Beviacqua, Ana Carina c. Ministerio de Salud y Banco de Drogas Neoplácias*, para 20.
91 *Campodónico de Beviacqua, Ana Carina c. Ministerio de Salud y Banco de Drogas Neoplácias*, para 20.
92 For an excellent development of the argument of the 'emptiness' of ESR jurisprudence that denies that socio-economic rights embody immediately enforceable individual claims in a South African context, see Pieterse (2007).
93 This claim has been made in relation to the extensive litigation and adjudication of the directly applicable right to health in Brazil (although not necessarily in relation to the right to health of the child, in particular). For more, see Henriques (2008) cited in Moreira Maués (2008) and Ferraz (2009).
94 Treatment Action Campaign, para 79.
95 Treatment Action Campaign, para 35.
94 Treatment Action Campaign, para 37.

95 Treatment Action Campaign, para 38.
96 For a more recent discussion of the situation with regard to prevention of MTCT services in South Africa, see Treatment Action Campaign (2007).
97 This case is discussed in Sepúlveda (2008).
98 See e.g. T-067/94 and T-068/94. For a discussion of these cases, see Courtis (2008b).
99 See e.g. T-165/95; SU-819/99. For more on these cases, see Sepúlveda (2008).
100 The ECtHR has largely dealt with the right to health in the context of Article 2 (the right to life) (*Calvelli and Ciglio v. Italy*, Judgment of 17 Jan. 2002), Article 3 (the right to freedom from torture and inhuman and degrading treatment or punishment) (*D v. St Kitts* (1997) 24 EHRR 423; *Dybeku v. Albania*, application no. 41153/06, judgment of 18 December 2007) and Article 8 (*Fadeyeva v. Russia*, Judgment 9 June 2005; *Guerra and Ors v. Italy*, Judgment of 19 February 1998).
101 See e.g. *Juvenile Reeducation Case v. Paraguay* Judgment of 2 September 2004, Inter-Am. C.H.R. (Ser. C) No. 112 (2004). For more, see Melish (2008: 388).
102 I am grateful to Christian Courtis for highlighting this line of argument.
103 Treatment Action Campaign, paras 97–98.
104 The Court has adopted an innovative and striking approach to employing international (non-Inter-American) human rights standards in its jurisprudence as a result of Art 29(b) of the Convention, which prohibits the Court from interpreting any provision of the American Convention in such a way as to restrict the exercise of any right recognised by virtue of the domestic laws of any State Party or any treaty ratified by that State Party. For more, see Melish (2008: 377–8).
105 See e.g. the Constitutional Court's rejection in Treatment Action Campaign (following *Grootboom*) of arguments based on the concept of the 'minimum core', reference to which is a recurring feature of the ComESCR's jurisprudence.
106 This body is due to be replaced by the African Court of Justice and Human Rights, following the adoption of the protocol of the Statute of the African Court of Justice and Human Rights by the Assembly of the African Union in July 2008.
107 Communication 241/2001. Decided at 33rd Ordinary Session of the African Commission (15–29 May 2003).
108 In June 2008, the Committee on the Rights of the Child endorsed the campaign to establish a communication procedure under the UN Convention on the Rights of the Child. December 2009 saw the first session of the Open-ended Working Group to explore the possibility of elaborating an Optional Protocol to the Convention of the Rights of the Child. For more, see http://www.crin.org/law/CRCcomplaints/#info

Bibliography

African [Banjul] Charter on Human and Peoples' Rights (1981), OAU Doc. AB/LEG/67/3 rev. 5.

African Charter on the Rights and Welfare of the Child (1990), OAU Doc. CAB/LEG/24.9/49.

Baimu, E. (2002) 'The Government's Obligation to Provide Anti-Retrovirals to HIV-Positive Pregnant Women in an African Human Rights Context: The South African Nevirapine Case', *African Human Rights Law Journal*, 2(1): 160–74.

Bandes, S. (1990) 'The Negative Constitution: A Critique', *Michigan Law Review*. 80: 2271–347.

Brinks, D. and Gauri, V. (2008) 'A New Policy Landscape: Legalizing Social and Economic Rights in the Developing World', in Gauri, V. and Brinks, D. *Courting Social Justice: Judicial Enforcement of Social and Economic Rights in the Developing World*. Cambridge: Cambridge University Press.

Budlender, G. (2002) 'A Paper Dog with Real Teeth', *Mail and Guardian*, 12 July 2002.

Butler, I. (2005) 'The Rights of the Child in the Case Law of the Inter-American Court of Human Rights: Recent Cases', *Human Rights Law Review*, 5(1): 151–67.

CESCR (1990) *The Nature of States Parties Obligations (Art. 2, Para. 1 of the Covenant). General Comment No. 3*, 5th Sess., Annex III at 86. U.N. Doc. E/1991/23.

—— (1998) *Substantive Issues Arising in the Implementation of the International Covenant on Economic, Social and Cultural Rights: The Domestic Application of the Covenant. General Comment No.9*, 19th Sess., Agenda Item 3. U.N. Doc. E/C.12/1998/24.

—— (1999) *Substantive Issues Arising in the Implementation of the International Covenant on Economic, Social and Cultural Rights: The Right to Education. General Comment No. 13*, 21st Sess., Agenda Item 3. U.N. Doc. E/C.12/1999/10.

—— (2000) *Substantive Issues Arising in the Implementation of the International Covenant on Economic, Social and Cultural Rights: The Right to the Highest Attainable Standard of Health. General Comment No. 14*, 22nd Sess., Agenda Item 3. U.N. Doc. E/C.12/2000/4.

Convention on the Elimination of All Forms of Discrimination Against Women (1981), G.A. res. 34/180, 34 U.N. GAOR Supp. (No. 46) at 193, U.N. Doc. A/34/46.

Convention on the Rights of the Child (1989) G.A. res. 44/25, annex, 44 U.N. GAOR Supp. (No. 49) at 167, U.N. Doc. A/44/49.

ComRC (2003a) *HIV/AIDS and the Rights of the Children. General Comment No. 3*, 32nd Sess., U.N. Doc. CRC/GC/2003/3.

—— (2003b) *Adolescent Health and Development in the Context of the Convention on the Rights of the Child. General Comment No.4*, 33rd Sess., U.N. Doc. CRC/GC/2003/4.

—— (2003c) *General Measures of Implementation for the Convention on the Rights of the Child. General Comment No. 5*, 34th Sess., U.N. Doc. CRC/GC/2003/5.

—— (2005a) *General Guidelines Regarding the Form and Content of Periodic Reports*, 39th Sess., U.N. Doc. RC/C/58/Rev.1.

—— (2005b) *Implementing Child Rights in Early Childhood. General Comment No. 7*, 40th Sess., U.N. Doc. CRC/C/GC/7/Rev.1.

—— (2006) *The Rights of Children with Disabilities. General Comment No. 9*, 43rd Sess., U.N. Doc. CRC/C/GC/9.

—— (2009) *Indigenous Children and Their Rights under the Convention. General Comment No. 11*, 50th Sess., U.N. Doc. CRC/C/GC/11.

Courtis, C. (2008a), 'Argentina – Some Promising Signs', in Langford, M. (ed.) (2008) *Social Rights Jurisprudence: Emerging Trends in International and Comparative Law*. New York: Cambridge University Press.

—— (2008b), 'The Right to Life and the Right to Health of Children with Disabilities before Courts: Some Latin American Examples', in Clements, L. and Read, J. (eds.), *Disabled People and the Right to Life: The Protection and Violation of Disabled People's Most Basic Human Rights*. London: Taylor and Francis.

De Vos, P. (1997) 'Pious Wishes or Directly Enforceable Human Rights?: Social and Economic rights in South Africa's 1996 Constitution', *South African Journal of Human Rights*, 13(1): 67–101.

Department of Health (2003) *National HIV and Syphilis Antenatal Sero-Prevalence Survey in South Africa: 2002*. South Africa: Department of Health.

Doek, J. (2001) 'Children and Their Right to Enjoy Health: A Brief Report on the Monitoring Activities of the Committee on the Rights of the Child', *Health and Human Rights*, 5(2): 155–62.

Ely Yamin, A. (2003) 'Not Just a Tragedy: Access to Medications as a Right under International Law', *Boston University International Law Journal*, 21: 325–371.

European Social Charter (1965), 529 U.N.T.S. 89.

Ferraz, O. (2009) 'The Right to Health in the Courts of Brazil: Worsening Health Inequities?' *Health and Human Rights*, 11(2): 33–45.

Forman, L. (2005) 'Ensuring Reasonable Health: Health Rights and the Judiciary, and South African HIV/AIDS Policy', *Journal of Law, Medicine and Ethics*, 33: 711–24.

Franklin A. and Sloper, P. (2006) 'Listening and Responding? Children's Participation in Health care within England', in Freeman, M. (ed.) *Children's Health and Children's Rights*, Leiden: Martinus Nijhoff.

Freeman, M. (1992) 'Taking Children's Rights More Seriously', in Alston, P., Parker, S. and Seymour, J. (eds.) *Children, Rights and the Law*. Oxford: Clarendon Press.

Friedman, A. and Pantazis, A. (2006) 'Children's Rights', in Woolman, S. *et al.* (eds.) *Constitutional Law of South Africa* 2nd edition. Cape Town: Juta.

García Méndez, E. (2007) 'A Comparative Study of the Impact of the Convention on the Rights of the Child: Law Reform in Selected Civil Law Countries', in UNICEF (ed.), *Protecting the World's Children*. New York: Cambridge University Press.

Heyns, C. (2000) 'Introduction to the Rights Concerning Health care in the South African Constitution'. in Bekker G. (ed.) *A Compilation of Essential Documents on the Right to Health*. Pretoria: Centre for Human Rights, University of Pretoria.

Hogan, G. (2001) 'Directive Principles, Socio-Economic Rights and the Constitution', *Irish Jurist*. 36: 174–98.

International Convention on the Protection and Promotion of the Rights and Dignity of Persons with Disabilities (2006), G.A. Res. 61/106, Annex I, U.N. GAOR, 61st Sess., Supp. No. 49, at 65, U.N. Doc. A/61/49.

International Convention on the Protection of the Rights of All Migrant Workers and Members of Their Families (1990), G.A. res. 45/158, annex, 45 U.N. GAOR Supp. (No. 49A) at 262, U.N. Doc. A/45/49.

International Covenant on Economic, Social and Cultural Rights (1966) G.A. res. 2200A (XXI), 21 U.N.GAOR Supp. (No. 16) at 49, U.N. Doc. A/6316.

Kinney, E. and Clark, B. (2004) 'Provisions for Health and Healthcare in the Constitutions of the Countries of the World', *Cornell International Law Journal*, 37: 285–355.

Liebenberg, S. (2004) 'Taking Stock: The Jurisprudence on Children's Socio-Economic Rights and Its Implications for Government Policy', *ESR Review*, 5(4): 2–6.

Maastricht Guidelines (1997), Guidelines on Violations of Economic, Social and Cultural Rights, Maastricht, 22–26 January 1997.

McGillivray, A. (1994) 'Why Children Do Have Equal Rights: In Reply to Laura Purdy', *International Journal of Children's Rights*, 2: 243–258.

Meier, B. M. and Fox, A. (2008) 'Development as Health: Employing the Collective Right to Development to Achieve the Goals of the Individual Right to Health', *Human Rights Quarterly* 30: 259–355.

Melish, T. (2008) 'The Inter-American Court of Human Rights: Beyond Progressivity' in Langford, M. (ed.) *Social Rights Jurisprudence: Emerging Trends in International and Comparative Law*. New York: Cambridge University Press.

Memorandum from WHO Legal Counsel (2008) (WHO Reference LEG:H.R., 2 August 2008), E/CN.4/1988/WG.1/WP.1/Rev.2.

Moreira Maués, A. (2008) 'The Limits of Litigation Strategies: The Case of Right to Health in Brazil', paper presented at Conference on The Local Relevance of Human Rights, University of Antwerp, October.

Nolan, A. (2009) 'Addressing Economic and Social Rights Violations by Non-State Actors through the Role of the State: A Comparison of Regional Approaches to the "Obligation to Protect" ', *Human Rights Law Review*, 9(2): 225–55.

Nolan, A., Porter, B. and Langford, M. (2007) 'The Justiciability of Social and Economic Rights: An Updated Appraisal', *NYU CHRGJ Working Paper Series No. 15 of 2007*. See www.chrgj.org/publications/docs/wp/NolanPorterLangford.pdf

Office of the High Commissioner for Human Rights (2001) 'Children's Rights' in Office of the High Commissioner for Human Rights, *Training Manual on Human Rights Monitoring*. Geneva: Office of the High Commissioner for Human Rights.

Pieterse, M. (2007) 'Eating Socioeconomic Rights: The Usefulness of Rights Talk in Alleviating Social Hardship Revisited', *Human Rights Quarterly*, 29(3): 796–822.

Piovesan, F. (2008) 'Brazil: Impact and Challenges of Social Rights in the Courts', in Langford, M. (ed.) *Social Rights Jurisprudence: Emerging Trends in International and Comparative Law*. New York: Cambridge University Press.

Purdy, L. (1994) 'Why Children Shouldn't Have Equal Rights', *International Journal of Children's Rights*, 2. 223–41.

Revised European Social Charter (1996), E.T.S. 163.

Sepúlveda, M. (2008) 'Colombia: The Constitutional Court's Role in Addressing Social Injustice' in Langford, M. (ed.) *Social Rights Jurisprudence: Emerging Trends in International and Comparative Law*. New York: Cambridge University Press.

Shung-King, M., Michelson L., Kaime,T., Proudlock, P., Vennekens-Poane, A. and Ndlovu, N. (2004) 'Children's Rights to Health' in Coetzee, E. and Streak, J. (eds) *Monitoring Child Socio-Economic Rights in South Africa: Achievements and Challenges*. Cape Town: IDASA.

Sunstein, C. (1993) *The Partial Constitution*. Cambridge, MA: Harvard University Press.

Tobin, J. (2005) 'Increasingly Seen and Heard: The Constitutional Recognition of Children's Rights', *South African Journal of Human Rights*, 21: 86–126.

Treatment Action Campaign (2007) 'Maternal health and prevention of mother-to-child transmission (PMTCT)', *Treatment Action Campaign Newsletter*, 29 November 2007. See www.tac.org.za/community/node/2124

UNICEF (2002) *A UNICEF Factsheet: Mother-to-Child Transmission of HIV*. New York: UNICEF.

van Wyk, C. (2003) 'The Enforcement of the Right of Access to Healthcare in the Context of HIV/AIDS and its Impact on the Separation of Powers', *Tydskrif vir Hedendaagse Romeins-Hollandse Reg*, 66: 389–407.

Viljoen, F. (2002) 'Children's Rights: A Response from a South African Perspective', in Brand, D. and Russell, S. (eds.) *Exploring the Core Content of Socio-economic Rights: South African and International Perspectives*. Pretoria: Protea Book House.

Wringe, C. (1981) *Children's Rights: A Philosophical Study*. London: Routledge & Kegan Paul.

8 The World Health Organization, the evolution of human rights, and the failure to achieve Health for All

Benjamin Mason Meier

1 Introduction

Human rights are heralded as a modern guide for public health. Cited by health advocates throughout the world, the human right to health – proclaimed seminally in the Universal Declaration of Human Rights (UDHR) and codified in the International Covenant of Economic, Social and Cultural Rights (ICESCR) as 'the right of everyone to the enjoyment of the highest attainable standard of physical and mental health' – has become a cornerstone of global health governance. As a normative framework for international public health, the right to health is seen as foundational to the contemporary policies and programs of the World Health Organization (WHO).

It was not always so.

This chapter traces the political history leading up to WHO's invocation of human rights for the public's health. With both the UDHR and WHO coming into existence in 1948, there was great initial promise that these two institutions would complement each other, with WHO – as a specialised agency of the United Nations (UN) – upholding human rights in all its activities. In spite of this promise, and early WHO efforts to advance a human rights basis for its work, WHO policy intentionally neglected the right to health during crucial years of its evolution, projecting itself as a technical organisation above 'legal rights'.

Where WHO neglected human rights – out of political expediency, legal incapacity and medical supremacy – it did so at its peril. After 25 years of shunning the development of the right to health, WHO came to see these legal principles as a political foundation upon which to frame its 'Health for All' strategy under the Declaration of Alma-Ata. But it was too late: WHO's constrained role in developing international human rights for health – specifically the transition from Article 25 of the UDHR to Article 12 of the ICESCR – had already set into motion a course for the right to health that would prove fatal to the goals of primary healthcare laid out in the Declaration of Alma-Ata (see Table 8.1).

This chapter evaluates the evolution of legal obligations for a human right to health, focusing on WHO's role in developing these obligations. Scholars have reached contradictory conclusions as to WHO's role in the advancement and

Table 8.1

UDHR (1948)	*ICESCR (1966)*	*Declaration of Alma-Ata (1978)*
Article 25: (1) Everyone has the right to a standard of living adequate for the health and well-being of himself and of his family, including food, clothing, housing and medical care and necessary social services, and the right to security in the event of unemployment, sickness, disability, widowhood, old age or other lack of livelihood in circumstances beyond his control.	Article 12: 1. The States Parties to the present Covenant recognize the right of everyone to the highest attainable standard of physical and mental health. 2. The steps to be taken by the States Parties to the present Covenant to achieve the full realization of the right shall include those necessary for: (a) The provision for the reduction of the stillbirth-rate and of infant mortality and for the healthy development of the child; (b) The improvement of all aspects of environmental and industrial hygiene; (c) The prevention, treatment and control of epidemic, endemic, occupational and other diseases; (d) The creation of conditions which would assure to all medical service and medical attention in the event of sickness.	I. The Conference strongly reaffirms that health, which is a state of complete physical, mental and social wellbeing, and not merely the absence of disease or infirmity, is a fundamental human right and that the attainment of the highest possible level of health is a most important world-wide social goal whose realization requires the action of many other social and economic sectors in addition to the health sector. V. Governments have a responsibility for the health of their people which can be fulfilled only by the provision of adequate health and social measures. A main social target of governments, international organizations and the whole world community in the coming decades should be the attainment by all peoples of the world by the year 2000 of a level of health that will permit them to lead a socially and economically productive life. Primary health care is the key to attaining this target as part of development in the spirit of social justice.

implementation of human rights – finding either that WHO had an influential presence in the evolution of human rights for health (Alston 1979) or that public health and human rights always 'evolved along parallel but distinctly separate tracks', joined for the first time at the advent of the HIV/AIDS pandemic (Gruskin *et al.* 2007: 449). Both of these accounts, however, present an incomplete history of global health governance, disregarding the vital human rights leadership displayed by WHO in its early years, and the consequences that resulted from WHO's subsequent renunciation of its authoritative role as a leading voice for health rights. Through legal analysis and historical narrative, this research examines WHO's early contributions to and subsequent abandonment of the evolution of health rights. While other studies have examined the treaty language of the right to health (Roscam Abbing 1979; Toebes 1999), no previous study has examined the underlying WHO communications that framed international treaty negotiations (Thomas and Weber 2004). Employing archival research to clarify these communications, it becomes possible to analyse the processes of global health governance in translating health discourses into international legal norms through the development of a human right to health.

2 The foundations of human rights for health

The international codification of a right to health begins in the context of the Second World War. On 6 January 1941, US President Franklin Delano Roosevelt announced to the world that the postwar era would be founded upon four 'essential human freedoms': freedom of speech, freedom of religion, freedom from fear, and freedom from want (Roosevelt 1941). It is the final of these 'Four Freedoms' – freedom from want – that introduced a State obligation to provide for the health of its peoples. Rising out of the cauldron of war, and drawing on working-class struggles of the late nineteenth and early twentieth centuries, this freedom from want became enshrined in the lexicon of social and economic rights, seeking State obligations to prevent deprivations such as had taken place during the Depression and the War that followed (United Nations Conference on Food and Agriculture 1943). Elaborated at a 1944 postwar planning conference among the Allied Powers, these social and economic rights would take form in the development of State obligations for human rights, providing binding mechanisms for assessing and adjudicating principles of justice under international law (US Department of State 1944).

The Charter of the United Nations (UN Charter) became the first international legal document to recognise the concept of human rights. While not initially enumerated or elaborated, States raised human rights as one of the four principal purposes of the nascent UN, which would 'make recommendations for the purpose of promoting respect for, and observance of, human rights and fundamental freedoms for all' (UN 1945: Art 62). During the drafting of the UN Charter, however, States did not initially include any mention of health, either as a goal of the UN or as a human right (*Lancet* 1945). But for the efforts of the Brazilian and Chinese delegations to the 1945 UN Conference in San Francisco – inserting the word 'health' in the UN Charter, finding international health cooperation to be among the purposes of the UN's Economic and Social Council (ECOSOC), and advocating the establishment of an international health organisation – health would have received no mention in the creation of the UN, blunting the legitimacy of health in international law and the creation of WHO as a UN specialised agency (AJPH 1945). With this promise of international health and human rights cooperation in the UN Charter, it would fall to subsequent human rights treaties to codify a human right to health in international law.

In doing so, the rapid drafting and adoption of the Constitution of the World

Health Organization (WHO Constitution) would make it the first international treaty to find a unique human right to health. During an International Health Conference in June 1946, delegates adopted WHO Constitution pursuant to the UN Charter, thereby establishing an Interim Commission to subsume within WHO all of the prior obligations of the League of Nations Health Organization, the Office International d'Hygiene Publique (OIHP), and the Health Division of the United Nations Relief and Rehabilitation Administration (UNRRA). To achieve these ends, the International Health Conference established three organs through which to implement the goals of the new organisation: (a) The World Health Assembly, the legislative policy-making body of WHO, made up of representatives from each member state; (b) the Executive Board, an executive program-developing subset of the World Health Assembly; and (c) the WHO Secretariat, carrying out the decisions of the aforementioned organs through the elected Director-General and appointed WHO staff (WHO 1946). Recognising a necessity to facilitate international cooperation through global health governance, representatives of 61 States signed WHO Constitution on 22 July 1946, after which it remained open for signature until it came into force on 7 April 1948 (Goodman 1948).

In establishing the contours of a human right to health under WHO Constitution – a document far more extensive than those of its institutional predecessors (Masters 1947) – the Preamble declares that 'the enjoyment of the highest attainable standard of health is one of the fundamental rights of every human being', defining health positively to include 'a state of complete physical, mental, and social well-being and not merely the absence of disease or infirmity' (WHO 1946: Preamble). By expanding the mandate of international public health far beyond the 'absence of disease' envisioned by early international health treaties, the International Health Conference 'extended [WHO] from the negative aspects of public health – vaccination and other specific means of combating infection – to positive aspects, i.e. the improvement of public health by better food, physical education, medical care, health insurance, etc' (Štampar 1949). In meeting this expansive vision of underlying determinants of health, a vision commensurate with public health's contemporaneous focus on 'social medicine' (Sand 1934), the Preamble declares that 'governments have a responsibility for the health of their peoples which can be fulfilled only by the provision of adequate health and social measures' (WHO 1946: Preamble). Under such far-reaching legal principles, WHO Constitution created a veritable 'Magna Carta of health' (Parran 1946: 2), 'represent[ing] the broadest and most liberal concept of international responsibility for health ever officially promulgated' and encompassing the aspirations of WHO's mandate to build a healthy world out of the ashes of the Second World War (Allen 1950: 30).

Drawing on the negotiations for WHO Constitution, the UN proclaimed its UDHR on 10 December 1948, enacting through it 'a common standard of achievement for all peoples and all nations' (UDHR 1948). By defining a set of interrelated social welfare rights to underlie health, the nascent UN framed a right to health by which:

> Everyone has the right to a standard of living adequate for the health and well-being of himself and of his family, including food, clothing, housing and medical care and necessary social services, and the right to security in the event of unemployment, sickness, disability, widowhood, old age or other lack of livelihood in circumstances beyond his control.
>
> (UDHR 1948: Art 25(1))

In developing this right to a standard of living adequate for health, there was widespread international agreement that a human right to health included both the fulfillment of medical care and the realisation of underlying determinants of health – explicitly including public health systems for food, clothing, housing, and social services (UN 1950). This broad, rights-based vision of public health systems was in accordance with: (a) the expansion of European welfare policy, founded on the notion that 'social security cannot be fully developed unless health is cared for along comprehensive lines' (Beveridge 1942); (b) the development of human rights in the Americas, incorporating 'the right to the preservation of . . . health through sanitary and social measures relating to food, clothing, housing and medical care' (International Conference of American States 1948: Art XI); and (c) the Soviet Constitution, which established protections of medical care and 'maintenance in old age and also in case of sickness or disability' (Konstitutsiia SSSR 1936: Art 120). With this consensus on the underlying determinants of health, framed under the broad umbrella of 'social security', there was widespread expectation that this expansive declaratory language would soon be elaborated by specific human rights obligations.

3 The development of a right to health

This narrative chronicles the political dynamics of WHO in the evolution of human rights for health, from the UDHR to the immediate aftermath of the Declaration of Alma-Ata. In the midst of WHO's role in the codification of the 1948 UDHR in the 1966 ICESCR, WHO Secretariat walked away from its efforts to develop the international legal language of the right to health. When WHO sought to reclaim the mantle of human rights in the pursuit of its 'Health for All' strategy, its past obsolescence in rights-based strategies left it without the human rights obligations necessary to implement primary healthcare pursuant to the Declaration of Alma-Ata. In a chronological series of subparts, this research describes WHO's early influence on human rights (1948–1953), subsequent neglect of human rights (1953–1973), and ultimate rediscovery of human rights as the basis of its 'Health for All' strategy (1973–1979) – with these time periods corresponding with successive changes in WHO leadership and direction.

3.1 WHO influences human rights (1948–1952)

From the moment of its inception, WHO sought to pursue dual policy paths in its work: an extension of previous coordination in international disease prevention;

and an ambitious rights-based project in national health promotion, implemented programmatically through medical interventions for curative care and public health systems for underlying determinants of health (*Lancet* 1948). In the aftermath of the Second World War, medical technologies – in the form of new physician practices, newly discovered scientific therapies and global epidemiologic surveillance – had created unlimited possibilities to extend and improve life. As articulated by Brock Chisholm, WHO's first Director-General, 'I strongly believe that with all the marvellous tools which modern science and medicine have put at our disposal, we could make tremendous strides towards the attainment by "all peoples of the highest possible level of health"' (Chisholm 1951: 25). Notwithstanding this moment of exultation for the observed 'miracles' of modern medical care, global health discourse continued to emphasise the importance of underlying determinants of health, focused on the relation between economic conditions and physical well-being (Ryle 1948). Adopting the term 'healthcare' rather than 'medical care' as the basis of health discourse, public health practitioners sought to acknowledge that the full development of health requires both insurance for medical services *and* underlying conditions for, *inter alia*, adequate nutrition, housing, education, and social security (Grant 1948). It is in this undercurrent of social medicine – this understanding of the limits of technological progress, and correspondingly, the importance of national public health systems to address underlying determinants of health – that WHO concerned itself with what it considered an 'inseparable triad' for public health – 'the interdependence of social, economic and health problems' (WHO 1952). To address these interdependent determinants of health, WHO sought to coordinate international health policy, with Member States finding that 'under the leadership of the World Health Organization, the various national and international programs have become, in a very real sense, a single, unified movement with a common goal and common methods of attaining that goal' (van Zile Hyde 1953: 605). With a synoptic view of underlying determinants of health and a predilection for collaborative effort to attain its multi-sectoral health goals, WHO Secretariat sought to work with the UN to develop human rights for health.

In fulfilling its global health mission through human rights frameworks, WHO's early years are marked by its active role in developing human rights treaty language, working with States and UN agencies to expand human rights principles for public health through the codification of the UDHR into legally-enforceable covenants, first in the draft International Covenant on Human Rights and subsequently in the ICESCR. Following WHO's preliminary initiative to advance the civil and political rights implicated by human experimentation (Commission on Human Rights 1950), ECOSOC's Commission on Human Rights would take up legal obligations concerning economic, social and cultural rights in its 1951 session, giving WHO Secretariat its first opportunity to influence the development of a human right to health. With the UN reaching out to WHO on collaborative opportunities with the Commission on Human Rights, Director-General Chisholm responded enthusiastically in January 1951, quoting from the preambular language of WHO Constitution and 'welcom[ing] opportunities to co-operate with the Commission on Human Rights in drafting international conventions, recommendations and standards with a view to ensuring the enjoyment of the right to health' (WHO 1951a). To this cooperative end, Director-General Chisholm concluded that:

> It is clear that the whole programme approved by the World Health Assembly represents a concerted effort on the part of the Member States to ensure the right to health . . . I am well aware of the obligation of WHO to be guided by this fundamental relationship in planning its work with governments as well as with other international organizations.
>
> (WHO 1951a)

Based upon this general direction, WHO staff followed up on the Director-General's response by suggesting specific human rights treaty language well beyond the UDHR – on topics ranging from occupational health, to nutrition, to child welfare and maternal and child health clinics, to medical and nursing education and research, to international health policy (WHO 1951b).

To further this human rights cooperation, arrangements were made for WHO to direct negotiations on the right to health during the Commission on Human Rights' 1951 session (WHO 1951c). Having received notice of WHO's human rights initiative, the US Representative to WHO Executive Board wrote to the Director-General, expressing his scepticism toward the successful implementation of economic and social rights and his 'hope' that WHO recognise 'the problems inherent in attempting to draft enforceable rights for health services' (van Zile Hyde 1951). Overcoming this scepticism, WHO Secretariat suggested in April 1951 that the right to health should be couched in terms – drawn from WHO Constitution and language abandoned in compromises on the UDHR (UN 1950a) – that emphasised (a) a positive definition of health; (b) the importance of social measures as underlying determinants of health; and (c) the obligation of State health ministries for these underlying determinants:

> Every human being shall have the right to the enjoyment of the highest standard of health obtainable, health being defined as a state of complete physical mental and social well-being.
>
> Governments, having a responsibility for the health of their peoples, undertake to fulfil that responsibility by providing adequate health and social measures.
>
> Every Party to the present Covenant shall therefore, so far as it [sic] means allow and with due allowance for its traditions and for local conditions, provide measures to promote and protect the health of its nationals, and in particular:
>
> – to reduce infant mortality and provide for healthy development of the child;

> – to improve nutrition, housing, sanitation, recreation, economic and working conditions and other aspects of environmental hygiene;
> – to control epidemic, endemic and other diseases;
> – to improve standards of medical teaching and training in the health, medical and related professions;
> – to enlighten public opinion on problems of health;
> – to foster activities in the field of mental health, especially those affecting the harmony of human relations.
>
> (Commission on Human Rights 1951a)

The Commission on Human Rights met in June 1951 to draft legal provisions for – among other economic, social and cultural rights – the right to health (Commission on Human Rights 1951b). Director-General Chisholm opened this debate by challenging State delegates to define health in international human rights law, advocating adoption of the positive definition of health from WHO Constitution. In the shadow of his impassioned plea for health promotion, international consensus developed around WHO's approach – providing simultaneously for the general recognition of a right to health in an opening paragraph with an enumeration of state obligations in subsequent paragraphs. Framed by WHO's outline, the Commission on Human Rights concluded its session with the following draft right:

> The States Parties to this Covenant recognize the right of everyone to the enjoyment of the highest standard of health obtainable.
>
> With a view to implementing and safeguarding this right, each State party hereto undertakes to provide legislative measures to promote and protect health and in particular:
>
> 1. to reduce infant mortality and to provide for healthy development of the child;
> 2. to improve nutrition, housing, sanitation, recreation, economic and working conditions and other aspects of environmental hygiene;
> 3. to control epidemic, endemic and other diseases;
> 4. to provide conditions which would assure the right of all its nationals to a medical service and medical attention in the event of sickness.
>
> (Commission on Human Rights 1951c)

Although States had reverted from the expansive vision of 'complete' health to the delimited 'highest standard of health obtainable', the revised draft of the right to health was the most detailed of the draft economic, social and cultural rights, placing explicit obligations on states to progressively realise underlying determinants of health through public health systems.

While a right to health lacked the support of medical practitioners (e.g. World Medical Association 1951), WHO Secretariat continued to engage in constructive UN debates to develop the normative language of this legal right. In doing so,

WHO leadership in health rights proved influential, as the UN Division of Human Rights drew upon WHO's background documents in subsequent drafts of the Covenant (UN 1951), highlighting WHO's policy leadership in its catalogue of UN human rights activities (UN 1952). With WHO Secretariat receiving broad authorisation from its Executive Board to develop human rights standards for health and to implement those standards through national health legislation and global health reports (WHO 1951d), WHO returned to the 1952 session of the Commission on Human Rights to assist in the finalisation of the language of the right to health.

When the 1952 session of Commission on Human Rights reached the right to health – now incorporated in the draft ICESCR (Commission on Human Rights 1952a) – State delegates presented and adopted the following amendments in line with WHO's original vision, expanding:

- the first paragraph to include the definition of health from WHO Constitution, and
- the second paragraph to replace the obligation of 'legislative measures' with all 'those necessary for' realising underlying determinants of health (Commission on Human Rights 1952b).

As a result, and in correcting a translation error to replace 'obtainable' with 'attainable standard of health,' the draft text of the article on the right to health was amended to:

> The States Parties to the Covenant, realizing that health is a state of complete physical, mental and social well-being, and not merely the absence of disease or infirmity, recognize the right of everyone to the enjoyment of the highest attainable standard of health.
>
> The steps to be taken by the States Parties to the Covenant to achieve the full realization of this right shall include *those necessary* for:
>
> (a) The reduction of infant mortality and the provision for healthy development of the child;
> (b) The improvement of nutrition, housing, sanitation, recreation, economic and working conditions and other aspects of environmental hygiene;
> (c) The prevention, treatment and control of epidemic, endemic and other diseases;
> (d) The creation of conditions which would assure to all medical service and medical attention in the event of sickness.
>
> (Commission on Human Rights 1952c)

With the Commission unable to complete its drafting of the human rights covenants before the end of the session, ECOSOC authorised States to revisit the covenants at the Commission's 1953 session (ECOSOC 1952). However, between the 1952 and 1953 sessions, a change in leadership and health priorities would lead WHO to relinquish its leadership in health rights, and as a consequence, the right to health would be progressively weakened in the years to come.

3.2 WHO neglects human rights (1953–1972)

As the UN sought to expand its treaty framework for human rights – beginning with the transition from the UDHR to the ICESCR, and then extending these rights outward through international conventions – WHO eschewed the development of health rights under international law. With WHO adopting a medicalised view of health, it shifted away from the development of national health systems for underlying determinants of health and toward the provision of individual medical treatments then thought to be singularly necessary for achieving the 'highest attainable standard of health' (Pannenborg 1979). Turning its attention to purely technical enterprises, which it approached through a medical lens, WHO sought a vertical, disease-specific approach to international public health (Brockington 1958). This technical agenda – under the leadership of Director-General Marcolino Gomes Candau – focused largely (a) at the domestic level, in assisting countries through specific requests for medical assistance; and (b) at the international level, in coordinating communicable disease eradication for the control of malaria, tuberculosis, plague, cholera, yellow fever and smallpox. As explained by WHO's chief legal officer, 'a programme based on the notion of priorities has given way to one based on the needs of the countries themselves, expressed through their requests for advice and assistance' (Gutteridge 1963: 8). Rather than working with States to develop comprehensive public health systems, WHO Secretariat merely trained health ministries in medical techniques, with the new Director-General viewing WHO personnel simply as a 'catalyst', 'who, working on projects, pass on to their national counterparts the skill and knowledge needed to attack a specific health problem' (Candau 1957: 676). Thus, despite operating with more than triple its original staff and more than double its original funding, WHO's programme agenda shifted away from its previous emphasis on global health priorities for the disadvantaged (which included noncommunicable diseases and underlying determinants of health), delegating programs to regional health offices and decentralising leadership for health policy within the UN system (Ascher 1952).

Under such a medical framework, there was little room for the utilisation of human rights to develop and implement social measures to realise underlying determinants of health. Despite an understanding from the UN General Assembly that specialised agencies would take responsibility for creating detailed definitions of the human rights principles within their respective fields of action, WHO took no specific actions to explain these broadly defined rights for health promotion. When the 1953 session of the Commission on Human Rights sought to finalise the language of the right to health in the ICESCR, WHO communicated previously produced technical documents, many of which had no bearing on human rights norms (Commission on Human Rights 1953).

When specialised agencies were again asked to submit detailed comments on their human rights reporting procedures, WHO responded with far fewer comments relative to other agencies, requesting only that simpler reporting procedures be instituted, based on the notion that few States submit WHO reports for the Secretariat then to summarise for the Commission on Human Rights (WHO 1953).

In the ensuing years, WHO did not respond to repeated requests for comments on final drafts of the ICESCR (UN 1954), enabling the weakening of health protections as States resurrected debates on the inclusion of (a) a definition of health, (b) the idea of 'social well-being', and (c) the 'steps to be taken' by States, with Director-General Candau responding repeatedly that WHO had 'no comments to offer concerning the right to health' (WHO 1955). When the finalisation of the right to health moved to the UN General Assembly in 1957 (UN 1957a), WHO had lost credibility to affect policy within the UN Secretariat or among State delegations. As delegates summarily eliminated the definition of health and the reference to 'social well-being' from the right to health – under the contradictory rationales that the definition was either unnecessarily verbose or irreconcilably incomplete – WHO personnel made no attempt to prevent these deletions (UN 1957b). In limiting the 'measures to be taken' by States, UN representatives removed obligations for underlying determinants of health, replacing 'the improvement of nutrition, housing, sanitation, recreation, economic and working conditions and other aspects of environmental hygiene' with the vague 'improvement of all aspects of environmental and industrial hygiene' (UN 1957c, 1957d). Abandoning its previous efforts to strengthen health rights, WHO took little part in the concluding debates relative to other specialised agencies, and no amendments were offered to expand the obligations of this enfeebled right. On 30 January 1957, the General Assembly approved the right to health, leaving it substantively unchanged until the December 1966 adoption of the ICESCR:

1. The States Parties to the present Covenant recognize the right of everyone to the enjoyment of the highest attainable standard of physical and mental health.
2. The steps to be taken by the States Parties to the present Covenant to achieve the full realization of this right shall include those necessary for:
   (a) The provision for the reduction of the stillbirth-rate and of infant mortality and for the healthy development of the child;
   (b) The improvement of all aspects of environmental and industrial hygiene;
   (c) The prevention, treatment and control of epidemic, endemic, occupational and other diseases;
   (d) The creation of conditions which would assure to all medical service and medical attention in the event of sickness.

(UN 1957f: Art 12)

Although subsequent changes were made to strengthen other articles of the ICESCR, WHO made no additional comments on the right to health. Even once the ICESCR was completed, WHO claimed no ownership over the new Covenant's obligations on health, noting in meetings with UN staff that 'acceptance of WHO Constitution covers this matter fully in health terms and WHO could not press its Member States with respect to the covenants' (WHO 1972).

With States moving independently to adopt the ICESCR, WHO's continued silence on health rights in international law eliminated opportunities for health advocates to elaborate the scope and content of human rights in accordance with public health discourse, leaving this imprecise elaboration of the right to health as the seminal, final and definitive international legal obligation pursuant to this right. As seen in the following examples, WHO's neglect for human rights development continued to deny the right to health a place in evolving international legal frameworks:

- In 1959 debates on the Draft Declaration of the Rights of the Child, although the UN Secretariat welcomed WHO comments in the process, WHO representative to the Commission on Human Rights received instructions from WHO Headquarters to offer only 'general support' (WHO 1959a), leading the representative not to make any statement or offer any substantive comments (WHO 1959b).
- When the UN General Assembly began work in 1964 on a Draft Declaration on the Elimination of Discrimination against Women (UN 1964), WHO considered this to be outside its mandate, finding that the 'non-discrimination clause' in the Preamble of WHO Constitution did not refer to discrimination on account of sex (WHO 1964a) and responding that because it 'is not entrusted with responsibility for direct action to overcome such restrictions', it was 'not possible to derive from the work of WHO principles that might be incorporated into a draft declaration' (WHO 1964b).
- In developing a Convention on the Elimination of All Forms of Racial Discrimination in 1965, WHO responded dismissively that while legislation is outside its competence, its technical programs 'may be said to give effect to the principle of non-discrimination', blithely submitting that WHO's publications 'breathe a spirit of equality and are intended, by their universal treatment of many topics, by showing people as people wherever they may live, to help the advancement of human rights and the improvement of race relations' (WHO 1965). As a result, health discrimination and inequities in healthcare – while forming a contemporaneous impetus for Martin Luther King's invocation 'of all the forms of inequality, injustice in health care is the most shocking and inhumane' (Gordon and Assefa 2006: 697) – would not be a part of the international human rights debate.

In the midst of such non-cooperation in treaty development, WHO staff also engaged in a purposeful campaign to distance WHO from any UN responsibilities in implementing human rights (ECOSOC 1956), with Director-General

Candau's announcing to the UN beginning in 1957 that 'the Organization, not being entrusted with safeguarding legal rights, is not in a position to take a share in a report describing developments and progress achieved . . . in the field of human rights and measures taken to safeguard human liberty' (WHO 1957). Following over a decade of criticism by the Commission on Human Rights (WHO 1958a), with WHO requesting that the UN Secretariat not include a section on health in its human rights summaries (WHO 1958b), WHO then attempted to excise itself entirely from the human rights reporting process and measures of progress in the protection of human rights. Arguing that the UDHR dealt far more with 'social questions' than with health, WHO suggested that the UN would be the only appropriate reviewing agency for the UDHR, noting that 'the provisions contained in Article 25 of the Declaration, in their letter and spirit, go substantially beyond the competence of the World Health Organization' (WHO 1959c). With the UN declining to request future WHO comments on UN reports and WHO resisting all subsequent efforts to submit reports to the UN, the UN's 1968 review of specialised agency efforts in human rights includes only vague generalities on the right to health and includes the activities of every specialised agency except WHO (UN 1968a, UN 1968b).

3.3 WHO rediscovers human rights (1973–1980)

Given changes in health discourse, WHO would return to the promise of international human rights standards as a means to realise an improved standard of global health. The perceived emergence of new threats – in the form of heart disease, cancer, labor migration and exploitation, drug addiction, overpopulation and environmental harms – was shifting public health toward an emphasis on socio-economic determinants of health (Rosen 1974). Through this appreciation of the systemic conditions that structure health inequalities, public health practitioners reengaged underlying determinants of health, drawing on theories of social medicine and recognising a 'need for a shift in the balance of effort [to] modification of the conditions which led to disease rather than from intervention in the mechanism of disease after it has occurred' (McKeown 1976: 179). Given a growing gap between what could be done and what was being done to address underlying determinants of health, scholars and practitioners began to examine national health systems – including political institutions and financial distributions – as moving health rights beyond the purview of the physician and the dominion of medical services (Evang 1973). With the failures of prominent disease eradication programs (e.g. the global malaria campaign) and successes of national health promotion systems (e.g. China's 'barefoot doctors'), WHO's health goals and technical documents would transition from a persistent faith in a disease-specific approach to health to an increased emphasis on comprehensive 'primary healthcare' – healthcare in addition to underlying social, political, and economic determinants of health (WHO 1973). In translating these public health discourses into international legal norms, WHO came to recognise that human rights could bind States to realise primary healthcare. While a comprehensive approach to public health had long garnered technical support within WHO, only political support could bring these evolving health ideas to the fore of WHO policy (Brown *et al.* 2006). With health rights providing this political foundation, WHO – under Director-General Halfdan Mahler – would come to advocate for primary healthcare as a human right, and under its 'Health for All' strategy to primary healthcare, WHO would again take a leading role in developing health policy pursuant to a human right to health.

Concurrent with the expansion of the human rights movements, organisations and instruments, WHO sought to expand its influence by redefining its health goals to reflect human rights standards. Within the UN system, increased human rights coordination among specialised agencies buttressed WHO efforts, providing added collaborative opportunities for human rights advancement in health (UN 1974). After years of absence, WHO re-emerged in 1973 as a voice for social justice – at the Commission on Human Rights and in human rights seminars. In doing so, WHO leadership held out human rights as a force for health, using treaties, articles, and conferences to analyse the relevance of the right to health to public health practice and extolling human rights as a clarion call to the realisation of health for all.

WHO would embark on its 'Health for All' campaign as a means to advance primary healthcare, with specific public health targets to be achieved by the year 2000. Viewing health equity as a human rights challenge, Director-General Mahler noted as early as 1974 that 'in the context of the universal human right to a socially optimal standard of individual physical and mental health . . . the very sophistication of today's medical wisdom tends to prevent individual and community participation without which health often becomes a technological mockery' (Mahler 1975). This argument was extended in WHO's 1975 embrace of underlying determinants of health, wherein the Director-General's Annual Report argued that 'we must also remind ourselves that the urgent health problems of developing countries relate to poverty, to infection, to malnutrition and undernutrition, to lack of accessible potable water, and to multiple environmental hazards' (WHO 1975).

Framing this rights-based vision of global public health around underlying determinants of health and reflecting the 'basic needs approach' of contemporaneous human rights scholars through programs to meet 'basic health needs' (Djukanovic and Mach 1975), WHO Secretariat advocated for primary healthcare as a human right, and under its 'Health for All' strategy, the WHO would again take a leading role in developing rights-based health policy.

This 'Health for All' strategy, defined by the World Health Assembly in 1977 and regarded as WHO's 'main thrust' for developing the right to health (Taylor 1991), would seek 'the attainment by all citizens of the world by the year 2000 of a level of health that would permit them to lead socially and economically productive lives' (WHO 1977). In fulfilling this right through State obligations for primary healthcare, the World Health Assembly proclaimed government responsibility for 'a complex of economic and social measures which directly or indirectly promote the attainment of the highest possible level of health, through the establishment of a nation-wide system of health services' (WHO 1977). At the pinnacle of this WHO reengagement with human rights for underlying determinants of health, there was internal agreement that WHO had the constitutional authority to develop legal obligations for its 'Health for All' strategy (Vigne 1979), which it pursued through the 1978 Declaration of Alma-Ata.

With the 'Health for All' strategy providing rights-based policy reflective of public health discourse, the Declaration of Alma-Ata would provide international consensus for national primary healthcare systems consistent with WHO's vision of health and human rights. As WHO was participating for the first time in celebrations of the anniversary of the UDHR, as the ICESCR was entering into force, and as WHO was preparing its first progress report on the right to health (ECOSOC 1980), WHO and UNICEF convened an international conference to frame a human rights agenda for achieving WHO's 'Health for All' strategy (Taylor and Jolly 1988). To design the contours of this agenda – moving the human right to health from vertical hospital-based technologies to horizontal primary healthcare – WHO sought to bring together interdisciplinary public health and development actors to evaluate national health systems. With representatives from 134 State governments, this International Conference on Primary Health Care adopted the Declaration on Primary Health Care (a document that has come to be known as the 1978 Declaration of Alma-Ata), affirming that primary healthcare would be the key to addressing underlying determinants of health pursuant to the right to health.

Drawn from the rights-based language of WHO Constitution, Article I of the Declaration of Alma-Ata outlines that:

> health, which is a state of complete physical, mental and social well-being, and not merely the absence of disease or infirmity, is a fundamental human right and that the attainment of the highest level of health is a most important world-wide social goal whose realization requires the action of many other social and economic sectors in addition to the health sector.
>
> (WHO 1978)

To realise this right, the Declaration of Alma-Ata focuses on primary healthcare, from which it derives a collective right to

> essential health care made universally accessible to individuals and families in the community by means acceptable to them, through their full participation and at a cost that the community and the country can afford to maintain at every stage of their development in the spirit of self-reliance and self-determination.
>
> (WHO 1978)

In reifying the goals of WHO's 'Health for All' strategy, the Declaration of

Alma-Ata sought to narrow health inequalities within and between States, encouraging States to work toward establishing a New International Economic Order, and prioritising disadvantaged groups in achieving 'equity-oriented targets'. Under this approach, the Declaration of Alma-Ata adopted a holistic view of underlying determinants of health, seeking social justice in the distribution of health resources in line with the interconnectedness of human rights in the realisation of public health.

From this definition of health as a human right, the Declaration of Alma-Ata found that realisation of the right to health requires 'intersectoral' government Policy in the social and economic sectors to achieve health equity. To frame programmatic obligations for addressing underlying determinants of health – creating a national system of primary healthcare based on individual and collective participation in the planning and implementation of health policy decisions – the Declaration of Alma-Ata promoted a reorientation of national health strategies to incorporate and fund public health in line with the needs of each nation. In framing these national health needs in the context of economic development, the Declaration expanded upon the provisions outlined in the ICESCR, enumerating specific rights-based government obligations for essential aspects of primary healthcare, including:

(a) education concerning prevailing health problems;
(b) promotion of food supply and proper nutrition;
(c) an adequate supply of safe water and basic sanitation;
(d) maternal and child healthcare, including family planning;
(e) immunization against major infectious diseases;
(f) prevention and control of endemic diseases;
(g) appropriate treatment of common diseases and injuries; and
(h) the provision of essential medicines

(WHO 1978: §VII).

Thus, despite giving flexibility to national policy based upon States' varying stages of development, the Declaration of Alma-Ata guides States in creating health systems, emphasising underlying determinants of health rather than individual curative treatments (Leary 1993).

By laying out criteria for States in developing primary healthcare, and declaring these criteria to be human rights – rights that would have priority over other national goals – the Declaration of Alma-Ata presented a unifying framework for advancing public health under the aegis of the right to health (MacDonald 2008). Subsequent to the Declaration of Alma-Ata, WHO invited States in January 1979 to use the Declaration as the basis of national policies to meet the goals of 'Health for All' (WHO 1979). Yet, despite the development of the right to health in the Declaration of Alma-Ata, WHO's past neglect of human rights had created insurmountable obstacles to the evolution of the right to health – obstacles that ultimately contributed to the failure of WHO's 'Health for All' strategy and the abandonment of the Declaration of Alma-Ata.

4 The failure of 'Health for All'

Where the human right to health did not reflect WHO's expansive definition of health – with the right narrowed in the course of its evolution from underlying determinants of health to medical care – the 'Health for All' campaign would not find support in human rights frameworks. Without international law to support human rights obligations for underlying determinants of health, States could credibly find WHO's 'Health for All' strategy, with a focus on social and economic development, to be beyond the purview of WHO's organisational mandate (Starrels 1985). Although there existed a movement to implement the 'Health for All' strategy through primary healthcare, the obligations of the Declaration of Alma-Ata represented an illusory success for public health advocacy, with the Declaration failing to create sustainable frameworks for international health law and national health policy (Battista 1981).

When international legal frameworks moved from the UN system to international economic institutions at the end of the 1970s, there were no commensurate health rights in law to challenge these new institutional realities and prevent the collapse of the 'Health for All' strategy. With global health governance encumbered by neo-liberal economic policy, the Declaration of Alma-Ata suffered from medical reductionism in its obligations (Cueto 2004), reducing the breadth of primary healthcare to 'selective primary healthcare' (Walsh and Warren 1979). Steeped in the provision of medicine and health technology, this medicalisation of the right to health was incorporated into the 1981 WHO Global Strategy for 'Health for All by the Year 2000' (WHO 1981). Rather than proposing effective public health systems to facilitate underlying determinants of health, WHO focus would shift to 'health services systems' to address the provision of medical care (Roemer 1984). In this return to a focus on vertical health programming – through which international economic institutions sought efficient healthcare expenditure as a means to economic growth – developing States reduced health expenditures, and health inequalities widened (Horwitz 1983). By 1988, WHO conceded the impossibility of its initial primary healthcare goal, removing the language of 'by the Year 2000' from its 'Health for All' campaign (WHO 1988).

Despite WHO's efforts to reclaim the legal standards of the right to health in its 'Health for All' strategy, rigid international legal paradigms leave human rights fixed in outmoded models of health, codified in weak international legal standards that cannot easily evolve to encompass underlying determinants of health. WHO Constitution envisioned an expansive role for human rights protection and promotion in realising the highest attainable standard of health, but WHO failed to live up to this role. Given WHO's longstanding (a) reluctance to politicise health policy, (b) incapacity to create legal frameworks for health rights and (c) grounding in medical practice, these vicissitudes in institutional leadership for human rights ultimately limited WHO's ability to carry out its public health mission under the right-based 'Health for All' strategy.

First, WHO had long sought to avoid politicising its public health work, disengaging from national healthcare and global health policy debates where those issues presented international relations conflicts. Given the State welfare obligations inherent in a human right to health, the Cold War posed normative and budgetary challenges to the development of health rights in international law (Hoole 1976; Mingst 1990). Compounding these constraints, a decentralised structure prevented WHO Secretariat from creating uniform health policy, allowing national governments to manipulate WHO regional offices in the pursuit of short-term medical interventions rather than underlying determinants of health (Berkov 1957; Jacobson 1974). Despite the quixotic vision of a universal organisation devoted to achieving health equity through non-political policy, 'efforts to place health goals above power politics were pointedly rejected' (Lee 2009: 24). While some have faulted WHO for engaging in political advocacy under its 'Health for All' strategy (Siddiqi 1995), this narrative reveals that public health is inherently political, with WHO failing to achieve its health goals where these goals were not crafted in the political terms of human rights.

Second, in spite of WHO's efforts to concretise human rights through its 'Health for All' strategy, it was hobbled in these efforts by its inability to engage with the language of legal rights, set standards under international agreements or develop models for national legislation. The reticence of WHO Secretariat toward human rights – never developing personnel devoted to human rights or involving its legal staff in rights-based communications – limited WHO's contributions to human rights institutions and treaties (Taylor 1992; Lakin 2001). Even when WHO came to develop human rights principles under its 'Health for All' strategy, it did so ineffectually, engaging in superficial statements unsuited to the implementation of legal standards (Nielsen 1999). Where WHO had sought to address health issues in the absence of its constitutionally endowed legal authorities (Burr 1988), the inherent limitations of this approach became transparent in the failure to achieve rights-based reform through the Declaration of Alma-Ata, with legal advocates thereafter recognising the importance of international law and national health legislation to the creation of global health policy (Fuenzalida-Puelma and Connor 1989). While WHO possesses invaluable technical expertise in health, giving it preeminent legitimacy in developing public health standards to address underlying determinants of health, this history shows that WHO must be competent to frame these normative processes pursuant to legal frameworks if it is to bind States meaningfully to realise the right to health.

Third, WHO Secretariat elevated medical practice over health rights, finding that its pragmatic approach to selective medical care was incompatible with a rights-based approach to underlying determinants of health. Given ambiguities in the language of the right to health – ambiguities largely caused by a lack of WHO participation in the development of legal norms – the right to health was left open to shifting definitions on the very object of the right, with the medical establishment holding sovereign authority to define the policies necessary to realise health (Taylor 1991). As medical practitioners abandoned public health in the aftermath of the Second World War – a unique and unrepresentative moment in the history of ideas surrounding health – WHO would institutionally support this medicalised agenda, with the right to health regressing to a right to the individual medical technologies and services then thought to be singularly necessary to bring about the 'end of disease' (King 1974). With its technical agenda long focused on the provision of medicines and the training of medical practitioners, WHO's medical staff gave scant attention to underlying determinants of health under the Director-General's 'Health for All' strategy (Litsios 2005). In implementing this strategy through the Declaration of Alma-Ata, WHO Secretariat would not concern itself with the human rights necessary to support an expansive public health approach to primary healthcare.

With these institutional impediments stymieing the evolution of a human right to health, WHO leaders could not bring States to accept their obligations for underlying determinants of health pursuant to the 'Health for All' strategy. Unlike other specialised agencies, WHO viewed its mission solely through a functional lens, and '[f]ulfilling its mandate was not done from a rights perspective nor with the aim of setting standards to be met by states' (Jamar 1994: 45). Where WHO had focused on health as a set of functional problems rather that as a human right, it failed to achieve both, undercutting its own health goals by denying them a foundation in human rights norms. This enduring neglect for international legal approaches to health has led the right to health to fall from the UDHR's promise of lexical rigidity to its current state of aspirational fluidity, rarely legislated or litigated to realise underlying determinants of health (Chapman and Russell 2002).

5 The enduring legacy of WHO neglect

As a result of the medicalisation of primary healthcare and the downfall of WHO's 'Health for All' strategy, a limited individual right to health – interpreted predominantly as a right to healthcare – has confined rights-based advocates to pressing for discrete medical services in response to problems demanding widespread change through public health systems. Given WHO's abnegation of global health governance for human rights, this framework for the right to health has set up an obligation that few States can fulfil, and which has proven inadequate to addressing growing socio-economic disparities in underlying determinants of health (Meier and Mori 2005). With responsibility for the provision of health services passing to partnerships of public, private and not-for-profit actors, neither States nor international organisations are held to account under this atomised right to individual healthcare (Stuttaford 2004).

Following the fall of the Declaration of Alma-Ata – with the hegemony of the neo-liberal economic paradigm necessitating a return to the 'Health for All' strategy – WHO's weaknesses in rights-based approaches to health have been most painfully felt by those in greatest need (Tarantola 2008). The neo-liberal economic paradigm – including policy prescriptions for privatisation, deregulation and decentralisation – has led to the dismantling of national health systems and the reorienting of economic development to the detriment of public health, exacerbating health inequalities within and between countries (Chen and Berlinguer 2001). In the wake of neo-liberal economic reforms, exposing developing States to exorbitant national debt repayments and insalubrious structural adjustment programs, the broad definition of primary healthcare laid out in the Declaration of Alma-Ata has been replaced with one that focuses on curative interventions in the context of national health system retrenchment and reduced social welfare expenditure (McMichael and Beaglehole 2000). Rather than opposing this paradigm under the legal mantle of health rights, 'WHO has fallen victim to neo-liberal globalization' (Katz 2007), forced into public-private partnerships for individual healthcare instead of primary healthcare for the public's health (MacDonald 2005). Evincing this paradox between healthcare policy and underlying determinants of health, WHO's Director-General was left to concede that although '[n]ever have so many had such broad and advanced access to healthcare . . . never have so many been denied access to health' (Millen *et al.* 2000: 4).

Without access to international legal standards, WHO could be denied a seat at the development table, excluding it from the global socio-economic institutions most crucial to realising improvements in public health (Meier and Fox 2008). Given WHO's inability to apply human rights to reclaim global health governance and to alleviate the harmful ramifications of neo-liberal economic policies (Kirby 1999), health advocates, not accustomed to working with WHO to develop human rights norms, abandoned legal obligations for health, relegating themselves to the non-binding 'commitments' of the UN's Millennium Development Goals (UN 2000) and UNAIDS' and WHO's '3 by 5' programme for the distribution of HIV medications (WHO 2004). Yet these efforts, much like previous hortatory goals – celebrated in their creation but abandoned in their codification – have failed to achieve programmatic specificity and legal accountability, enabling further regression from the universal standards of 'Health for All'.

In the absence of WHO leadership for health rights, it has fallen to the UN's human rights institutions – the Committee on Economic, Social and Cultural Rights (CESCR) and Special Rapporteur on the Right to Health (UN 2003) – to do what WHO could not: interpret the right to health in an expansive way that would set legal standards for addressing underlying determinants of health. Given past WHO neglect in developing these legal norms under the right to health, such UN interpretations required an explicit acknowledgement of the 'dynamic definition of the right to health' (CESCR 1994: 7), and an attempt to reinterpret the right to health commensurate with evolving health discourses (CESCR 2000). To the extent that these UN efforts have faced criticism for exceeding the limits of their legal mandate for norm clarification (Gorove 2004), constraining these interpretations in influencing State health policy, these obstacles to international legal obligations for underlying determinants of health can be traced back to the foundations of WHO's ill-fated movement for health and human rights.

6 Conclusion

Only by appreciating the rich political history of WHO involvement with human rights are we able to recognise the squandered opportunities for WHO leadership in advancing a rights-based approach to health – and to learn from those lost opportunities. After decades without enforceable legal obligations under the right to health, with repeated criticism of WHO for its lack of human rights coordination, the UN's 'cross-cutting approach' to human rights has paved the way for WHO to mainstream human rights in its public health policies (UN 1997). WHO has only begun to institutionalise this cross-cutting approach, most prominently through the creation of its Department of Ethics, Trade, Human Rights and Health Law, which has collaborated with organisations, scholars, and advocates to advance consensus at the intersection of health and human rights. After a decade under this new UN approach, however, this WHO human rights department has faced attrition in its budget and prominence, and nascent WHO health policies have faced criticism for their disconnection from the path of human rights. As these challenges continue to confound rights-based approaches to health, WHO's 2008 World Health Report, 'Primary Health Care – Now More Than Ever', notes striking public health inequities within and between countries and calls for a return to the primary healthcare approach of the 'Health for All' campaign (WHO 2008). Given WHO's inconstant commitment to human rights, it remains to be seen whether WHO will adhere to this evolving rights-based imperative or revert to its previous institutional neglect of human rights for the public's health.

Bibliography

AJPH (1945) 'Summary of actions related to public health during United Nations conference in San Francisco', *American Journal of Public Health* 35: 1106–7.

Allen, C. E. (1950) 'World health and world politics', *International Organization* 4(1): 27–43.

Alston, P. (1979) 'The United Nations' specialized agencies and implementation of the International Covenant on Economic, Social and Cultural Rights', *Columbia Journal of Transnational Law* 18: 79–118.

Ascher, C. S. (1952) 'Problems in the World Health Organization's program', *International Organization* 6(1): 27–50.

Battista, M. E. (1981) 'An enforceable human right to health: A new role for WHO'. Sao Paulo Conference on the Law of the World, 16–21 August. Washington: World Peace Through Law Center.

Berkov R. (1957) *The World Health Organization: A Study in Decentralized International Administration*. Geneva: E. Droz.

Beveridge, W. (1942) *Social Insurance and Allied Services: Report by Sir William Beveridge*. London: Inter-Departmental Commission on Social Insurance and Allied Services.

Brockington, F. (1958) *World Health*. Harmondsworth: Penguin.

Brown, T. M., Cueto, M. and Fee, E. (2006) 'The World Health Organization and the transition from "international" to "global" public health', *American Journal of Public Health* 96(1): 62–72.

Burr, S. (1988) 'Health human rights and international law', *American Society of International Law Proceedings* 82: 122–123.

Candau, M. G. (1957) 'World health catalysts', *American Journal of Public Health* 47(6): 675–81.

Chapman, A. and Russell, S. (eds.) (2002) *Core Obligations: Building a Framework for Economic, Social, and Cultural Rights*. New York: Intersentia.

Chen, L. C. and Berlinguer, G. (2001) 'Health equity in a globalizing world', in Evans, T. (ed.) *Challenging Inequities in Health: From Ethics to Action*, Oxford: Oxford University Press.

Chisholm, B. C. (1951) 'Is the World Health Organisation succeeding in its work?', in Pollak, S. W. (ed.) *Uphill: Nine Leading Figures on UN's Progress and Difficulties*. London: United Nations Association 24–33.

Commission on Human Rights (1950) Sixth Session. Compilation of the Comments of Governments on the Draft International Covenant on Human Rights and on the Proposed Additional Articles. E/CN.4/365. 22 March.

—— (1951a) Draft International Covenant on Human Rights and Measures of Implementation. Suggestions Submitted by the Director-General of the World Health Organization. Seventh Session. Item 3(b). UN Document E/CN.4/544. 18 April 1951.

—— (1951b) Seventh Session E/CN.4/SR.223. 13 June 1951.

—— (1951c) Report of the Seventh Session. E/1992. 45.

—— (1952a) Draft International Covenant on Human Rights and Measures of Implementation. E/CN.4/650. 10 March 1952.

—— (1952b) E/CN.4/L.79/rev.1.

—— (1952c) Draft International Covenants on Human Rights and Measures of Implementation. Article—* of the draft covenant on economic, social and cultural rights: Text adopted by the Commission at its 296th meeting, on 15 May. E/CN.4/666/Add.9. 16 May.

—— (1953) Tenth Session. Draft International Covenants on Human Rights and Measures of Implementation. Existing Procedures for Periodic Reporting to Specialized Agencies. E/CN.4/590/Add. 5. 9 December.

CESCR (1994) Summary Record of the Forty-Second Meeting, 6 December 1993. E/C.12/1993/SR.42. 23 November.

—— (2000) Substantive Issues Arising in the Implementation of the International Covenant on Economic, Social and Cultural Rights: The Right to the Highest Attainable Standard of Health. General Comment No. 14, 22nd Sess., Agenda Item 3. U.N. Doc. E/C.12/2000/4.

Cueto, M. (2004) 'The Origins of Primary Health Care and Selective Primary Health Care', *American Journal of Public Health* 94: 1864–74.

Djukanovic, V. and Mach, E. P. (1975) *Alternative Approaches to Meeting Basic Health Needs in Developing Countries*. Geneva: World Health Organization.

ECOSOC (1952) Res. 440 (XIV). Official Records of the Economic and Social Council. Fourteenth Session. Supp. 4 (Annex I). E/2256. 30 July.

—— (1956) Resolution 624B(XXII). Periodic reports on human Rights and studies of specific rights or groups of rights. 1 August.

—— (1980) E/1980/24.

Evang, K. (1973) 'Human rights: health for everyone', *World Health* 3–11.

Fluss, S. S., Gutteridge, F. (1990) 'Some contributions of the World Health Organization to legislation', in Lambo, T. A. and Day, S. B. (eds.) *Issues in Contemporary International Health*. New York: Plenum Medical Book Co.

Fuenzalida-Puelma, H. L. and Connor, S. S. (1989) *The Right to Health in the Americas: A Comparative Constitutional Study*. Washington: Pan American Health Organization.

Goodman, N. M. (1948) 'First World Health Assembly', *Lancet* 14 August, 252: 265–66.

Gordon, R. I. and Assefa, B. (2006) 'A tale of two initiatives: Where propaganda meets facts in the debate over America's healthcare', *Seattle Journal for Social Justice* 4: 693–744.

Gorove, K. (2004) 'Shifting norms in international health law', *American Society of International Law Proceedings* 98: 18–19.

Grant, J. B. (1948) 'International trends in healthcare', *American Journal of Public Health* 38: 381–97.

Gruskin, S., Mills, E. J. and Tarantola, D. (2007) 'History, principles, and practice of health and human rights', *Lancet* 4 August, 370: 449–454.

Gutteridge, F. (1963) 'The World Health Organization: Its scope and achievements', *Temple Law Quarterly* 37(1): 1–14.

Hoole, F. W. (1976) *Politics and Budgeting in the World Health Organization.* Bloomington: Indiana University Press.

Horwitz, A. (1983) 'Changing concepts of health and health services: New opportunities for nutrition promotion', *Bulletin of the Pan American Health Organization* 17(1): 61–76.

International Conference of American States (1948) Resolution XXX. Art. XI.

Jacobson H. K. (1974) 'WHO: Medicine, regionalism, and managed politics', in Cox, R. W. and Jacobson H. K. (eds.) *The Anatomy of Influence: Decision Making in International Organization*, New Haven: Yale University Press.

Jamar, S.D. (1994) 'The international human right to health', *Southern University Law Review* 22: 1–62.

Katz, A. (2007) Letter from Alison Katz to WHO Director-General Margaret Chan. January 2007 (copy on file with author).

King, M. (1974) 'Personal healthcare: The quest for a human right', in *Human Rights in Health* London: Elsevier 227–38.

Kirby, M. (1999) 'The right to health fifty years on: Still skeptical?', *Health and Human Rights* 4(1): 6–25.

Konstitutsiia SSSR (1936) Art. 120; reprinted in Georgadze, M. (ed.) (1982) *USSR, Sixty Years of the Union 1922–1982: A Collection of Legislative Acts and Other Documents.* Moscow: Progress Publishers 229–59.

Lakin, A.E. (2001) 'The World Health Organisation and the right to health'. PhD Dissertation. King's College. London, England.

Lancet (1945) 'Health and the nations', *Lancet*, 11 August, 246: 177.

—— (1948) 'International health or world health?' *Lancet*, 14 August, 252: 260.

Leary, V. (1993) *Implementation of the International Covenant on Economic, Social and Cultural Rights – Day of General Discussion on the Right to Health*, E/C.12/1993/WP.27.

Lee, K. (2009) *The World Health Organization.* London: Routledge.

Litsios, S. (2005) 'The health, poverty, and development merry-go-round: the tribulations of WHO', in Gunn, S. W., Mansourian, P. B., Davies, A. M. and Piel, A. (eds.). *Understanding the Global Dimensions of Health.* New York: Springer: 15–33.

MacDonald, T. H. (2005) *Health, Trade and Human Rights.* Oxford: Radcliffe Publishing.

—— (2008) *Health, Human Rights and the United Nations: Inconsistent Aims and Inherent Contradictions?* Oxford: Radcliffe Publishing.

Mahler, H. (1975) 'Further thoughts on WHO's mission', *WHO Chronicle* 29(7): 254.

Masters, R. D. (1947) *International Organization in the Field of Public Health.* Washington: Carnegie Endowment.

McKeown, T. (1976) *The Role of Medicine: Dream, Mirage, or Nemesis?* London: Nuffield Provincial Hospitals Trust.

McMichael, A. J. and Beaglehole, R. (2000) 'The changing global context of public health', *Lancet*, 5 August, 356: 495–99.

Meier, B. M. and Fox, A. M. (2008) 'Development as health: employing the collective right to development to achieve the goals of the individual right to health', *Human Rights Quarterly* 30: 259–355.

Meier, B. M. and Mori, L. M. (2005) 'The highest attainable standard: advancing a collective human right to public health', *Columbia Human Rights Law Review* 37: 101–47.

Millen, J., Irwin, A. and Kim, J. Y. (2000) 'Introduction: what is growing? Who is dying?', in Millen, J., Irwin, A., Kim, J. Y. and Gershman, J. (eds.) *Dying for Growth: Global Inequality and the Health of the Poor*. Monroe: Common Courage Press.

Mingst, K. A. (1990) 'The United States and the World Health Organization', in Karns, M. P. and, Mingst, K. A. (eds.) *The United States and Multilateral Institutions: Patterns of Changing Instrumentality and Influence*. Boston: Unwin Hyman.

Nielsen, H. K. (1999) *The World Health Organisation: Implementing the Right to Health*, Copenhagen: Europublishers.

Pannenborg, C. O. (1979) *A New International Health Order: An Inquiry into the International Relations of World Health and Medical Care*. Alphen aan den Rijn: Sijthoff and Noordhoff.

Parran, H. (1946) *Remarks at Concluding Meeting of International Health Conference*. UN Doc. E/H/VP/18. at 2.

Roemer, M.I. (1984) 'Analysis of health services systems – a general approach', in Pannenborg, C. O. (ed.) *Reorienting Health Services: Application of a Systems Approach*. New York: Plenum Press.

Roosevelt, F. D. (1941) *President Franklin Roosevelt's 6 January 1941 State of the Union Address*. The Public Papers of Franklin D. Roosevelt, Vol. 9.

Roscam Abbing, H. D. C. (1979) *International Organizations in Europe and the Right to Health Care*. Deventer: Kluwer: Deventer, the Netherlands.

Rosen, G. (1974) *From Medical Policy to Social Medicine: Essays on the History of Health Care*. Baltimore, MD: Johns Hopkins Press.

Ryle, J. A. (1948) *Changing Disciplines: Lectures on the History, Method and Motives of Social Pathology*. London: Oxford University Press.

Sand, R. (1934) *L'Économie Humaine par la Médecine Sociale*. Paris: Rieder.

Siddiqi, J. (1995) *World Health and World Politics: The World Health Organization and the UN System*. Columbus: University of South Carolina Press.

Štampar, A. (1949) 'Suggestions relating to the Constitution of an International Health Organization', *WHO Official Records*. 1(Annex 9).

Starrels, J. M. (1985) *The World Health Organization: Resisting Third World Ideological Pressures*. Washington: Heritage Foundation.

Stuttaford, M. (2004) 'Balancing collective and individual rights to health and health care', *Law, Social Justice and Global Development Journal*. See http://www2.warwick.ac.uk/fac/soc/law/elj/lgd/2004_1/stuttaford/

Tarantola, D. (2008) 'A perspective on the history of health and human rights: from the Cold War to the gold war', *Journal of Public Health Policy* 29: 42–53.

Taylor, A. L. (1991) '*The World Health Organization and the right to health*', unpublished thesis, Columbia Law School; New York.

—— (1992) 'Making the World Health Organization work: a legal framework for universal access to the conditions for health', 18 *American Journal of Law and Medicine* 301–346.

Taylor, C. and Jolly, R. (1988) 'The straw men of primary healthcare', *Social Science and Medicine* 26: 971–86.

Thomas, C. and Weber, M. (2004) 'The politics of global health governance: whatever happened to "health for all by the year 2000"?' *Global Governance* 10(2): 187–205.

Toebes, B. C. A. (1999) *The Right to Health as a Human Right in International Law*. Antwerp: Intersentia.

UDHR (1948) Universal Declaration of Human Rights, Art 7, G.A. Res. 217A(III), U.N. GAOR, 3d Sess., at 71, U.N. Doc. A/810.

UN (1945) United Nations Charter, signed at San Francisco, 26 June, entered into force on 24 October, 1945. Preamble.

—— (1950a) *United Nations. These Rights and Freedoms*. UN Department of Public Information.

—— (1951) Memorandum from UN Division of Human Rights G. Brand to UN Division of Human Rights Assistant Director E. Schwelb. Some Further Reactions on the Articles on Economic, Social and Cultural Rights and Their Implementation Adopted by the Commission on Human Rights at Its Seventh Session. 9 June.

—— (1952) Activities of the United Nations and the Specialized Agencies in the Field of Economic, Social and Cultural Rights. E/CN.4/364/Rev.1. January.

—— (1954) Memorandum from UN Division of Human Rights Acting Director Egon Schwelb to UN Department of Social Affairs Acting Principal Director John P. Humphrey. Draft International Covenants on Human Rights – Implementation of GA Resolution of 4 December 1954. 9 December.

—— (1957a) Report to the General Assembly on the Human Rights Convention. A/2929.

—— (1957b) A/C.3/L.589.

—— (1957c) A/C.3/L/593.

—— (1957d) A/C.3/SR.746.

—— (1957e) Memorandum from UN Division of Human Rights Director John P. Humphrey to UN Under-Secretary for Economic and Social Affairs Philippe de Seynes. 747th Meeting of the Third Committee. SO 221/9(1). 31 January.

—— (1964) General Assembly Resolution 1921 (XVIII).

—— (1968a) *The United Nations and Human Rights*. New York: United Nations.

—— (1968b) General Assembly. International Year for Human Rights. Measures and Activities Undertaken in Connexion with the International Year for Human Rights. Report of the Secretary-General. A/7195. 24 September.

—— (1974) Annual Report of the Administrative Committee on Co-ordination 1973–74. E/5488.

—— (1997) Renewing the United Nations: A Programme for Reform. Report of the Secretary-General. U.N. GAOR. 51st Session. UN Doc. A/51/950.

—— (2000) Millennium Development Goals. See http://www.un.org/millenniumgoals/index.html.

—— (2003) The Right of Everyone to the Enjoyment of the Highest Attainable Standard of Physical and Mental Health: Report of the Special Rapporteur, Paul Hunt. U.N. ESCOR, Commission on Human Rights, 59th Sess., Agenda Item 10. U.N. Doc. E/CN.4/2003/58. 13 February.

United Nations Conference on Food and Agriculture (1943) Declaration, Hot Springs. May 1943. *American Journal of International Law [Supp]* 37(4): 159–192.

US Department of State (1944) *The United Nations, Dumbarton Oaks Proposal for a General International Organization*. Washington, DC: US Government Printing Office.

van Zile Hyde, H. (1951) Letter from US Representative to WHO Executive Board H. van Zile Hyde to WHO Director-General Brock Chisholm. 28 March.

—— (1953) 'The nature of the World Health Organization', *Public Health Reports* 68(6): 601–605.

Vigne, C. (1979) 'Droit à la santé et coordination', in The Right to Health as a Human Right: Workshop, The Hague,27–29 July 1978. Alphen aan den Rijn: Sijthoff and Noordhoff.

Walsh, J. A. and Warren, K. S. (1979) 'Selective primary healthcare: an interim strategy for disease control in developing countries', *New England Journal of Medicine* 301(8): 967–74.

WHO (1946) Constitution. Geneva: World Health Organization.

—— (1951a) Letter from WHO Director-General Brock Chisholm to UN Assistant Secretary-General H. Laugier. SOA 317/1/01(2). 12 January.

—— (1951b) Letter from WHO Division of Co-ordination of Planning and Liaison William P. Forrest to UN Assistant Secretary-General Henri Laugier. SOA 317/1/01(2). 8 February.

—— (1951c) Letter from WHO Director General to UN Secretary General. 7 March. Available at ECOSOC E/1880/Add3.

—— (1951d) Executive Board. Eighth Session. EB8/39. 2 June.

—— (1952) 'Work of WHO 1952 – Annual Report of the Director-General to the World Health Assembly and to the United Nations', *Official Records of the World Health Organization*, 45. E/2416

—— (1953) Letter from WHO Director-General M. G. Candau to UN Assistant Secretary-General Georges-Picot. CC 4–6 HUMAN Rights OER. 9 November.

—— (1955) Letter from WHO Director of Offices of External Relations and Technical Assistance to UN Under Secretary of the Department of Economic and Social Affairs. SOA 317/1/01(2). 18 January.

—— (1957) Letter from WHO Director-General M. G. Candau to UN Deputy Under-Secretary for Economic and Social Affairs Martin Hill. SOA 317/15/01(2). 19 February.

—— (1958a) Memorandum from WHO P. Bertrand to WHO P. Dorolle. Participation de L'OMS aux Rapports Périodiques sur les Droits de L'Homme. 23 July.

—— (1958b) Memorandum from WHO B. Howell to WHO. P. Bertrand. Periodic Reports on Human Rights. Notes of Conversation with Mrs. Bruce of the UN Department of Human Rights – 4 July 1958. 7 July.

—— (1959a) Memorandum from PHA Section to WHO Assistant Director-General P. M. Kaul. Human Rights Commission, 15th Session, Right of the Child. 28 January.

—— (1959b) Memorandum from WHO Director, Liaison Office with United Nations to WHO Deputy-Director General. Report on the Fifteenth Session of the Commission on Human Rights. 21 April.

—— (1959c) Letter from WHO Deputy Director-General P. Dorolle to UN Division of Human Rights Director J. Humphrey. 24 February.

—— (1964a) Memorandum from LEG Director F. Gutteridge to P. Dorolle. Discrimination Against Women. 12 February.

—— (1964b) Letter from WHO Deputy-Director P. Dorolle to UN Division of Human Rights Director John P. Humphrey. N64/180/5(2). 17 February.

—— (1965) Letter from WHO Assistant Director-General L. Bernard to UN Director of the Division of Human Rights John P. Humphrey. 16 December.

—— (1972) Notes for the Record. Meeting with Mr. Marc Schreiber, Director, United Nations Division of Human Rights – Friday, 5 May 1972. 4N64/372/1. 29 May.

—— (1973) Interrelationships between Health Programmes and Socioeconomic Development, Geneva: World Health Organization.

—— (1975) Director-General Report, OR 229, pp. 7–9.

—— (1977) WHA 30.43.

—— (1978) Primary Health Care: Report of the International Conference of Primary Health Care Alma-Ata, USSR, September 6–12 1978. Geneva: World Health Organization.
—— (1979) WHO EB63.R21.
—— (1981) *Global Strategy for Health for All by the Year 2000*, Geneva: World Health Organization.
—— (1988) *World Health Assembly. Strengthening Primary Health Care.* WHA Res. 41.34. 13 May.
—— (2004) *Treating 3 Million by 2005: Making It Happen: The WHO Strategy*. Geneva: WHO.
—— (2008) *World Health Report: Primary Health Care – Now More than Ever*. Geneva: World Health Organization.
World Medical Association (1951) Letter from World Medical Association Secretary-General Louis H. Bauer to UN Secretary-General Trygvie Lie. 9 October.

9 The human right to health in an age of market hegemony

Paul O'Connell[1]

1 Introduction

Recognition that individuals and communities enjoy a human right to health has, progressively, come to be widely accepted at the international, regional and domestic levels. First with the post-Second World War consensus on human rights, and subsequently through the reinvigorated health and human rights movement, which emerged in response to the HIV/AIDS pandemics in the early 1990s, a consensus has emerged on the centrality of health as a basic human right and on the concomitant obligations of States to respect, protect and fulfil the various aspects of this most basic of rights (Gruskin and Tarantola 2005). Notwithstanding the widespread diffusion of the language of the right to health, the modern era of globalisation has been characterised by 'bourgeoning health inequalities' on many levels (Meier 2007: 545). This chapter seeks to contribute to explaining this disjuncture by problematising the relationship between the right to health and the economic, social and political doctrines that have characterised the era of globalisation. We begin by briefly highlighting some of the central principles of the right to health as recognised in international human rights law, before then going on to set out the current context within which the right to health is asserted through a discussion of the nature of contemporary globalisation, noting in particular the centrality of neo-liberal ideology and 'market solutions'. Following this, we consider the tensions between the assertion of the right to health and the 'common sense' of market hegemony, before concluding that a substantive commitment to the right to health may very well require a conscious break with the logic of contemporary globalisation.

2 The human right to health

It was not until the twentieth century, following the atrocities of the Second World War, that the concept of human rights in general, and the right to health in particular, gained widespread institutional support. Two noteworthy milestones in the recognition of the right to health in international human rights law were the adoption of the Constitution of the World Health Organization (WHO) in 1946, which provides that the 'enjoyment of the highest attainable standard of health is one of the fundamental rights of every human being without distinction of race, religion, political belief, economic or social condition'; and subsequently the Universal Declaration of Human Rights (UDHR) in 1948, Article 25 of which states that 'everyone has the right to a standard of living adequate for the health and wellbeing of himself and his family, including food, clothing, housing and medical care'. These moral and aspirational obligations were subsequently transformed into binding legal norms with the adoption of the International Covenant on Economic, Social and Cultural Rights (ICESCR) in 1966. Article 12 of the ICESCR, which Gross calls 'the foremost international legal document addressing the right to health' (Gross 2007: 293), guarantees 'the right of everyone to the enjoyment of the highest attainable standard of physical and mental health'. It also sets out an illustrative list of specific measures to be taken by States in order to achieve the full realisation of this right, the most pertinent for present purposes being the obligation on States to create the 'conditions which would assure to all medical service and medical attention in the event of sickness'.

2.1 The right to health in general

It can be seen from this expansive statement that the 'right to health is one of the most extensive and complex human rights in the international lexicon' (Hunt 2007: 8), extending far beyond the provision of medical services to encompass, as it must, all of the underlying determinants of health. However, for the purposes of the discussion here, the focus will be limited to that aspect of the right to health which gives rise to an entitlement to healthcare, understood in its simplest terms as clinical and therapeutic measures that health professionals and medical systems provide for sick people.[2] In what follows, we will examine how the normative content of this aspect of the right to health has been delineated at an international level, through the work of both the Committee on Economic, Social and Cultural Rights (CESCR), the body established to monitor compliance with the ICESCR, and the subsequent and supplementary work of the UN Special Rapporteur on the Right to Health. Particular attention will be given to the principles of non-discrimination and non-retrogression, both of which are central to the right to health.

At the outset, it should be said that the right to health, belonging to the class of socio-economic rights, has traditionally been one of the 'poor cousins' within the international human rights regime. One of the consequences of this historical dispensation is that the right to health, in common with most other socio-economic rights, suffers from a relative dearth of jurisprudence to clarify its nature and content. In order to overcome this deficiency as it relates to socio-economic rights in general, the CESCR has developed the practice of adopting 'General Comments' to clarify the normative character of the various rights guaranteed in the ICESCR. In relation to the right to health, the most important of these to date is General Comment 14, which represents 'perhaps the most successful attempt to infuse concrete substance into the right to health' (Gross 2007: 300), and which clarifies the normative character of the right to health under Article 12

ICESCR, setting guidelines on the nature of States' obligations with respect to this right, and identifying potential violations of it. The principles established initially in General Comment 14 have subsequently been reinforced and otherwise elaborated upon by the work of the Special Rapporteur on the Right to Health.

After reaffirming the importance, in general terms, of the human right to health, General Comment 14 proceeds to delineate the normative content of the right to health under Article 12 ICESCR. First and foremost, the CESCR point out that the right to health does not amount to a right to be healthy *per se*, but instead entails a 'right to the enjoyment of a variety of facilities, goods, services and conditions necessary for the realization of the highest attainable standard of health' (UN-CESCR 2000: para 9). The right to health is then defined in expansive terms, encompassing an entitlement to, *inter alia*, safe, potable water and adequate sanitation, an adequate supply of food, nutrition and housing, as well as timely and appropriate healthcare (UN-CESCR 2000: para 11). Furthermore, all of these aspects of the right to health must comply with four essential criteria: availability, accessibility, acceptability and quality. Availability requires that functioning public health facilities, goods and services, as well as programmes, are available in sufficient quantity within the State. Acceptability means that all health facilities, goods and services must, *inter alia*, be 'respectful of medical ethics and culturally appropriate', while quality requires that all health facilities, goods and services are 'scientifically and medically appropriate and of good quality' (UN-CESCR 2000: para 12).

The requirement of accessibility is given the greatest attention in General Comment 14, and is also the most pertinent of the criteria for the purposes of the present discussion. In the context of the right to health, accessibility has four overlapping dimensions to it: (a) health facilities, goods and services 'must be accessible to all, especially the most vulnerable or marginalized sections of the population, in law and in fact, without discrimination'; (b) health facilities, goods and services must be physically accessible, in the broadest sense of that term; (c) all health facilities must be economically accessible, in the sense that '[payment] for health-care services . . . has to be based on the principle of equity, ensuring that these services, whether privately or publicly provided, are affordable for all, including socially disadvantaged groups'; (d) the requirement of accessibility entails an element of information accessibility, encompassing 'the right to seek, receive and impart information and ideas concerning health issues' (UN-CESCR 2000: para 12).

2.2 The principles of non-discrimination and non-retrogression

Pursuant to Articles 2(2) and 3 ICESCR, the principle of non-discrimination is central to the normative character of the right to health under Article 12. The CESCR points out that:

> With respect to the right to health equality of access to health care and health

> services has to be emphasized. States have a special obligation to provide those who do not have sufficient means with the necessary health insurance and health-care facilities, and to prevent any discrimination on . . . prohibited grounds in the provision of health care and health services, especially with respect to the core obligations of the right to health.
>
> (UN-CESCR 2000: para 19)

In this context, the CESCR goes on to note that '[inappropriate] health resource allocation can lead to discrimination that may not be overt' (UN-CESCR 2000: para 19). In this manner, the Committee acknowledges that *de facto* discrimination in access to healthcare services resulting from ostensibly benign policies can contravene the non-discrimination facet of the right to health under Article 12 ICESCR.

Having delineated the normative character of the right to health, the CESCR then considers the legal obligations placed on States in order to fulfil their obligations under the Covenant. The Committee first notes that the concept of progressive realisation, contained in Article 2(1) ICESCR, in no way diminishes States' obligations with respect to the right to health; rather, 'progressive realization means that States parties have a specific and continuing obligation to move as expeditiously and effectively as possible towards the full realisation of Article 12' (UN-CESCR 2000: para 31). One consequence of this general obligation is that 'any retrogressive measure taken in relation to the right to health' is presumptively impermissible (UN-CESCR 2000: para 32). In relation to the more specific obligations placed on States, the CESCR, in common with its practice in relation to other rights, states that the right to health imposes three levels of obligation on States Parties: the obligations to respect, protect and fulfil. The CESCR further elaborates on this typology in the following terms:

> The obligation to *respect* requires States to refrain from interfering directly or indirectly with the enjoyment of the right to health. The obligation to *protect* requires States to take measures that prevent third parties from interfering with article 12 guarantees. Finally, the obligation to *fulfil* requires States to adopt appropriate legislative, administrative, budgetary, judicial, promotional and other measures towards the full realization of the right to health.
>
> (UN-CESCR 2000: para 33)

Interestingly, in further elaborating on the nature of States' obligations, the CESCR points out that the obligation to protect the right to health requires States to, among other things, ensure that 'privatization of the health sector does not constitute a threat to the availability, accessibility, acceptability or quality of health facilities' (UN-CESCR 2000: para 35).

The CESCR then sets out certain 'core obligations' of the right to health, which are subject neither to the idea of progressive realisation nor to resource constraints; the most important of which, for present purposes, is the obligation on States to 'ensure the right of access to health facilities, goods and services on a non-discriminatory basis, especially for vulnerable and marginalized groups' (UN-CESCR 2000: para 43). Having established the normative character of the right to health and States' obligations concomitant thereto, the CESCR provides an illustrative list of potential violations that emerge from the interaction of the two. The most important examples given, at least in so far as the present discussion is concerned, are; (a) that a denial of access to health facilities, goods or services to particular individuals or groups resulting from either *de jure* or *de facto* discrimination will constitute a violation of the ICESCR (UN-CESCR 2000: para 50); and that (b) 'insufficient expenditure or misallocation of public resources which results in the non-enjoyment of the right to health by individuals or groups, particularly the vulnerable or marginalized', will also be considered a violation of the Covenant (UN-CESCR 2000: para 52). These last two examples capture the ideas of non-discrimination and non-retrogression, and emphasise their centrality to the right to health.

The Special Rapporteur picks up on the various key points developed by the CESCR; in particular, the centrality of the principle of non-discrimination permeates all of the Special Rapporteur's reports. Indeed, in his first report he notes that '[n]on-discrimination and equal treatment are among the most crucial components of the right to health', and as a consequence, 'international human rights law proscribes any discrimination in access to healthcare [on] prohibited grounds . . . which has the intention or effect of impairing the equal enjoyment of the right to health' (Hunt 2003: 8). Later in the same report, he notes that the States' obligations to ensure access, without discrimination, to all health facilities, goods and services is of increased relevance in the case of 'the most vulnerable [and] marginalized sections of the populations'. In a subsequent report, the Special Rapporteur argues that the very essence of the right to health is 'an effective and integrated health system', which 'must be accessible to all, not just the wealthy but also those living in poverty' (Hunt 2006: 5). Also in his most recent report, the Special Rapporteur stresses that equality and non-discrimination 'are among the most fundamental elements of international human rights, including the [right to health]' and that ensuring equal and non-discriminatory access to healthcare services, with a proverbial preferential option for the socially excluded, is one of the core obligations imposed on States (Hunt 2008: 11, 14).

In similar terms to the CESCR, the Special Rapporteur also stresses the importance of the principle of non-retrogression with respect to the right to health. In particular, in his most recent report he notes that:

> [An] . . . implication arising from progressive realization is that at least the present level of enjoyment of the [right to health] must be maintained. This is sometimes known as the principle of non-retrogression. Although rebuttable in certain limited circumstances, there is a strong presumption that measures lowering the present enjoyment of the right to health are impermissible.
>
> (Hunt 2008: 14)

It can therefore be seen, from both the work of the CESCR and the Special

Rapporteur, that the principles of non-discrimination and non-retrogression are central elements of the international human right to health. In the next section, we will digress slightly to spell out the context of neo-liberal global hegemony, before then going on to consider the extent to which the principles and policies characteristic of the era of globalisation impact on individual and community enjoyment of the right to health.

3 The triumph of 'the market'

The last quarter of the twentieth century and the early years of this century were defined, in many respects, as the era of globalisation (Held and McGrew 2002). The language of globalisation was (and remains) ubiquitous, with a concomitant burgeoning of scholarly literature and increased public consciousness of the term. Without delving too deeply into the ongoing debates and controversies about the precise nature, contours and definitions of globalisation here, it will be accepted, *arguendo*, that the current era of globalisation has been, first and foremost, an era of neo-liberal global hegemony. The point is made cogently by Jan Aart Scholte, who notes that:

> Neoliberalism has generally prevailed as the reigning policy framework in contemporary globalization . . . Most governments . . . have promoted neo-liberal policies towards globalization, especially since the early 1980s . . . agencies such as the IMF, the WTO and the [OECD] have continually linked globalization with liberalization. Champions of neoliberal globalization have also abounded in commercial circles, particularly in the financial markets and among managers of transborder firms. Business associations like the International Organization of Employers and the World Economic Forum . . . have likewise figured as bastions of neo-liberalism. In the mass-media, major business-orientated newspapers . . . have generally supported neoliberalism. In academic quarters, mainstream economists have extolled the virtues of global free markets . . . Given this widespread hold on centres of power, neoliberalism has generally ranked as policy orthodoxy in respect of globalization. Indeed in the late twentieth century neoliberal ideas gained widespread unquestioned acceptance as 'commonsense'
>
> (Scholte 2005: 39)

In light of this assessment, we can say that, in truth, the age of globalisation is better understood as being an age of market hegemony: an era in which all of the governments of the world, whether through ideological commitment or under the pressures of market discipline, embraced and implemented orthodox neo-liberal policy prescriptions (O'Connell 2007). With this understanding, we can now fruitfully move on to look at the impact of neo-liberal hegemony on the right to health; however, before that we will take the time to spell out what we mean by neo-liberalism, and what has contributed to it emerging as the 'common sense' world view over the last quarter century.

Neo-liberalism is a multifaceted phenomenon, constituting an ideological world view, a set of policy prescriptions and, most fundamentally, a political project, which privileges the economic interests of small, economically powerful sections of society, both domestically and globally. As a political project, it is essential to stress that the ascendancy of neo-liberal common sense was not, as is often implied, a natural and neutral phenomenon. Rather, it was the result of an inherently political project, as Leys notes:

> Globalisation was . . . a political project to defeat 'socialism'. Both the US and the British economies had experienced slow growth and declining international competitiveness in the 1960s. In both countries politics became polarised, between defenders of the post-war 'settlement' . . . in which the state played the role of both manager of the economy and provider of social services and social security . . . and those who feared that private capital risked losing its power and authority. One side of the successful campaign to roll back socialism . . . was to attack its domestic base in the labour movements through anti-union measures and higher unemployment, privatisation and reduced taxes on capital. The other side was to end controls over capital movements and reduce trade barriers, exposing the domestic workforce to competition from lower-paid workers in countries with weaker regulatory regimes – at the same time making it hard, if not impossible, for any future government to reverse these changes. The result of capital mobility was this the rapid formation of a global economy that quickly generated market forces which impinged on national states and governments much more powerfully, and led to domestic deregulation in response.
>
> (Leys 2001: 12)

Thus the era of globalisation, or in truth the era of neo-liberal market hegemony, has fundamentally been a project to both increase profit rates for capital and to assert the class power of the owners of capital (Harvey 2005).

At the level of ideology, neo-liberalism espouses a hard-edged interpretation of the classic *laissez-faire* thinking of figures such as Hobbes, Locke and Adam Smith, rebottled for the twentieth century by Hayek, Nozick, Friedman and others (Macpherson 1987; Hayek 1986; Nozick 2001). This world view holds that the centre of the moral universe is the rational, self-centred, utility-maximising individual; an individual who asks nothing of society and seeks nothing in return. From this vantage point, the collectivity of organised society and the State are necessary evils and should be ordered so as to impinge as little as possible on the autonomy of the individual. The State should protect the institution of private property, put in place the necessary framework for the operation of a free-market economy, and punish transgressions against private property; other than these limited roles, the State's functions should be strictly circumscribed (Harvey 2005: 64–7).

This ideological predisposition, in the modern era, has led to a specific set of policy prescriptions. Namely, 'taxation structures that favour capital accumulation over income redistribution, industrial policies that minimize the presence of the state in private industry, and retrenchment in welfare spending' (Prasad 2006: 4–5). Furthermore, and of particular relevance to the present discussion, neo-liberalism has championed privatisation as a central policy prescription. This essentially entails the transfer of hitherto publicly owned property, industries or services to the private sector, in exchange for the purported dual benefits of greater efficiency and reduced public spending (Herman 1995). However, the real objective behind the push to privatisation and commodification has been 'to open up new fields for capital accumulation in domains hitherto regarded off-limits to the calculus of profitability' (Harvey 2005: 160). The focal point for neo-liberals, particularly in the UK and US, was a rejection of the postwar compromise, which placed limits on corporate activity and also provided for a relatively strong welfare State.

The *raison d'être* of neo-liberalism, at least rhetorically, is to roll back this social State (Prasad 2006), although as Navarro notes, the neo-liberal rhetoric of rolling back the State belies the fact that that neo-liberal globalisation has relied heavily on strong, activist States – augmenting the manner and reasons for which the State intervenes, but not, in truth, diminishing the State's power. What neo-liberal globalisation has really been about is rolling back the State's involvement in social provision (education, healthcare, etc.) and opening up these fields to profit-making, while at the same time strengthening the State's coercive capacities and its pro-capital, market-friendly regulatory functions (Navarro 2007). This means that, contrary to some common wisdom, the nation State has not been rendered impotent in the era of globalisation, rather the State is 'constrained to use its power to advance the process of commodification' (Leys 2001: 2).

It is interesting to note that in the context of the current global economic crisis some authors are claiming that '[capital's] reign has come to an end in a vicious crash, with ruined lives, bankrupt nations, and the free market model in tatters' (Andrews 2009: 60). Such pronouncements about the demise of neo-liberalism should, however, be viewed with a healthy degree of scepticism, in light of the fact that international financial institutions, such as the International Monetary Fund (IMF), consider the departures from free-market orthodoxy, and massive government interventions necessitated by the current economic crisis, to be aberrant steps – necessary in the short term before a return to business as usual (Collyns 2008: 19–20; Blanchard 2008: 10). It is also notable that US President Barak Obama has appointed as one of his chief advisers in addressing the crisis Paul Volcker, who was also one of the leading lights in the ascendancy of neo-liberalism (Harvey 2005: 1–2). Furthermore, talk of the demise of neo-liberalism turns, in many respects, on one's understanding of what 'neo-liberalism' means. If you view it simply as the collection of policy prescriptions that characterised the last 20 years or so (deregulation, privatisation, etc.) then we may very well witness a retreat from some aspects of these policy prescriptions, at least in the short-term. If, on the other hand, you accept Harvey's contention that neo-liberalism is ultimately a catch-all term for the global realignment of class forces, the privileging and strengthening of the ruling classes *vis-à-vis* the working class (Harvey 2005), the current crisis may well be considered as enhancing and strengthening neo-liberalism; through driving down workers' wages and demands, through multiple austerity plans resulting in budget cuts, for example in health, which in turns open the way for greater reliance on private sector provision.

The context, then, in which the right to health is asserted, advanced, denied and undermined is not one of some abstract 'global village'. Rather, the operative context remains one in which the logic of the market is advanced as the only viable means through which human interaction on all of its levels can be pursued. With respect to healthcare, the prescriptions of privatisation and commodification are presented as the common-sense solutions to address people's healthcare needs and demands, while the reality is that these policy prescriptions serve, first and foremost, to open up new avenues of profit realisation for both domestic and global economic elites. Appreciating this context will assist us in understanding the disjuncture between the rhetoric of the right to health and systemic denials of the right to health, and it is to concrete examples of this disjuncture that we now turn.

4 The right to health and market hegemony

The real-world fortunes, then, of the various aspects of the right to health are determined in this context of market hegemony. In this section, I want to highlight a number of areas in which the market paradigm conflicts with the human right to health – one somewhat esoteric and abstract, but no less important, and two practical. The tensions highlighted by these arguably irreducible problems raise questions about the extent to which the right to health can genuinely be realised in a context of market hegemony, or whether, instead, a substantive commitment to the protection of the right to health poses a challenge to the politico-economic doctrines that have dominated national, regional and supranational policy fora for the last two decades or more. Ultimately, the discussion in this section allows us to view the common sense of neo-liberalism through the optic of the human right to health, and thereby consider the extent to which commitment to the latter is compatible with the logic of the former.

4.1 Competing ethical foundations

The first issue we examine is a foundational conflict between the differing ways in which healthcare and access to medical facilities and treatments are viewed – on the one hand from the perspective of the right to health, and on the other hand how they are viewed through the optic of the market. The right to health is, at the very least, grounded on 'equal enjoyment of the right . . . specifically, the right to receive medical care . . . on a needs-basis' (Gross 2007: 305). In contrast, the neoliberal push to privatisation of healthcare views it as a service or commodity like any other, to be produced and provided for a profit (Leys 2001). Herman notes that privatisation and commodification are overlapping categories (Herman 1995: 3); consequently, the transfer of the provision of medical services from the public to the private sector not only entails a change in 'who' delivers the service, but more fundamentally involves a re-definition of 'what' is being provided. Healthcare, in this context, goes from being an essential public good and human right, available without arbitrary discrimination on the basis of medical need, to a market commodity or service, available, to differing degrees and at different levels of quality, to those who can pay. As Leys puts it:

> the provision of a service to fulfil collectively determined socio-political purposes ends up as a drive to find mass-produced goods that can be sold profitably. The collective needs and values that the service was originally created to serve are gradually marginalised and finally abandoned.
>
> (Leys 2001: 4)

This shift involves a fundamental redefinition of what healthcare is, and the terms on which it should be available, and it is a shift that does not sit easily with healthcare understood from the perspective of the right to health. For Pellegrino, 'health and medical care do not fit the conceptual model of commodities' because they 'center too much on the universal human needs which are much more fundamental to human flourishing than any commodity *per se*' (Pellegrino 1999: 251). He goes on to pose the contrast between the market conception of healthcare and what we might call the human rights compliant conception, in the following terms:

> The contrasts between business and professional ethics are striking. Business ethics accepts health care as a commodity, its primary principle is non-maleficence, it is investor- or corporate-centred, its attitude is pragmatic, and it legitimates self-interest, competitive edge, and unequal treatment based on unequal ability to pay. Professional ethics, on the other hand, sees health care not as a commodity but as a necessary human good, its primary principle is beneficence, and it is patient-orientated.
>
> (Pellegrino 1999: 254)

Similarly Aeyal Gross notes that it is only when the right to health is treated as inconsequential that 'health becomes a commodity or good – something that is purchased with money by those who wish to and have the means to do so' (Gross 2007: 291).

What the zealous push to privatisation and commodification fails to realise, or is incapable of realising, is that:

> Many public services, like health and education, have been publicly provided because they have been produced "for the benefit of the public". This reflects the egalitarian idea that everybody, regardless of income or foresight, should have access to a decent standard of these services, and that all in society benefit from a healthy and well-educated population.
>
> (Glyn 2006: 44–45)

This egalitarian idea predates the contemporary ascendancy of the discourse of human rights, however it is very much congruent with the fundamental principles underlying the right to health, and it is also fundamentally at variance with the operative logic of neo-liberalism. Paul Farmer sums the issue up in the following terms: '[we] thus find ourselves at a crossroads: health care can be considered a commodity to be sold, or it can be considered a basic social right. It cannot comfortably be considered both of these at the same time' (Farmer 2005: 175). This is thus the first, and most basic, level at which we see tension between the currently dominant ideological discourse and political practice and a commitment to the right to health.

4.2 *Unequal access to privatised healthcare*

The second major area of concern is the question of equal access to medical care. As Paul Farmer notes, 'inequalities of access and outcome constitute the chief drama of modern medicine' (Farmer 2005: 164). In common with the general neo-liberal push towards privatisation and commodification of heretofore non-market spheres of activity, there has been a generalised push towards greater private sector involvement in the provision of healthcare throughout the world. Indeed, healthcare is somewhat of a special case from the perspective of the dominant classes pushing neo-liberalism, because of the increased opportunities for profit accumulation presented by the healthcare sector (Filc 2005). The purported advantages of this policy prescription are greater efficiency, reduced demands on the public purse and, as the commodification processes becomes more entrenched, an emphasis on 'consumer choice'. This push to privatisation, however, has potentially serious consequences for the idea of access to healthcare enjoyed on a non-discriminatory basis, which is at the heart of the international human right to health. As Aeyal Gross notes, 'a major challenge to health rights is the maintenance of a public health system with equal access in the face of the transfer of medical services to private or semi-private processes, where they become available for a fee' (Gross 2007: 331). Privatisation, thus, represents one of the primary sites of conflict between the ideal of the human right to health and the logic of market hegemony.

We begin our discussion in this context, as we must, with an examination of the US healthcare system. Due to the fact that the US has historically relied on for-profit provision as a central element of its healthcare system – far more so than any other developed country (Oberlander 2006) – it provides the primary 'test case' for an assessment of the likely impact of privatisation on access to healthcare. The most immediately striking feature of health, in general, in the US is the fundamental inequality that marks it, as one commentator notes:

> [in the US today] the most advantaged portions of the population . . . experience levels of longevity and health that approach the current biologically attainable maxima . . . In contrast, the least advantaged . . . experience levels of health and life expectancy only somewhat better than humankind prior to the industrial and medical revolutions of the past seven centuries.
>
> (House 2001: 524)

While this chasm between health levels correlates with race, gender, disability and a number of other indicia, the salient feature that marks both differences in health, quality of life, etc., and inequalities in access to healthcare is social class (Blacksher 2008). Put simply, the US free-market model provides the highest attainable standard of health, but only for those who can afford it.

With respect to access to healthcare services, the US model of delivery means that timely access to the best medical care is available to those who can pay for it, primarily through the medium of private health insurance. Because of this, the clearest indicator of the extent to which the US healthcare system provides effective access to its services is an assessment of the levels of health insurance coverage. This, of course, brings us to the great scandal of the US healthcare system: the numbers of uninsured. Estimates of America's uninsured vary, but a recent study by Rowland and Shartzer argues that a snapshot of 2006 would show 47 million Americans – or 18 per cent of the population under the age of 65 – without health insurance (Rowland and Shartzer 2008: 619). The authors of this report stress, however, that health insurance coverage is not a static matter, and that in the two-year period from 2004–2005 as many as 82 million people, or one-third of the American population under the age of 65, would have been without health insurance for at least one month (Rowland and Shartzer 2008: 620). This is not merely inequitable in an abstract sense: as the authors note, in 2006 as many as 22,000 'excess deaths' occurred as a result of individuals not having medical insurance and therefore being unable to access essential medical care (Rowland and Shartzer 2008: 618). Vicente Navarro goes even further, and argues that as many as 100,000 people die in the US every year due to lack of access to essential medical care (Navarro 2007: 16).

Irrespective of which of these startling figures is more accurate, the key point is that tens of millions of Americans are denied equal access to essential medical care, due to the for-profit basis of US healthcare provision, and this is literally a matter of life and death for tens of thousands of people every year. Some commentators will be quick to argue that these inequalities are a result of excessive interference in the market, or some other external force preventing the market from working its magic (US Federal Trade Commission and US Department of Justice 2004). However, Jonathan Oberlander argues strongly against this view – for him:

> the problem in U.S. health policy is not with politicians distorting the market, but with the market itself . . . Markets ration by price and ability to pay, and the American experience demonstrates that they are predictably regressive in their distributional implications for medical care.
>
> (Oberlander 2006: 262)

He concludes that continued reliance on for-profit solutions in the delivery of healthcare services will lead to growing numbers of uninsured, spiralling health costs (putting the lie to the claims of cost-efficiency associated with neo-liberal policy prescriptions) and greater inequality in access to healthcare services. For

Oberlander, this is 'the inescapable conclusion of the history of U.S. health policy' (2006: 263).

The significance of the US example is that its model of healthcare delivery, with greater involvement of for-profit corporations, for example, has been pushed (by corporations themselves, their trade representative bodies, the US government and international financial institutions) and generally adopted throughout both the developed and developing world in the era of global neo-liberal hegemony (Maarse 2006; Martinsen and Vrangbæk 2008; and Farmer 2005). In consequence, countries such as Ireland, where the Minister for Health has zealously pushed the privatisation agenda, have seen the exacerbation of access problems latent in their public healthcare system. In that case, it is claimed, as is the norm, that greater private-sector involvement in the form of private hospital co-location on the grounds of public hospitals, State funding for public patients to purchase certain acute medical services from private providers, and various other vehicles, will result in more efficient and more cost-effective delivery of health services (Harney 2005; Redmond 2005). However, the reality is that the pursuit of these policies has been seen to be both un-economical on its own terms, and furthermore as contributing to increased inequality in access to essential services and undermining the quality of services available in public hospitals (O'Connell 2005).

Indeed, a recent report, published jointly by a non-profit health provider and an independent research centre, concluded that in Ireland, 'the operative logic of health policy in recent years, with its favouring of private sector provision, would seem [to be leading] to greater inequity' (Adelaide Hospital Society and Jesuit Centre for Faith and Justice 2007: 17). Similarly, Pollock has argued that the steady move in the UK from the ideal of a universal, comprehensive and free medical service, as embodied in the NHS at its inception, to a user-pays, US-style market system of provision has resulted in 'inequities of all kinds [being] aggravated, not reduced, and new inequities . . . created' (Pollock 2005: 35). Similarly, countries such as South Africa, Tanzania, Guatemala (O'Connell 2005) and Israel (Filc 2005; Gross 2007) have seen greater inequality in access to healthcare concomitant with greater private sector, for-profit involvement.

On a more fundamental level, the problem with the market-model of healthcare provision is that it not only results in increased inequality of access, but also that it normalises and rationalises such inequality. As Pellegrino puts it:

> Inequalities in distribution of services and treatments are not the concerns of free markets. Denial of care for patients who could not pay were not unknown in the past. But they were not legitimated as they are in a free market system where patients are expected to suffer the consequences of a poor choice in healthcare plans, or a decision to go uninsured or to pay only for a plan with lesser levels of coverage. In this view, inequities are unfortunate but not unjust . . . Some people simply are losers in the natural and social lottery.
>
> (Pellegrino 1999: 252)

The logic of profit maximisation in the context of healthcare provision tends strongly towards the sort of exclusion characteristic of the US model, and the increased levels of inequality and *de facto* discrimination in access experienced by countries that have more recently embraced the neo-liberal orthodoxies of privatisation and commodification. Again the point is made succinctly by Pellegrino, when he notes that 'there is no room in a free market for the non-player, the person who can't "buy in" – the poor, the uninsured, the uninsurable' (Pellegrino 1999: 253). And this logic of exclusion is fundamentally at odds with the principles of equality and non-discrimination at the heart of the right to health. Furthermore, in the countries that are moving from a more egalitarian or universal model of healthcare delivery, such as the UK and to a lesser extent Ireland, the adoption of these neo-liberal policies can reasonably be considered as retrogressive, and therefore similarly in violation of international human rights norms.

4.3 Intellectual property rights, patents and access to essential medicines

Access to essential medicines is an essential human right, derived both from the right to health and from the right to life as recognised in various international human rights treaties (Forman 2007). However, in the contemporary era the importance of this right has been challenged by the assertion of the priority of intellectual property rights, specifically in the patenting of essential medicines. Unequal access to healthcare services is therefore not the only problem thrown up by the market-driven domination of health. Another equally important and deleterious consequence of market hegemony is the problem of denial of access to essential medicines due to the prioritising of intellectual property rights over individual and group health needs. An immanent tension subsisted between the assertion of intellectual property rights, which are by their nature exclusionary, and human rights in the context of access to essential medicines, which is by its nature inclusive. This latent tension became very real with the adoption of the WTO Agreement on Trade-Related Aspects of Intellectual Property Rights (TRIPS). Coupled with the explosion of the HIV/AIDS pandemics, particularly in the developing world, the entry into force of this agreement, '[requiring] patents in everything from seeds to drugs, [made] intellectual property law literally an issue of life and death' (Chander and Sunder 2007: 566).

Prior to the adoption of the TRIPS agreement, many countries, particularly developing countries where lack of access to essential medicines is particularly acute, did not provide stringent patent protection for medicines, or provided only short-term patents, in 'large part because they took the view that the health sector met a basic need and thus should be protected from full commercialization' (Cullet 2005: 181). The TRIPS agreement, however, requires all signatories to provide stringent and extensive protection for various copyright and patent claims, including allowing for the grant of patents in all fields of technology (TRIPS Arts 27.2–3) and the grant of patents for at least 20 years (TRIPS Art 33). The stated reason for such patent protection is to incentivise research and innovation through rewarding inventors for their work (Cullet 2005: 182); the reality, of course, is that the greater insistence on the priority of intellectual property rights is in order to maximise the profits of transnational pharmaceutical companies (Shahmanesh 2007). As Cullet points out, patented drugs are far more expensive than their generic counterparts, thus realising significant profits for the patent holders (Cullet 2005: 182). But, because of the centrality of cost as a determinant of access to essential medicines, particularly in developing countries:

> the introduction of process and product patents on drugs is likely to influence access to drugs to a significant extent. There will be abrupt rises in price . . . and greater emphasis on private sector research and development. Together, these are likely to create a situation where drugs become both less accessible and less affordable.
>
> (Cullet 2005: 189)

Indeed the current data on denial of access to essential medicines is truly staggering: at present some two billion people, or one-third of the world's population, are unable to gain routine access to essential medicines. This problem is more pronounced in certain regions of the world, for example in sub-Saharan Africa, which has the highest global concentration of HIV sufferers, 72 per cent of the people requiring access to antiretroviral drugs are denied it purely, or primarily, because they cannot afford the patented drugs (Forman 2007: 337–8). In an effort to address these access problems, the governments of a number of countries, notably South Africa and Brazil, sought to use the flexibilities in the TRIPS agreement to create an exception, in the context where their countries were facing major public health crises, to the general rules so that they could make generic HIV/AIDS drug treatments available (Lazzarini 2003).[3] These initiatives, however, were met with hostility from both the pharmaceutical industry and certain Western governments, most notably the US government (Forman 2007). Ultimately, both disputes were resolved in favour of the respondent States, and subsequently the WTO issued the Doha Declaration in 2001. This declaration provided that the TRIPS agreement would not be used to prevent Member States from taking steps necessary to protect public health, including, as in this case, the issuing of compulsory licences for the manufacture of generic drugs deemed necessary to tackle a public health crisis (WTO 2001).

Despite the fact that the TRIPS agreement has these in-built flexibility mechanisms to allow governments, through compulsory licensing or parallel imports, to respond to pressing domestic healthcare problems by sidestepping the stringencies of the other TRIPS obligations, and despite the fact that these flexibilities were validated and reinforced through the Doha declaration, they remain underutilised. This is due to the pressure placed on governments, particularly but not exclusively in developing countries, to provide stringent and extensive protection for the intellectual property claims of multinational corporations, both by those corporations themselves and by Western governments – particularly the US government – through both the threat of litigation and trade sanctions (Forman 2007: 342; Gross 2007:334–5; Sell 2007).

Furthermore, the TRIPS flexibilities have been obviated by the negotiation of bi-lateral trade agreements between the US and both developed and developing countries, referred to as TRIPS-plus agreements, which include intellectual property protections even more demanding than those contained in the TRIPS agreement itself (Forman 2007; Gross 2007), such as 'data exclusivity provisions . . . prohibitions of parallel importation . . . highly restrictive conditions for issuing compulsory licences . . . expanded subject matter requirements . . . and . . . patent term extensions' (Sell 2007: 59). Following an in-depth examination of 14 such agreements, Krikorian and Szymkowiak conclude that all of these agreements:

> contain TRIPS-Plus provisions, and . . . are systematically more restrictive than the WTO standards. Therefore, these agreements increase the barriers to access to generic medicines, either by intensifying such IP protections as the existence and duration of exclusivity or by reducing the use of flexibilities such as compulsory licences and parallel imports.
>
> (Krikorian and Szymkowiak 2007: 408)

In a similar vein, Harvey and colleagues have argued that the TRIPS-plus trade agreement reached between the US and Australia has the very real potential to undermine the Australian Pharmaceutical Benefits Scheme, which is designed to make essential medicines readily available to all Australians (Harvey *et al.* 2004). The net consequence is that, notwithstanding the pious words of the Doha declaration, the 'global imposition of stringent patent rights [plays] a direct role in the high loss of life due to inaccessible medicines' (Forman 2007: 343).

Similar to the impact of greater privatisation of healthcare provision, more stringent intellectual property rules can be seen to be contrary to both the principles of non-discrimination and non-retrogression. At the level of discrimination, the patenting of essential medicines inevitably results in a marked increase in their cost, thereby rationing access on the basis of ability to pay; this in turn fundamentally reduces the ability of the poor and socially excluded to gain ready access to essential medicines. With respect to the principle of non-retrogression, it can be seen that many countries, for example India, had hitherto refused to grant extensive protection of patent rights with respect to essential medicines, in an effort to provide some limited form of equality of opportunity to access such medicines. Compliance with the terms of the TRIPS requires a break with these sort of practices and, due to the attendant higher prices of patented drugs, this 'directly implies a reduction in access to drugs and thus a step back in the implementation of the right to health' (Cullet 2005: 197). We therefore see two concrete examples of the logic of neo-liberal market hegemony, privatisation and commodification, contributing directly to substantial, widespread and entrenched denials of the right to health. Taken with the general, more foundational conflict between the right to health and the market conception of health discussed above, this raises serious questions about the compatibility of the two.

5 Conclusions

Alicia Yamin has recently noted that health is 'perhaps the most radical of subjects for human rights' (Yamin 2008: 1); we could go a little further and say that in the current global conjuncture health is also one of the most subversive of human rights. Indeed, the foregoing discussion of the impact of neo-liberal globalisation on the right to health provokes serious questions about the compatibility of a commitment to realising the promise of the right to health with the economic, social and political orthodoxies that prevail today. It raises the fundamental question of whether a substantive commitment to the right to health can be sustained in the confines of this market hegemony, or whether instead the right to health requires 'deep changes in the basic economic and political systems that currently define our lives' (Mercer 2004: 170), in order for its promise to be realised. Solomon Benatar and his colleagues have argued that:

> There is a . . . contradiction between the global accumulation of medical knowledge (capital) and the provision of stable conditions for the (social) reproduction of facilities to deliver accessible, appropriate and affordable healthcare . . . This contradiction is being locked in by neo-liberal constitutional governance mechanisms with damaging effects on the provision of healthcare for the majority of the world's population.
>
> (Benatar *et al.* 2009: 357)

Consequently, they argue, the realisation of health for all (of the right to health) is contingent on a paradigm shift in global, regional and domestic economic, political and social practices (Benatar *et al.* 2009: 371). Put bluntly, the promise of the right to health will remain rhetorical and unfulfilled in a world where market hegemony prevails.

There is, of course, nothing to be gained from imagining or believing that the language of human rights, or of the right to health, can act as a panacea for all of the social ills and inequities induced by the era of neo-liberal globalisation and the logic of market hegemony (Meier 2007; Gross 2007). However, by the same token we cannot deny that the language of human rights provides one form of emancipatory discourse for responding to the commonsense of neo-liberalism. Whether consciously or not, once we begin to use the language of human rights, and for present purposes of the right to health, we embrace a foundational value system that, at the very least, requires social solidarity, equal access to essential services on the basis of need, and a prioritising of collective welfare over individual or sectoral private interests for its realisation (Leys 2001). All of these values are completely anathema to the logic of neo-liberalism, consequently a commitment to the former raises serious questions about the extent to which it can be pursued in the context of market hegemony.

Notes

1 Thanks to Shivaun Quinlivan and the editors of the present volume for comments on an earlier draft of this chapter; while the chapter no doubt benefited from their careful and considered input, responsibility for any remaining shortcomings rests solely with the author.

2 While this chapter focuses primarily on the question of healthcare, and problematises the relationship between the human right to health and neo-liberal hegemony in this context, this focus is in no way intended to diminish or discount the equally important role of the underlying determinants of health (access to water, decent nutrition, education, shelter etc.) and the ways in which both the commodifying logic and inequalities engendered and exacerbated by the era of neo-liberal globalisation have undermined these, see Meier (2007) and Benatar *et al.* (2009). Rather, the focus of this chapter is limited simply because doing justice to the wider context would require a chapter (or possibly several) of its own.

3 In particular these governments relied on the public health exception provided in TRIPS Article 8, the provision allowing for the granting of compulsory licences in Article 31 and, to a lesser extent, the provision allowing for parallel imports in Article 6 (Cohen-Kohler *et al.* 2008: 236–9).

Bibliography

Adelaide Hospital Society and Jesuit Centre for Faith and Justice (2007) *The Irish Health Service: Vision, Values, Reality*, Dublin.

Andrews, M. (2009) 'Burying Neoliberalism', *Dissent*, 56(3): 57–62.

Benatar, S., Gill, S. and Bakker, I. (2009) 'Making Progress in Global Health: The Need for New Paradigms', *International Affairs*, 85: 347–71.

Blacksher, E. (2008) 'Healthcare Disparities: The Salience of Social Class', *Cambridge Quarterly of Healthcare Ethics*, 17: 143–53.

Blanchard, O. (2008) 'Cracks in the System: Repairing the Damaged Global Economy', *Finance and Development*, December: 8–10.

Chander, A. and Sunder, M. (2007) 'Is Nozick Kicking Rawls's Ass? Intellectual Property and Social Justice', *UC Davis Law Review*, 40: 563–79.

Cohen-Kohler, J. C., Forman, L and Lipkus, N. (2008) 'Addressing Legal and Political Barriers to Global Pharmaceutical Access: Options for Remedying the Impact of the Agreement on Trade-Related Aspects of Intellectual Property Rights (TRIPS) and the imposition of TRIPS-Plus Standards', *Health Economics, Policy and Law*, 3: 229–56.

Collyns, C. (2008) 'The Crisis Through the Lens of History', *Finance and Development*, December: 18–20.

Cullet, P. (2005) 'Patents and Medicines: The Relationship between TRIPS and the Human Right to Health', in Mann,J., Gruskin, S., Grodin, M. and Annas, G. (eds.) *Perspectives on Health and Human Rights*, London: Routledge.

Farmer, P. (2005) *Pathologies of Power: Health, Human Rights and the New War on the Poor*, London: University of California Press.

Filc, D. (2005) 'The Health Business under Neo-liberalism: The Israeli Case', *Critical Social Policy*, 25: 180–97.

Forman, L. (2007) 'Trade Rules, Intellectual Property, and the Right to Health', *Ethics and International Affairs*, 21: 337–57.

Gevers, S. (2004) 'The Right to Health Care', *European Journal of Health Law*, 11:29–34.

Glyn, A. (2006) *Capitalism Unleashed*, Oxford: Oxford University Press.

Gross, A. M. (2007) 'The Right to Health in an Era of Privatisation and Globalisation: National and International Perspectives', in Barak-Erez, D. and Gross, A. M. (eds.) *Exploring Social Rights: Between Theory and Practice*, Oxford: Hart.

Gruskin, S. and Tarantola, D. (2005) 'Health and Human Rights', in Gruskin, S. (ed.) *Perspectives on Health and Human Rights*, London: Routledge.

Harney, M. (2005) 'New Plan for Private Hospitals Will Benefit Everybody', *Irish Times*, 24 August 2005: 14.

Harvey, D. (2005) *A Brief History of Neoliberalism*, Oxford: Oxford University Press.

Harvey, K., Faunce, T., Lokuge, B. and Drahos, P. (2004) 'Will the Australia–United States Free Trade Agreement Undermined the Pharmaceutical Benefits Scheme?', *Medical Journal of Australia*, 181: 256–9.

Hayek, F. A. (1986) *The Road to Serfdom*, London: Ark Paperbacks.

Held, D. and McGrew, A. (2002) *Globalization/Anti-Globalization*, Cambridge: Polity Press.

Herman, E. S. (1995) *The Triumph of the Market*, Boston: South End Press.

House, J. S. (2001) 'Relating Social Inequalities in Health and Income', *Journal of Health Politics, Policy and Law*, 26: 523–532.

—— (2003) Report of the UN Special Rapporteur on the Right to Health (E/CN.4/2003/58).

—— (2004) Report of the UN Special Rapporteur on the Right to Health (E/CN.4/2004/49).

—— (2005) Report of the UN Special Rapporteur on the Right to Health (E/CN.4/2005/51).

—— (2006) Report of the UN Special Rapporteur on the Right to Health (E/CN.4/2006/48).

—— (2007) Report of the UN Special Rapporteur on the Right to Health (A/HRC/4/28).

—— (2008) Report of the UN Special Rapporteur on the Right to Health (A/HRC/7/11).

Krikorian, G. P. and Szymkowiak D. M. (2007) 'Intellectual Property Rights in the Making: The Evolution of Intellectual Property Provisions in US Free Trade Agreements and Access to Medicine', *Journal of World Intellectual Property*, 10: 388–418.

Lazzarini, Z. (2003) 'Making Access to Pharmaceuticals a Reality: Legal Options Under TRIPs and the Case of Brazil', *Yale Human Rights and Development Law Journal*, 6: 103–38.

Leys, C. (2001) *Market-Driven Politics: Neoliberal Democracy and the Public Interest*, London: Verso.

Maarse, H. (2006) 'The Privatization of Health Care in Europe: An Eight-Country Analysis', *Journal of Health Politics, Policy and Law*, 31: 981–1014.

Macpherson, C. B. (1987) *The Rise and Fall of Economic Justice and Other Essays*, Oxford: Oxford University Press.

Martinsen, D. S. and Vrangbæk, K. (2008) 'The Europeanization of Health Care Governance: Implementing the Market Imperatives of Europe', *Public Administration*, 86: 169–84.

Meier, B. M. (2007) 'Advancing Health Rights in a Globalized World: Responding to Globalization through a Collective Human Right to Public Health', *Journal of Law, Medicine and Ethics*, 35: 545–55.

Mercer, M. A. (2004) 'Shall We Leave It to the Experts?', in Fort, Mercer and Gish (eds.) *Sickness and Wealth: The Corporate Assault on Global Health*, Cambridge, MA: South End Press.

Morone, J. A. (2000) 'Citizens or Shoppers? Solidarity under Siege', *Journal of Health Politics, Policy and Law*, 25: 959–68.

Navarro, V. (2007) 'Neoliberalism as a Class Ideology: Or, the Political Causes of the Growth of Inequalities', in Navarro (ed.) *Neoliberalism, Globalization and Inequalities: Consequences for Health and Quality of Life*, New York: Baywood Publishing.

Nozick, R. (2001) *Anarchy, State and Utopia*, Oxford: Blackwell Publishing.

Oberlander, J. (2006) 'The Political Economy of Unfairness in U.S. Health Policy', *Law and Contemporary Problems*, 69: 245–64.

O'Connell, P. (2005) 'The Human Right to Health and the Privatisation of Irish Health Care', *Medico-Legal Journal of Ireland*, 11(2): 76–82.

—— (2007) 'On Reconciling Irreconcilables: Neo-liberal Globalisation and Human Rights', *Human Rights Law Review*, 7(3): 483–509.

Pellegrino, E. D. (1999) 'The Commodification of Medical and Health Care: The Moral Consequences of a Paradigm Shift from a Professional to a Market Ethic', *Journal of Medicine and Philosophy*, 24: 243–66.

Petersmann, E. U. (2000) 'The WTO Constitution and Human Rights', *Journal of International Economic Law*, 3: 19–25.

Pollock, A. M. (2005) *NHS plc: The Privatisation of Our Health Care*, new edn, London: Verso.

Prasad, M. (2006) *The Politics of Free Markets*, Chicago: University of Chicago Press.

Redmond, M. (2005) 'Healthcare System Needs the Private Sector Treatment', *Irish Times*, 31 October 2005: 14.

Rowland, D. and Shartzer, A. (2008) 'America's Uninsured: The Statistics and Back Story', *Journal of Law, Medicine and Ethics*, 36: 618–28.

Schlesinger, M. (2006) 'Markets as Belief Systems and Those Who Keep the Faith', *Journal of Health Politics, Policy and Law*, 31: 417–21.

Scholte, J. A. (2005) *Globalization: A Critical Introduction*, 2nd edn, London: Palgrave Macmillan.

Sell, S. (2007) 'TRIPs-Plus Free Trade Agreements and Access to Medicines', *Liverpool Law Review*, 26: 41–75.

Shahmanesh, M. (2007) 'Neoliberal Globalisation and Health: A Modern Tragedy', *Critique*, 35(3): 315–38.

UN-CESCR (2000) *General Comment No.14 – The Right to the Highest Attainable Standard of Health (Article 12 of the International Covenant on Economic, Social and Cultural Rights)* (E/C.12/2000/4).

US Federal Trade Commission and US Department of Justice (2004) *Improving Health Care: A Dose of Competition*, Washington DC: USFTC/USDOJ.

WTO (2001) *Doha Ministerial Declaration*. 20 November. WT/MIN(01)/DEC/1.

Yamin, A. E. (2008) 'Will We Take Suffering Seriously? Reflections on What Applying a Human Rights Framework to Health Means and Why We Should Care', *Health and Human Rights*, 10: 1–16.

Index

Printed in the USA/Agawam, MA
November 19, 2010
555222.040